RISK AND SAFETY MANAGEMENT IN THE LEISURE, EVENTS, TOURISM AND SPORTS INDUSTRIES

D1332493

RISK AND SAFETY MANAGEMENT IN THE LEISURE, EVENTS, TOURISM AND SPORTS INDUSTRIES

M.J. Piekarz

University of Worcester, UK

I.S. Jenkins

University of Iceland, Iceland

P.F. Mills

Quality Leisure Management. Ltd., UK

www.cabi.org

CABI is a trading name of CAB International

CABI	CABI
Nosworthy Way	745 Atlantic Avenue
Wallingford	8th Floor
Oxfordshire OX10 8DE	Boston, MA 02111
UK	USA
Tel: +44 (0)1491 832111	
Fax: +44 (0)1491 833508	Tel: +1 800 552 3083 (toll free)
E-mail: info@cabi.org	E-mail: cabi-nao@cabi.org
Website: www.cabi.org	

A catalogue record for this book is available from the British Library, London, UK.

Library of Congress Cataloging-in-Publication Data

Piekarz, Mark.
  Risk and safety management in the leisure, events, tourism and sports industries/Mark Piekarz, Ian Jenkins and Peter Mills.
     pages cm
  Includes bibliographical references and index.
  ISBN 978-1-78064-449-3 (pbk. : alk. paper) 1. Leisure industry--Risk management. 2. Sports administration--Risk management. 3. Tourism--Risk management. 4. Special events industry--Risk management. I. Jenkins, Ian (Ian S.) II. Mills, Peter (Peter F.) III. Title.
  GV188.P4 2015
  790.06'9--dc23
                                               2015000782

ISBN-13: 978 1 78064 449 3

Commissioning editor: Claire Parfitt
Assistant editor: Alexandra Lainsbury
Production editor: James Bishop

Typeset by SPi, Pondicherry, India.
Printed and bound in the UK by Gutenberg Press Ltd, Tarxien, Malta.

Contents

Preface

This is a book about risk analysis, assessment and decision making. It examines and explains how risk-related concepts, theories and tools can be applied to analyse past and current operational conditions, in order to try and assess what could happen in an uncertain future. The purpose of doing this is simple: it should be done to help practitioners ensure risks, as they relate to safety, operations, projects and strategy, are effectively managed, not simply removed. This book is designed for those people, from students to practitioners, who do not want to simply replicate past practices, but to understand why certain concepts and practices are used and how they can be improved.

While many writers and practitioners may view risk as simply a chance of a loss or injury occurring which needs to be removed or reduced, the preference in this book is to use a broader-based definition of risk, whereby it is viewed as something that not only creates threats, but also opportunities. There are a number of reasons for adopting this balanced approach. The first is that for many adventure, sport and touristic activities, risk can be a vital component in creating memorable and satisfying experiences, where to avoid all risk would be to destroy the essence of the activity. Second, in many fields of business, risk is never just understood as negative and something to be avoided. For example, in relation to financial management and entrepreneurship, risk has always been intimately related with making profits and loss. Another example relates to project management theories and practices, where there is encouragement to consider how risks can create both opportunistic and threatening risks, such as how a spell of good weather can mean project schedules can speed up, or bad weather can create delays or cancellations. Indeed, an increasing number of writers on project risk management state that, without risk, there can be little reward for undertaking the project. Finally, there is the ongoing debate about the role of risk in society and the problems of removing all risk from life, such as the discussion about childhood development and the possible impacts of how too much regulation and control of play environments can impede learning, development and reduce the quality of childhood.

So this book adopts the balanced or *symmetric* view of risk, whereby the focus is not a simplistic reaction to remove risk. Instead, the emphasis is on using various concepts, theories and tools relating to *risk* and *risk management* to try and help people make better management decisions that deal with negative, *downside* risks, or seize opportunistic, *upside* risks. It is a process that can be used for different levels of management, for different industries, in different countries, as the core strands of risk management can be distilled and adapted to all these areas. It is a book about decision making in an immediate context, or making more long-term strategic plans.

The difficulty is that there is no clear agreement about what risk is, or what the management of it involves in relation to the adventure, sport or tourist sectors. True, there is in theory a generic international standard of risk that has been developed by the International Organization for Standardization (ISO), which defines risk as 'the effect of uncertainty on objectives' (ISO, 2009: 1). This body also argues that this standard is relevant for any organization, industry, sector and country. Evidence can be found that some organizations have adopted this definition, particularly in Australia, New Zealand and to a lesser extent, the UK. For example, the Australian and New Zealand handbook for managing risk in sport and recreation defines risk in relation to the impact on objectives, noting that risk can be both positive or negative (Standards Australia/Standards New Zealand, 2010: 2); similarly, UK Sport, in its document on staging major sporting events, defines risk as 'any factor that may prevent you from fulfilling your objectives' (UK Sport, 2005: 43). Yet these examples are still far short of providing evidence that the international standard has universally filtered down to all adventure, event, sport and tourism operators around the world, because for each example where one can find an organization that adopts a symmetric approach to risk, one can find more that do not.

The result is that there are many inconsistencies in the application of concepts, terms and practices between the different sectors, countries and even within single organizations. This in turn means that many good practices may not be properly transferred between organizations and sectors, together with impeding the effective communication of risk to staff, customers and other key stakeholders in a business or organization.

In relation to the concepts of *safety* and safety *management*, these are intimately related to risk management but are not terms that should be used interchangeably. Safety is a critical element in risk management. Although it can often focus on operational-related issues, it is vital that it is also considered strategically, in terms of the leadership given by senior managers and recognizing that when accidents do occur, they can have profound strategic reverberations that can affect the future viability of the organization itself.

All these issues therefore help establish the key aims of this textbook, which are:

- to explain the underpinning concepts, theories and tools of risk, safety and risk management as they relate to the adventure, event, sport and tourism industries;
- for students and practitioners to develop a clear risk culture, or philosophy of risk, that can shape how they view and approach safety, operational, project and strategic risk management;

- for students and practitioners to gain an appreciation of the variations in definitions and approaches, in order to develop more effective risk practices that can be clearly communicated to staff, customers and other key stakeholders; and
- to enable students and practitioners to develop and implement effective risk control measures.

For many reading this book, the definitions used for risk, risk management and its various associated key concepts may run against their previous understanding and approaches, leading to the cry of 'that's not risk' or 'it's not done that way'. Yet this is the key to understanding why this book is necessary. It does not try to provide definitive definitions or approaches; rather it explains why there are variations in risk processes, together with identifying examples of good practice, in order to help with both regulatory compliance and good management decision making.

STRUCTURE OF THE BOOK AND THEORETICAL UNDERPINNINGS

In order to explain the underlying principles of risk management as they relate to the adventure, events, sport and tourism sectors, a wide variety of materials are used from a number of scientific disciplines and subject fields. In this textbook, one will find literature drawn from the disciplines of economics, sociology, anthropology and business management, with additional materials used from more specific subject areas of adventure, leisure, sport and tourism. Furthermore, an important aspect to this book is that it takes an international approach in relation to the theories, concepts and case studies scrutinized, focusing on all the key industry sectors.

In Chapter 1, how students and practitioners encounter risk is explored. It explains why practitioners working in the adventure, event, sport or tourism sectors can find it impossible not to engage with risk management concepts and practices. This is because of a mixture of legal regulations, good management practice and that risk is an inherent part of these activities which needs to be managed, not removed. It also briefly defines the different sectors and how risk is relevant to these areas.

In Chapter 2, risk is examined as both a culture and a practical management process. An important part of the discussion is an explanation of how the many different risk definitions can be placed in various cultural paradigms; simply put, this means that the risk definition people use can influence what is viewed as a risk and how they approach risk management. Particular attention is given to the contrasting risk paradigms where risk is viewed as the chance of harm, injury or loss, compared with definitions that define risk as both positive and negative, embedded in a complex system. The discussion about the practical process of risk management compares a variety of examples from different fields, identifying the key features of any risk process. From this chapter, various key concepts are identified and are utilized in many of the subsequent chapters.

In Chapter 3, the key theories that underpin risk and risk management are examined. It explains why certain concepts and practices are often used in risk management, exploring the historical scientific foundations of some of the key theories. It pays particular attention to the theory of probability, why it is used and some of the problems that students and practitioners should be aware of.

In Chapter 4, the practical tools that can be used to analyse risks are examined. A distinction is made between a risk theory and a risk tool, whereby tools are the practical methods that can be used to collect data and information, analyse it, then develop some form of assessment and control mechanism. A variety of tools are explored, ranging from simple mind mapping, to more complex scenario writing exercises. In essence, this is about turning the theory into practical analysis.

In Chapter 5, the focus is on the control measures that can be taken to deal with risk. It offers a reminder that the reason for analysing and assessing risk is to help practitioners make decisions. It also illustrates how practitioners and managers will have a range of options in terms of *what* they decide to do with risks, *how* they employ resources and *how* they implement control measures, which is represented as a jigsaw or mosaic of management options. It is stressed that controlling risk is not simply about removing risks, but managing them effectively, which in relation to safety is clarified by being done *as reasonably as practicable*.

In Chapter 6, the vital necessity of documenting and recording information in paper or electronic documents is explained. This chapter pays particular attention to designing forms and using assessment criteria. As before, the wide variety of practices are examined to help students and practitioners interpret the many possible approaches. Various practical tips are given for how to approach form design and use checklists to help with the implementation and monitoring of control measures. It also briefly explores aspects of crisis management.

In Chapter 7, the many factors and theories that influence risk behaviours are examined. The importance of understanding this is explained through the people who need to do the risk analysis and assessment, together with the key stakeholders and customers who use the services. A number of the themes touched on in Chapter 5 are returned to, highlighting the subjective nature of interpreting risk situations and events, which can influence the assessment of risk, or the participation in the activity.

In Chapter 8, the concept of tort and its importance in risk management are examined. The necessity for students and practitioners to understand tort is stressed and gives an additional insight into why risk is often considered in asymmetric terms. In essence, tort relates to the idea of a wrong having been done and the law. The chapter examines the various types of tort and its importance for managers when approaching risk management.

In Chapter 9, a more intimate examination is conducted in relation to safety risk management. The legal compliance to engage with risk and hazard management is examined in relation to health and safety legislation from around the world. It is illustrated that the engagement with risk management practices is not always explicitly stated in regulations, but it most certainly is always implied.

In Chapter 10, a number of key themes and theories relating to safety management are looked at in more detail. It is linked with Chapter 3 and the key theories of risk management, but brings in a number of additional theories and tools that can be used.

In Chapter 11, a range of case studies from each of the sectors are briefly examined. These are reflected and explored in relation to the main theories, concepts and themes discussed in all of the previous chapters. They are designed not only to help explain and illustrate how theories can be applied, but also to provide some important examples for students and practitioners to learn from.

Chapter 12 is a concluding chapter, which gives a short review of the key themes discussed in this book, together with a short reflection of the book aims.

In all chapters a series of text box inserts are given that highlight key theories, themes or case studies. In addition, a number of quick reflective tasks are given to help focus on some of the key points being discussed in the chapter. In each of the chapters, the final section explores and applies a number of key themes and concepts discussed in that chapter in relation to a variety of sector case studies.

REFERENCES

ISO (2009) *Risk Management – Principles and Guidelines*. International Organization for Standardization, Geneva, Switzerland.

Standards Australia/Standards New Zealand (2010) *HN 246: 2010: Guidelines for Managing Risk in Sport and Recreation Organizations*. Standards Australia, Sydney, Australia and Standards New Zealand, Wellington.

UK Sport (2005) Major Sports Events – The Guide. Available at: http://www.uksport.gov.uk/publications /major-sports-events-the-guide-april-2005 (accessed 24 June 2013).

chapter 1

The Risk Encounter for the Different Industry Sectors

CHAPTER OBJECTIVES

- To explain why risk management is important for practitioners to understand.
- To explain why managers in different industry sectors, at all levels of management, cannot avoid risk management.
- To define the key industry sectors, illustrating their relationship with each other and the importance of risk.

Key concepts

Risk and risk management; levels of management; defining adventure, leisure, events, sport and tourism.

1.1 INTRODUCTION

This chapter explores why risk management is difficult to avoid for practitioners and managers in the adventure, event, leisure, sport and tourism sectors. A representative model is developed to illustrate the variety of ways that risk and risk management are both encountered and utilized. Particular distinctions are made between those who help deliver services and those who plan services. Finally, a brief overview is given explaining what the different industry sectors are, how they relate to each other and some of the key reasons why it is vital to understand risk management in those sectors.

1.2   THE RISK ENCOUNTER

For someone working in the adventure, event, leisure, sport or tourism industry, it can be difficult to avoid risk management. By appreciating the factors that make risk unavoidable, it helps clarify the importance of understanding and using risk management theory and practices. These factors can be summarized as:

- *Risk is an inherent part of life.* Living involves constant exposure to risk and making decisions about risk. To cross a road, to take a new job, to play a sport, to go on holiday, to drive a car, all carry risks, with Box 1.1 offering more examples of how mundane objects and activities can generate risks. By recognizing the ubiquity of risk and the need to deal with it, this helps draw out an important feature about risk: that it involves assessing options and taking actions, which can be done in a matter of seconds, months or even years. In short, as Bernstein (1998: 12) observes, to take risks is to be human.
- *Risk is an inherent part of adventure, sport and tourism activities.* If there is no risk in many sport, adventure and travel activities then the essence of the activity and what creates the enjoyment and satisfaction can be lost. Just think where sport would be without physical contact, contests or if there was never any uncertainty about the outcome of games? Alternatively, consider the value of many adventurous activities in terms of the reflection on the learning, or the sense of achievement gained, if there was no surprise, challenge or

---

Box 1.1. Risk is everywhere!

Bill Bryson gives this humorous reflection on the risks we are exposed to from mundane objects, which helps remind us that risks are everywhere, but that we accept them because of the benefits they bring. He says:

> Here's a fact for you. According to the latest Statistical Abstract of the United States, every year more than 400,000 Americans suffer injuries involving beds, mattresses or pillows. Think about that for a minute. That is more people than live in greater Coventry. That is almost 2,000 bed, mattresses or pillow injuries a day. In the time it takes you to read this article, four Americans will somehow manage to wound themselves by the bedding… consider this interesting fact: almost 50,000 Americans are injured each year by pencils, pens and other desk accessories. How do they do it? I have sat many an hour at a desk and would have greeted almost any kind of injury as a welcome diversion… Consider this one. In 1992… more than 400,0000 people in the United States were injured by chairs, sofas and sofa beds. Does it tell us something trenchant about the design of modern furniture or merely that Americans are exceptionally careless sitters? … But the people I would really like to meet are the 142,000 hapless souls who receive emergency injury room treatment for injuries inflicted by their clothing. What can they be suffering from? Compound pyjama fracture? Sweatpants hematoma? I am powerless to speculate. (Bryson, 1999: 23)

arousal of emotion? Even in relation to travel, risk can play a vital role in the quality of the experience and it is of interest that the origin of the word *travel* derives from the French word *travail*, which means an arduous or painful journey, but one which still brings rewards.

- *Risk management can help organizations remain market oriented.* Marketing as a function is often misunderstood as simply advertising and selling. In fact the essence of marketing is about understanding customer needs and wants, whereby people are increasingly seeking more intense experiences. Risk can play a vital role in creating these memorable, intense experiences (explained in Chapter 7), which practitioners need to understand if they are to be market oriented (i.e. focusing on what customers need and want), rather than product oriented (i.e. focusing on the service or product offered, rather than the benefits it brings).

- *Risk is an essential part of entrepreneurial activity.* In business, risk is often viewed as essential, whereby Bernstein (1998) makes the blunt point that if there is no risk, there is no profit. Recognizing this is important in relation to adventure, sport and tourism activities as it can remind people who design services and products that taking risks may be necessary not only for the quality of the experiences, but also to make a financial profit.

- *Risk is part of management.* Merna and Faisal (2005: 35), citing Handy (1999), look at the necessity of risk in management, saying 'risk management is not a separate activity from management, it is management'. They go on to argue that a symptom of poor management is the constant reaction to events; in contrast, effective management attempts to deal with uncertainty by anticipating future events that can generate risk, then developing plans to deal with them.

- *Risk is part of the language of problem solving.* A simple scan of news stories can quickly reveal many instances where the language of risk is used in all spheres of work and life, ranging from education, health, business and even war. This widespread usage gives an indication of the value of using risk theories and concepts. It should, however, be appreciated that common usage of the term 'risk' does not mean consistency in understanding or application; hence, a more detailed examination of what risk can mean is given in Chapter 2.

- *Risk management is part of legal compliance.* For the developed world at least, it can be difficult to find a country that does not have a number of legal and regulatory guidelines which deal with work or occupational health and safety. While they may not always directly refer to the term 'risk' or 'risk management', implicit in these many regulatory guidelines is a legal requirement to conduct some form of assessment in order to identify hazards and risks that people may be exposed to. There can also be regulatory guidelines that deal with corporate governance and have a more strategic risk focus.

Yet there are problems. Despite the common usage and application of the concepts of *risk*, *risk management* and the *management of risks* (explained in more detail in Chapter 2), what can be so striking are the variations in definition and application. This leads to the problem that managers working at different levels of management, such as the health and safety, project or safety level, can encounter variations in the words, concepts and practices utilized. The result can be confusion. As will be explained in Chapter 2, these variations are not necessarily because operational safety, project or strategic risk management as used in the different sectors, or even countries, have different theoretical underpinnings; rather that it can reflect an insular development within the subject field or sector and the terminology or descriptors utilized.

It is also important to note that the growth of risk management practices is not the same as saying that there are more risks or dangers. For people in the developed world, improved sanitation, immunizations, health and safety legislation, etc. have made profound impacts on populations, life expectancy and the quality of life. Yet there is little doubt that the practice, language and literature on risk management have grown significantly over recent years; so much so that Furedi (2002) argues this now means a discrete risk industry has developed, which he considers is not necessarily always a good thing.

The challenge is for managers is to try and understand what is the *tolerability of risks* (TOR) (Gardiner, 2005: 175), or the *minimum risk environment* (MRE). The UK Health and Safety Executive (HSE) makes the important point that 'tolerable' risk does not necessarily mean 'acceptable' risk. Its goes on to say that a willingness by society to live with a risk is done so as to secure certain benefits, but in the confidence that the risk is one worth taking and that it is properly controlled (HSE, 2001: 3). For example:

- people are willing to tolerate the risk of a flight to gain the benefits of relaxing on a holiday;
- people will tolerate the risk of injury when playing sport to gain various health benefits;
- people will tolerate the risks of an event, such as travel delays and frustrations, to experience moments that can be intensified by sharing them with thousands of others;
- an entrepreneur may mortgage his/her house to raise the capital for a new business venture, which could mean a family home could be lost, but is done so because of the financial rewards that may be gained; and
- people may undertake a physically demanding adventure expedition to test themselves and gain a sense of achievement, even though it may be fraught with many physical dangers.

In all of these examples a degree of risk is 'tolerated' because of the personal or financial gains and benefits that may be made; the risks will be 'accepted' because there is a belief that the negative risks will be properly controlled by others, or because people have confidence in their ability to overcome the challenges and deal with the risks. Of course, what is deemed as tolerable can vary considerably between individuals, groups and countries, as will be discussed in Chapter 7 and as illustrated in Box 1.2. This also connects to the discussion in Chapter 5 in relation to what is *reasonably practicable* in terms of controlling the risks.

Box 1.2. Different risk tolerances?

An interesting observation can be made about how different countries tolerate and accept risk. In the USA for example, resorting to litigation (legal action) after accidents to try and gain compensation can be a common practice, which has also developed in the UK. Using litigation to seek financial compensation is epitomized by such slogans as 'where there is blame, there is a claim', with legal practices advertising their services that encourage people to put in claims with the promise of 'no win, no cost.' While there is no doubt that many claims are fully justified, particularly where there have been clear breaches in occupational or work health and safety guidelines, some would argue that the growth in a compensation culture is also leading to a risk-averse *society*, which is not necessarily beneficial for the individual, society or the economy. In the UK for example, the 2010 government report entitled *Common Sense, Common Safety* (Lord Young of Graffham, 2010) looked at the issue of health and safety regulation and the concern that it was being over-zealously applied, leading to such problems as 'uninspiring play spaces that do not enable children to properly experience risk, or school trips cancelled because of concerns over health and safety' (Lord Young of Graffham, 2010: 37). A key theme of the report was to try and move towards a risk–benefit analysis approach to the management of risk.

Collins and Collins (2013: 74) explain and outline the advantages of adopting a risk benefit approach in relation to sport and adventure, whereby they argue that teachers, coaches and leaders across sports should generate all assessments built around a 'justification' of stated risks against the benefits shown to flow from them. The key point is that risk should not just be approached from a risk avoidance view, but from one where the benefits of risks are also identified and can therefore be exploited.

In other countries, such as New Zealand, Australia, France or Switzerland, where the culture of litigation is not as strong, the tolerability of risk can appear much higher in comparison with the UK and USA. These differences between countries are partly reflected in how risk may be defined: while in the UK and USA it can be more common to find the definition of risk used that focuses on harm or loss, in Australia and New Zealand they tend to adopt the more neutral, ISO definition of risk as one impacting on objectives, which can be both good and bad (discussed in Chapter 2).

So what is *risk* and *risk management*? The answer is not a simple one, which is why a more considered approach is taken in Chapter 2. For now it will be sufficient to say that in this book the focus is on the control of risks, in order to deal with negative, threatening downside risks or to seize positive, opportunistic upside risks, all of which are explored in more detail in Chapter 2.

1.3   WHO NEEDS TO CONSIDER RISK MANAGEMENT?

To convey the variety of ways that people working in the adventure, event, leisure, sport and tourism sectors encounter risk, it can be useful to show how different work roles may utilize or encounter risk management practices, concepts and theories. This 'encounter' is represented in Fig. 1.1, which distinguishes between the roles and the factors that shape risk practices. The critical point to emphasize here is that everyone in an organization will either conduct some form of risk analysis and assessment, or will be affected by risk management practices.

In relation to the *roles*, a simple distinction can be made between *deliverers* of services and *planners* of services (see Fig. 1.1). The type of role can affect what type of risk management process needs to be engaged with and applied.

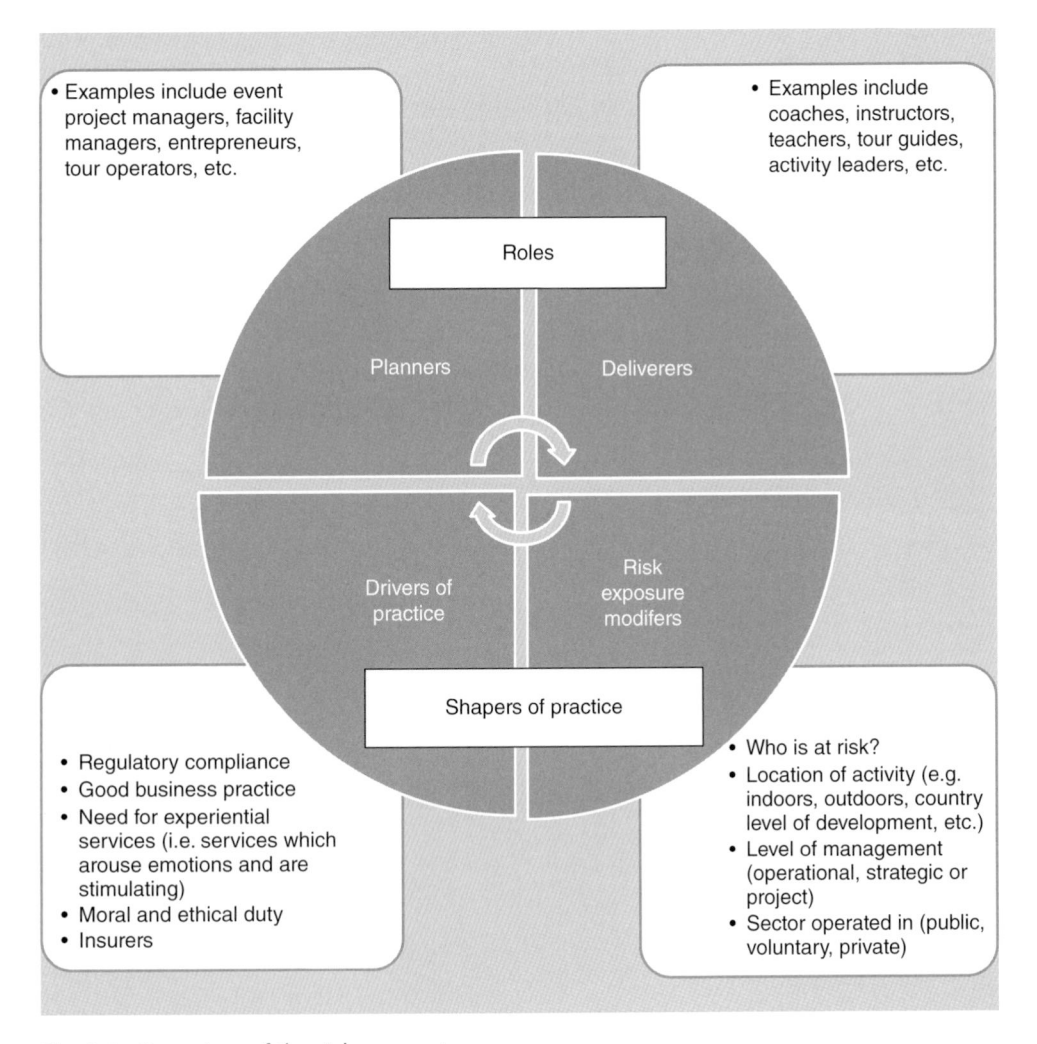

Fig. 1.1. Overview of the risk encounter.

The *deliverers* describes jobs such coaches, teachers, activity assistants, tour guides, instructors, volunteer helpers and event stewards. Deliverers are characterized by their direct involvement with participants and the responsibilities they have for controlling risks relating to safety and service operations. All these roles need to consider legal regulatory compliance, along with a constant assessment of risks as activities are being conducted (*dynamic risk management* discussed in Chapter 5). These people work primarily at an operational level of management, which refers to day-to-day decision making and management. Hence tour guides, coaches and teachers would all have to do preliminary, formal risk assessments, ensuring that they comply with regulations, such as using staff who are suitably qualified and checked, or ensuring proper maintenance of equipment has been done. This formal process is one which would require information being recorded on paper or as an electronic document. As the activities take place, if the conditions alter, such as the changes in the weather, the leader of the activities would have to make judgements on how the hazards and risks are changing. For these type of assessments, it is not realistic (or desirable) to stop and record information, as decisions must be made to deal with the immediate dynamic conditions as they change.

The *planners* describes roles such as project managers, event organizers, company owners, managing directors, line managers and boards of governors. Planners are characterized by being more remote from operational service activities and day-to-day safety. For planners, they are primarily operating in what can be described as *project* and *strategic* levels of management. Strategic management is defined by the scale and complexity of the resources that need to be coordinated, dealing in timescales of months and years. Project risk management falls between operational and strategic management in terms of the timescales and resources that may need coordinating, but is distinguished by having clearly defined start and end points. While in the early stages of projects, the risks may be more strategic in focus, as the project nears completion, the attention on risks becomes operationally concentrated, such as how periods of good weather allow schedules to be advanced, or bad weather may create schedule delays.

For planners, while at times there is a need to explicitly engage with risk management, very often risk management is an implicit part of planning activities. To put it another way, because the term 'risk' is not stated or used, this does not mean that risk management is not being engaged with. For example, SWOT (which stands for Strengths, Weaknesses, Opportunities and Threats) and PEST analysis (which stands for Political, Economic, Social and Technological) are two common tools used in both project and strategic management. While these tools do not explicitly refer to 'risk', they are, for all intents and purposes, also methods for identifying and assessing hazards and potential risks.

The need for deliverers and planners to engage with risk management is influenced by the *shapers of practice*, represented in Fig. 1.1. This has two key elements. The first relates to the *drivers of practice*, which considers such things as regulatory compliance, the desire for effective management, offering services which give satisfaction and, just as importantly, out of a sense of morality and behaving ethically. The second area relates to the *risk exposure modifiers*, which considers how different factors can affect the risk analysis and assessment done. This includes such things as the nature of the clients, the type of organization or the sector operated in, all of which are returned to in more detail in Chapter 2, Section 2.3.4.

This mix of planners, deliverers, drivers and exposure modifiers all take places within four key levels or areas of service management, which can often overlap, and can be summarized as:

- *The health and safety level.* For many countries, such as the USA, the UK and Australia, legislation relating to work or occupational health and safety can mean that there can be a legal requirement to engage with some form of risk or hazard assessment exercise. Implicit in these pieces of legislation from around the world is the duty of care that employees, employers and participants have to each other in ensuring that working environments − whether this is a playing field, a city tour, travelling for business, a mountain side, etc. − are safe and healthy places to operate in as far as is reasonably practicable. In short, health and safety legislation can form a unifying linking strand between countries and sectors, which has driven the need to adopt proper risk management practices.

- *The operational management level.* This is intimately related to safety risk management, but can consider a broader range of issues, such as what factors can lead to the risks of services being cancelled, or customers receiving a poor-quality service. There is no specific legal requirement to adopt risk management practices at an operational level, but it is intimately related to good management and implementing effective quality control systems, so that good services are consistently delivered that meet or exceed customers' expectations.

- *The project management level.* Cagno *et al.* (2007: 2) and the Project Management Institute (PMBOK, 2004) argue that risk analysis has become increasingly important in project management. Again, there is no formal legal requirement to engage with risk management in project management, but it is seen as good practice, where if a project fails because of failures to identify risks and manage them, there could be scope for litigation if the issue is related to safety, or the organization could have its reputation damaged, which may affect its future viability.

- *The strategic management level.* At a strategic level, the need to engage with risk management is embedded in practices and regulations relating to good corporate governance (i.e. the rules and regulations that shape how a business or organization is managed and directed). Regulations have now been developed in different countries (e.g. in the USA, the 2002 Sarbanes-Oxely Act passed in 2002; or in the UK, the Turnbull Report) that try and ensure organizations and businesses are governed or managed properly, whereby there is an effective system of managing and reporting risks to the key stakeholders and encouragement to adopt an appropriate risk culture and robust risk practices. This has been in response to the failings of various large banks or corporations, but with the reverberations going far beyond these sectors, which can be just as relevant to many sport, adventure, tourism or event organizers.

1.4   SECTOR DEFINITIONS AND RISK CONTEXTUALISATION

The adventure, event, leisure, sport and tourism sectors are significant parts of the global economy. Whether they can be regarded as a single industrial sector as a whole, or should be considered industries in their own right, is not to be gone into here. Instead, these sectors will be defined, showing their similarities and differences, along with any more specific considerations to risk management.

Although *leisure* is not always explicitly focused on in this book, it is useful to examine, as it can form a linking thread between the other sectors. The simplest definition of leisure describes it as time free from obligated activities, with 'obligated activities' often used to refer to employment or work. Such a simple definition is fraught with difficulties, particularly in relation to what is meant by 'obligation' and how changing work patterns, such as with the growth in voluntary work, challenge many traditional preconceptions of just what work, or a job, entails. For some, such as Torkildsen (2005), the preference is to understand leisure as a state of being, or how it makes people feel, and the quality of the experiences; an important theme that also appears in some of the other sector definitions. Whatever definition decided upon, what should be clear is that leisure can encompass all the other industry sectors focused on in this book because they are so intimately related to notions of free time and the different experiences sought. So 'leisure' can include the person going rock climbing, watching a football game, going on holiday, visiting a theme park or engaging with a hobby.

Tourism is a huge global industry. While there is some dispute as to whether it is the world's largest industry, there is no denying that when one considers it includes transport, accommodation, visitor attractions and the food sectors, this means it can certainly be considered the world's largest service sector. An essential part of any tourism definition is that it includes an element of travel away from home, which to be defined as 'touristic' needs to either have a period away from home (e.g. 24 hours or more), or include a minimum distance travelled. As with leisure, what is of interest are those writers who focus on some of the more humanistic elements, where they emphasize the quality of experience and the arousal of emotions. Franklin (2003) is one of the writers who stress the importance of this cognitive and physical experiential element of tourism, arguing that tourism should not be reduced to acts of travel and the recreation at the end of it. He goes on to cite Saldanha who says:

> Don't tourists swim, climb, stroll, ski, relax, become bored perhaps, or ill… don't they go to places to taste, smell, listen, dance, get drunk, have sex? We can perhaps say that as the 1990s faded into the 2000s more people wanted to get their hands on the world, to taste it, feel it, smell it and importantly, do things with it and not just look at it. (Saldanha, 2002: 44)

While tourism can take place in leisure time, it is important to recognize that tourism has some distinct attributes, which means all tourism is not all leisure. Business tourism in particular is a huge and significant part of the tourism sector, but because of the obligated nature of the travel it would not be categorized as leisure or recreation. One can also consider how travel and tourism can form an important part of adventure, sport activities and attending events.

Risk in relation to tourism will manifest itself in a number of ways. As with leisure, risk can play an important role in shaping the quality of the recreational travel and holiday experience. It should also be considered in relation to how the perceived risk of travelling to different countries influences the decision to travel (discussed more in Chapter 7). Another important area of risk management that many tourist organizations should consider is the subject area of *political risk management*, which can be considered a discrete area of risk management in its own right.

Sport is obviously a key part of the leisure industry, as it is an activity that can be passively consumed as a spectator or actively participated in and played. It has also become a significant part of the tourism sector, particularly in relation to sport events, which range from mega-events such as the Olympics or the football World Cup, to the numerous smaller events that people can travel to.

Risk in relation to sport can again be considered as an inherent part of the attraction to both play and watch. An important part of sport games is the uncertainty of outcome and the risks involved, which can range from the obvious physical risks to the more complex emotional risks generated when a commitment is given as a fan. Sport is also a key element of a huge gambling industry, which is founded on the notions of risk and probability, and which also has some useful allegorical properties in illustrating again that risk can bring both losses and potential gains.

The *adventure* sector can overlap with all of the different sectors already discussed, such as activities that are done in leisure time, the huge growth in adventure tourism, or the growth in adventure sports. There are, however, some areas of adventure that do not fit neatly into the tourism, sport or leisure category, such as the areas which deal with education, management training, or even exploration and record setting. Of all the sectors discussed, adventure has the most intimate relationship with the concept of risk. This is because for an activity to be deemed as 'adventure' it should involve a challenging (physical or mental) journey of discovery which provokes strong emotional experiences, while also having elements of the unknown and involve dealing with risks. It is a concept that should not just be associated with tough and dangerous physical activities, but also about arousing intellectual curiosity.

The inherent risks involved with adventure and outdoor activities is one of the reasons why Collins and Collins (2013) argue that risk management is an essential part of the coach's and outdoor professional's skill set, whereby he/she must optimally manage the inherent risk. It is the taking of risks that creates the basis for learning experiences, which can be reflected upon and learnt from.

Event management can overlap with sport, tourism and leisure, but it also has some unique elements which can separate it from those sectors. A key defining feature of an event is that there should be a coherent focus of activities, with a specific start and end point. To do this involves project management, which will run through many phases, from its inception, planning, execution and evaluation. Furthermore, UK Sport (2005: 41), in its guide on staging major sport events, notes how risk management is both an explicit and implicit part of the event management project process because of the types of activity involved and, as it argues, the unusually large and diverse number of risks.

As will be illustrated in Chapter 9, in certain countries, some of the sectors have specific legislation that helps shape how risk and safety management must be approached. This can be particularly true in the area of sport events and stadiums; in the UK, for example, there are specific pieces of legislation, which must be understood, where risk management, although not always stated in the primary piece of legislation, has become an implicit and integral part of the process of legal compliance.

1.5 CONCLUSION

Risk for people working in the adventure, event, leisure, sport and tourism industries is impossible to ignore. This is because of a mixture of the need to comply with legal regulations, the value of risk management practices to help deal with uncertainty and the fact that risk is an essential part of many activities.

It is something used at all levels of management. The people working at an operational level, which focuses more on short-term decision making, have particular responsibilities for ensuring good-quality services and that experiences are delivered safely, effectively and efficiently. Failing to deal with dangerous situations or practices can indicate either that poor risk assessments have been done, or that the control measures are inadequate or not properly implemented. Even customer dissatisfaction can indicate weaknesses in the quality management practices and systems, whereby the risks have not been properly managed.

For those operating at the strategic level, the need to consider risk can relate to good governance and strategic planning. To try and identify and report on any key medium- to long-term risks that can affect the future viability of a business can be part of regulatory compliance in many countries; but it is also a core foundation for any strategic planning process, whereby opportunistic, upside or threatening, downside risks generated by competitors, or the external business environment all need to be identified, analysed, assessed and controlled.

Finally, project risk management can be both strategic and operational in its focus, whereby medium- to long-term risks must be identified as to how they can impact on a project, then also on the operational stages, whereby the project is managed on a day-to-day basis. These levels are particularly pertinent for the event management sector.

In terms of variations from around the world, while the regulations differ, some of the underlying principles of risk management can be remarkably similar: the difference is that they may utilize different descriptions or vary in the extent that a risk management process is explicitly stated or implied. One of the reasons why risk management has grown in terms of its practice is that it can offer many useful ways in which managers can deal with uncertainty. In this sense, good practice and use of theoretical concepts have the capability of transcending differences between the different industry sectors and, crucially, between different countries. This is what is explored in more detail in the next chapter.

DISCUSSION QUESTIONS AND TASKS

1. Identify how many potential hazards and risks you may have been exposed to in one day that could affect your health, finances and sense of wellbeing.

2. How did you try and avoid or deal with some of these hazards and risks?

3. Choosing two different sectors of your choice, compare and contrast the need to engage with risk management by examining a range of documents and websites.

4. For a country of your choice, compare the approaches to risk in occupational health and safety guidelines with those of strategic corporate governance regulations.

REFERENCES

Bernstein, P. (1998) *Against the Gods: The Remarkable Story of Risk*. Wiley, Chichester, UK.

Bryson, B. (1999) *Notes from a Big Country*. Transworld Publishers, London.

Cagno, E., Caron, F. and Mancini, M. (2007) A multi-dimensional analysis of major risks in complex projects. *Risk Management* 9, 1–18.

Collins, L. and Collins, D. (2013) Decision making and risk management in adventure sports. *Quest* 65, 72–82.

Franklin, A. (2003) *Tourism: An Introduction*. SAGE Publications, London.

Furedi, F. (2002) *Culture of Fear: Risk Taking and the Morality of Low Expectation*. Continuum, London.

Gardiner, P.D. (2005) *Project Management: A Strategic Management Approach*. Palgrave Macmillan, Basingstoke, UK.

Handy, C. (1999) *Beyond Certainty: The Changing Worlds of Organizations*. Harvard Business School, Boston, Massachusetts.

HSE (2001) Reducing Risks, Protecting People, HSE's Decision-Making Process. Available at: http://www.hse.gov.uk/risk/theory/r2p2.pdf (accessed 20 August 2014).

Lord Young of Graffham (2010) *Common Sense, Common Safety*. HMSO, London.

Merna, T. and Faisal, F.A. (2005) *Corporate Risk Management: An Organizational Perspective*. Wiley, Chichester, UK.

PMBOK (2004) *A Guide to the Project Management Body of Knowledge*, 3rd edn. Project Management Institute, Newtown Square, Pennsylvania.

Saldanha, A. (2002) Music tourism and factions of bodies in Goa. *Tourism Studies* 2, 43–62.

Torkildsen, G. (2005) *Leisure and Recreation Management*. Routledge, London.

UK Sport (2005) Major Sports Events – The Guide. Available at: http://www.uksport.gov.uk/publications/major-sports-events-the-guide-april-2005 (accessed 24 June 2013).

FURTHER READING

Examples of country-specific websites relating to health and safety

Canadian Centre for Occupational Health and Safety (CCOHS), available at: http://www.ccohs.ca/ccohs.html

Safe Work Australia, available at: http://www.safeworkaustralia.gov.au/sites/swa/pages/default

WorkSafe New Zealand, available at: http://www.business.govt.nz/worksafe/

UK Health and Safety Executive (HSE) has many interesting and relevant sections on risk management, available at: http://www.hse.gov.uk

US federal government, via the Department of Labor and the Occupational Safety and Health Administration (OSHA), available at: https://www.osha.gov/ (note that the federal structure in the USA means that more specific state legislation should also be scrutinized)

Examples of websites relating to project risk management

Joint Information Systems Committee (JISC) is a UK-registered charity that offers a range of services and information relating to digital technologies for UK learning institutions. It provides a range of invaluable information toolkits (infoNet) on project management and risk, available at: http://www.jiscinfonet.ac.uk/, with the risk-related section available at: http://www.jiscinfonet.ac.uk/infokits/risk-management/

Project Management Institute (PMI) is a professional membership association relating to project management. It has a range of services and key standards relating to best industry practice, available at: http://www.pmi.org/en.aspx

Sport Grounds Safety Authority (SGSA) is the UK government body responsible for carrying out various statutory functions (see the 1975 and 1989 Acts for examples), such as licences, or offering guidance on creating safe and enjoyable experiences for sport spectators, available at: http://www.safetyatsportsgrounds.org.uk/

Articles that can be of use in relation to strategic risk management

Clarke, C.H. and Varma, S. (1999) Strategic risk management: the new competitive edge. *Long Range Planning* 32, 414–424.

Richard Anderson & Associates (2014) Risk Management & Corporate Governance. Available at: http://www.oecd.org/corporate/ca/corporategovernanceprinciples/42670210.pdf (accessed 3 July 2014).

chapter 2

Risk Definitions, Cultures and Practical Processes

CHAPTER OBJECTIVES

- To examine and compare different risk definitions and how they can shape risk cultures.
- To explain what a risk culture is and how it can influence how risks are analysed and assessed.
- To explain the fourth-age risk paradigm, which views risks as both positive and negative and which need to be analysed as part of a complex system.
- To compare risk processes and identify the key features in a practical risk management process.

Key concepts

Risk culture and risk processes; symmetric and asymmetric risk definitions; paradigm shifts; hazards, causation factors and trigger events; risk probability/likelihood; risk outcome/consequences; risk analysis, risk assessment and risk management; closed and open systems.

2.1 INTRODUCTION

This chapter looks at risks in two important ways: *risk as a culture* and *risk as a practical management process*. Risk as a culture refers to the ways that an individual or organization defines risk, which in turn will influence both *what* is viewed as a risk and *how* it should be controlled. Risk as a process refers to the practical management steps that need to be taken to identify, analyse, assess and control risks.

The chapter begins by comparing different risk definitions to illustrate the many variations that can be found, together with identifying some of the key concepts that can be used to underpin any practical risk process. These key concepts are represented in Fig. 2.1, which shows the anatomy of risk. This is done to help managers and practitioners reflect on their own, or others', risk culture. The chapter then compares examples of the key practical process stages, drawn from different sectors and subject fields. These are then brought together (synthesized) to give a generic representation of the key process stages involved with any risk management process, which can be used at any level of management, in any industry sector, or in any country.

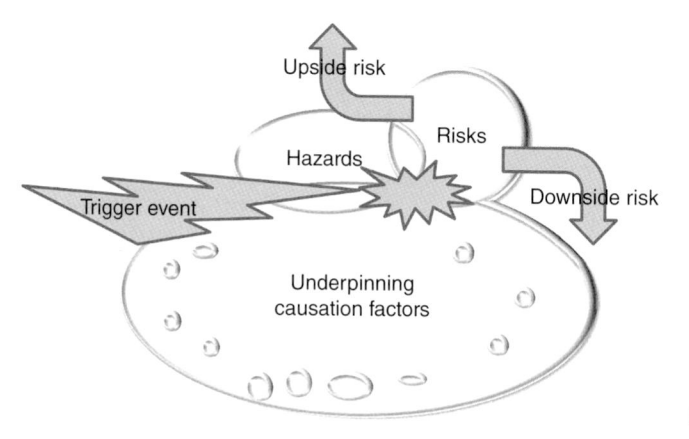

Fig. 2.1. Anatomy of risk.

2.2 THE MANY DEFINITIONS OF RISK

Risk and risk management, while they are difficult for managers to avoid, can be much harder to define. If one looks at various dictionary definitions of risk, it is often defined in relation to notions of danger and the chance of a loss or injury. While such a definition has simplicity, it has many limitations, particularly when analysing and assessing risks.

When examining other definitions of risk found from different sectors, or used for the different levels of management, what initially can be so striking are the apparent variations in definitions. To help illustrate these variations, a number of definitions of risk and risk management are compared and presented in Table 2.1.

Comparing these definitions, a number of observations can be made, which are:

- some definitions focus on the notions of harm and loss (sometimes called *asymmetric* definitions), while others refer to ideas of gains and benefits (*symmetric* definitions);
- risk can have an association with the concept of *chance, probability* or *likelihood*;
- risk can be associated with the *consequences* and *magnitude of outcome* or, for symmetric definitions, the *severity of outcome*;
- risk can be associated with the notion of *uncertainty*;

- some definitions present risk in relation to the concept of a *hazard*;
- risk can be regarded by some as an essential part of adventure, sport and business enterprise;
- risk management is used at all levels of management (operational, project and strategic); and
- definitions are not necessarily industry sector or country specific.

Table 2.1. Comparing risk definitions.

Asymmetric definitions (negative focus)	Symmetric definitions (positive and negative focus)
1. 'Risk is the chance, high or low, of somebody being harmed by the hazard, and how serious the harm could be.' (HSE, 2012) UK based	2. Risk is defined as '… the possibility of something happening that impacts on your objectives. It is the chance to either make a gain or a loss. It is measured in terms of likelihood and consequence.' (AS/NZS, 2009) New Zealand and Australia based
3. 'Risk is the potential to lose something of value, or simply the potential accident' (Brown, 1999: 274) UK based, adventure sector focused	4. 'Risk management is a rational approach to the problem of dealing with the risks faced by a business. It is about managing or optimising risks; it is not necessarily about eliminating them, because risk is inherent in adventure activities – and should remain so.' (Cloutier, 2002: 241) UK, Australia and USA
5. 'A risk is the likelihood that the harm a particular hazard can cause, will be realised.' (CIMSPA, 2014)	6. 'Risk management is a strategic process that will protect the assets and ensure the financial stability of an organization from the consequences of competitive business decisions. Risk management will reduce uncertainty and the potential for accidental or unanticipated loss and will provide the basis for maximizing opportunity.' (Fitzgerald, 2003: 2) Tourism and international in focus
7. 'Risk refers to uncertainty about and severity of the consequences (or outcomes) of an activity with respect to something that humans value.' (Aven and Renn, 2009: 1) Project focused	8. Project risk is '… an uncertain event or condition that, if it occurs, has a positive or negative effect on a project outcome.' (PMI, 2000; cited in Gardiner, 2005: 161) Project focused

There is not the scope to fully explain why the variations exist here, but an insight is given in Box 2.1. While one may expect variations because of the different countries or the industry sectors risk is written in, what is perhaps more surprising is that the differences are just as likely to be found *within*, as well as *between*, the different sectors and countries. For example,

---

Box 2.1. A brief history of risk and changing risk paradigms. (From Piekarz, 2009.)

As societies have changed over time, so too has our understanding of risk. These changes are sometimes categorized into four key periods, or *paradigm shifts* (i.e. a particular set of ideas and concepts as to how risk is viewed). These four key stages can be summarized as follows.

- *First age (pre-industrial)*. In this age, risk is linked to the growth of the maritime industry in the 17th century and focused on the *perils* that could compromise a sea voyage (Lupton, 1999: 5). Risk was viewed as an objective danger, or a neutral idea (Frosdick, 1997a: 33), or even as an act of god, which excluded the idea of human fault or responsibility.

- *Second age (industrial)*. The process of industrialization in the 19th century influenced how risks were understood, particularly as the science of probability and statistics were further refined and developed (Lupton, 1999: 6). The source of risk was extended not only to nature and acts of god, but also those generated by humans. The belief emerged that through science and mathematics the world could be better understood and predicted though calculations. Risk also became contrasted with uncertainty, which referred to a situation where probabilities could not be calculated. In terms of the management of risks, this was often analysed in a linear way, where simple patterns or sequences of causation could be identified (see the *domino theory* in Chapter 3), with controls focusing simply on avoiding or reducing risks.

- *Third age (post-industrial)*. Sadgrove (1997: 1) and Tarlow (2002: 207) argue that risk has more recently moved into a third, post-industrial age, whereby risk is characterized by the complexity in origin, creating both opportunities/upsides, as well as the more familiar threats/downsides. Paradoxically perhaps, while many organizations may view risk in a more neutral way, for the wider public risk has become more strongly associated with blame and notions of accountability or liability (Frosdick, 1997a: 36), having also become a tool of the legal system.

- *Fourth age*. Writers such as Tarlow (2002: 208) argue that for some areas of risk management, we are now entering a fourth age. Risk management in this age, he argues, becomes 'truly interdisciplinary' (Tarlow, 2002: 209), whereby it is necessary not only to understand the complexity of hazards and risks in terms of their origin, but also in relation to their complex interactions and impacts. Aspects of these new paradigms are not necessarily completely new. Lupton (1999: 148), for example, notes that in the field of economics there has always existed the notion of a 'good risk'. What is newer is the use of complexity theory, discussed later in Chapters 3 and 9.

---

if one looks at the two definitions relating to adventure (items 3 and 4 in Table 2.1), while Brown's (1999) definition has an asymmetric focus on loss, Cloutier's (2002) is more symmetric as it sees risk as both positive and negative. Not surprisingly, these variations in definitions can lead to confusion for people working in the different sectors, which can lead to risks being poorly analysed, assessed or communicated.

So what should one do? The first is to acknowledge and accept that these variations in definitions exist. The second is to try and identify some core conceptual strands or pillars that can be identified, defined and applied across an organization in a consistent manner, at all levels of management, in all industry sectors. Both of these issues are examined in more detail in the following sections of this chapter.

2.3 THE KEY CONCEPTS RELATING TO RISK AND RISK MANAGEMENT

While it should be recognized that many variations exist, in risk definitions, this does not mean that one should not strive for greater consistency in the use and application of relevant risk-related concepts and theories. This section therefore examines the key concepts that can be used and adapted to a variety of risk management situations, whether this is for a health and safety operational assessment for sport facilities, or a more strategic analysis of the external business environment for a tourism organization looking for future countries to invest in.

2.3.1 Risk is different from uncertainty

Knight (1921) is a key writer who explained the conceptual distinction between *risk* and *uncertainty*, arguing that risk is a product of uncertainty. The distinction between the two is that if the outcome of a project or event is not known, or highly biased because of a subjective viewpoint, then this can be categorized as uncertainty. Equally, if something approaches 100% probability, it becomes a reality rather than a risk (Irwin, 1998: 61).

It is important to appreciate the limitations of this distinction when actually making management decisions. Jablonowski (2001) makes the provocative point that it is difficult to distinguish between risk and uncertainty, saying:

> …managers could not come up with a credible probability for an event if they wanted to. What is more, they can do a perfectly accurate job of dealing with the domain of hazard risk without being able to (Jablonowski, 2001: 32)

Why is this case? Part of the reason relates to the complexity of decision making and gives an insight into why risk is increasingly represented as being embedded in a complex system, sometimes known as the *fourth-age risk paradigm*, explained in Box 2.1. Making a probability assessment on an outcome is possible if all of the outcomes are known, such as the chances of drawing a particular card from a pack of playing cards. In this case, the assessment is based on what can be described as a *closed system*, because all the possible outcomes are known or can be calculated, as there are only fifty-two playing cards to draw from. The difficulty is that many management decisions are not based on simple, closed systems, but on assessing *open* and *complex systems* whereby it is difficult to identify all possible hazards and risk outcomes. This complexity can increase as one moves from operational levels of management to project and strategic levels of management.

2.3.2   Risk is different from a hazard

Looking at examples of risk assessments from around the world, ranging from the USA to Australia and Europe, it is certainly common practice to utilize the concept of a *hazard* in forms designed to help assess risk (see Chapter 6). There can, however, sometimes be confusion between the concept of a hazard and a risk, with the two used interchangeably. It is recommended that they are used as distinct concepts as this allows for a more complex and subtle analysis. In the UK for example, the HSE (2001: 6) regards it as important to maintain a distinction between the two, because while the concept of a hazard is absent in the UK Health and Safety at Work Act, the courts have ruled that risk 'means the possibility of danger' rather than 'actual danger'.

The HSE (2012) goes on to define a hazard as 'anything that may cause harm, such as chemicals, electricity, stairs, sports equipment, working from ladders, noise etc.' For other writers, the preference is to focus on hazards as the *source* of the risk, rather than the *cause*. On first examination there may seem to be little difference between referring to the hazard as the cause or the source, but there are actually some important reasons why a distinction should be made. A simple example to illustrate these differences can be used in relation to the game of golf: sand bunkers and water features are referred to as hazards, where the risk can relate to the ball landing in these hazards resulting in shots being dropped, which can ultimately mean a game is lost. In theory, these hazards could be removed, but that would affect the enjoyment of the game and the development and testing of skills. In terms of causation, it is too simplistic to say the hazards caused the ball and game to be lost, as these outcomes are dependent on the interaction of factors, such as those relating to the shot played, the ability of the player and other environmental factors, such as weather conditions. Those who view the hazard as the source of the risk present hazards as neither good nor bad, whereby risks can be generated only by *interaction* with the hazard, as represented earlier in Fig. 2.1 below. The range of hazard categories is further explored in Chapter 6, with a table summarizing the key hazards appearing in Chapter 11.

2.3.3   Risk involves the concept of chance, likelihood and probability, but is different from frequency

Many risk definitions have two central concepts, or pillars (Klinke and Renn, 2001: 161). The first relates to the concept of a *chance* event happening. Chance can be refined by making a judgement of how likely it is to occur, or the probability of occurrence. In theory, the concept of *probability* is the more precise statement of chance, where it can be derived from mathematical modelling and be described in numerical terms, or given a percentage value, such as having a 50% probability of getting heads when flipping a coin. *Likelihood* can be a less precise term and is often expressed more by qualitative statements, such as describing risk events as having a 'high', 'medium' or 'low likelihood' of occurrence. The preference in this work is to use the term likelihood, to reflect the reality that many people making decisions on risk in relation to adventure, sport, events and tourism do so based not on complex mathematical modelling, but more on their own experience and judgement, which is returned to in Chapter 7.

The terms frequency and probability are sometimes used interchangeably in some work, but it is recommended that they are understood as distinct concepts. *Frequency* refers to the number of times an event may have taken place in the past, which can then be used to make an assessment of the probability or likelihood of the event occuring in the future (returned to in Chapter 3).

2.3.4   Risk involves the severity of outcome, consequence or impact of the event

The second key pillar of risk relates to the concept of an *outcome*, which can alternatively be described as *severity*, *consequences*, *magnitude* or *impact*. In relation to risk assessments that focus on work health and safety, it can be common to use the term severity, focusing primarily on the harm or injuries that can occur to identified groups or people. In other areas of risk management, or for those organizations that adopt the symmetric ISO (2009) definition of risk, the preference can be to use one of the other more neutral terms, such as outcome or consequence, with a broader focus not only on *who* can be exposed to injuries, but also *what* can be impacted upon. For example, SPARC (2004) extends the range to consider not only people, but also such factors as reputation, finances and competiveness.

In terms of consequences and who and what is exposed to risk, this can be considered in relation to three key dimensions of risk exposure (returned to in Chapters 6 and 9). The key dimensions are:

- *What assets/components are exposed to risks.* This can relate to key stakeholders (participants, staff, sponsors, community, etc.), buildings, equipment, operational schedules, finances, reputation or brand, and market or league position.
- *How are these assets exposed.* This can relate to physical harm, emotional harm, physical damage to equipment or buildings, loss of building or equipment, operational time delays, financial losses or gains, imprisonment, competiveness slippage or gains, credibility or reputation lost or enhanced.
- *Degree of risk exposure.* This relates to relative stake of investment, client attributes (e.g. children compared with adults), the time invested and degree of captive investment (i.e. a building, such as a hotel, in a country cannot be moved, whereas some services have no physical investment in buildings or equipment).

So, while for health and safety assessments the primary focus is on people, it is of interest how easy it is to extend the analysis to consider a broader range of factors, which is a critical part of project and strategic assessments. What is argued in this book is that when engaging with the risk process, consideration should be given to a broader range of exposure areas for three key reasons, which are:

- *Saving time.* If time is being spent reflecting and analysing the risk of an activity for a work-related safety risk assessment, then it can make sense to extend the analysis to other areas of risk to ensure quality is maintained and objectives achieved.
- *More effective communication.* Attempting to use a broadly similar risk approach for all levels of management can mean the communication of risk to key stakeholders is easier.
- *Risk–benefit approach.* Using the term severity tends to skew the focus towards the negative outcomes such as injuries, damage and loss (the asymmetric risk definitions) and may encourage simple risk avoidance behaviour; yet as discussed in Chapter 1, it is important that the benefits of undertaking the risks are understood, together with giving a broader consideration to what may be impacted on.

2.4 BRINGING THE CONCEPTS TOGETHER: THE ANATOMY OF RISK MODEL

From the discussion so far, certain preferences have been identified for which concepts should be used in risk management practices. These concepts can be represented in a simple model to help illustrate how they relate to each other, shown in Fig. 2.1. It is framed within a fourth-age risk paradigm or risk culture: this means that risk is considered in terms of likelihood and outcomes, with outcomes presented in relation to possible upside or downsides risks (the two arrows in Fig. 2.1), categorized around the exposure categories identified in Section 2.3.4, such as physical impacts, financial impacts, etc.

The model also uses the concept of a *neutral hazard*, whereby risks are generated when people and activities *interact* with these hazards (the star burst symbol in Fig. 2.1). These hazardous events are sometimes described as *perils* (Fitzgerald, 2003: 29); a term more frequently used in the insurance industry, but will not be used here because of the skew it can give towards the negative risks. The reason for representing the source and cause separately is to allow for a deeper analysis of the potential hazards and risks, whereby risks are considered as embedded in a complex array of system factors (sometimes known as the *recipe of chaos*).

The model also utilizes the concept of a *trigger*, *spark* or *catalyst* event (the lightning symbol in Fig. 2.1). McKerlvey and Andriani (2010) elaborate on this concept of a *trigger event* in their discussion about how risk events 'incubate', smouldering away unnoticed, but then needing a triggering event that acts as the tipping point to initiate a crisis event.

The relationship of these conceptual elements can be illustrated by using a simple analogy of a forest fire. The fire can be regarded as the hazard, which has the potential to be a source of various risks for people. The underlying hazardous *causation conditions or factors* can be a long, dry summer, which dries out the forest, creating large amounts of combustible materials that create the hazardous conditions. The catalyst or trigger could be a lightning strike or a dropped cigarette, with the consequence that a hazardous event occurs: the actual forest fire. This fire can be a source of various risks when the fire bisects (the *point of interaction*) with people, generating risks such as loss of life or property. The hazardous event can be analysed in terms of likelihood of occurrence and assessed in terms of outcomes, which in this case could relate to the cost of a home being burnt down, or the physical dangers presented to individuals. Any control measures that a park authority may have in place can affect the likelihood of certain risks and the severity of the outcomes; for example: do they let forest fires burn as they are a necessary part of the ecosystem? Have they placed fire breaks to help minimize the potential damage? Can they evacuate people quickly? Although such an event may be viewed in negative terms, it should be noted that forest fires are in fact a necessary part of many forest ecosystems and so produce many upsides, such as allowing new growth to develop.

2.5 COMPARING THE PRACTICAL PROCESSES OF RISK MANAGEMENT

Having established a number of the key conceptual constructs which can be used in risk management and which can help form a risk culture, next comes the practical process of risk management. As with the risk definitions, many variations in terminology can be found, so it is important to briefly identify and clarify a number of key terms and concepts as they are used in this book. To do this, a number of examples of how the different risk management process stages can be represented are presented and compared in Table 2.2.

The intention of Table 2.2 is to show both the variations in terminology, together with identifying if there are core elements that are relevant for the different levels of risk management, whether this relates to a safety assessment or a project one. When comparing these examples a number of important observations can be made, which are:

- All of the examples have a process stage (somewhere) that involves *identifying* hazards and risks.
- There is usually a stage relating to the analysis and assessment of risks.
- *Risk analysis* can be considered as the process that involves the deeper exploration of different factors in relation to causation, triggers, hazard interactions, etc., which can be done using a variety of analytical tools (see Chapter 4).
- *Risk assessment* or evaluation is the part of the process where the analysis is interpreted in order to try and give some form of measurement to the risks, often in relation to likelihood and impacts (see Chapter 6).
- The examples highlight the need to develop clear *controls, responses, formulate strategies* or ways to *treat* the risks. Although this is sometimes also called *risk management*, the preference here is not to use it to refer to a single process stage, but as the term that denotes and

Table 2.2. Comparison of risk process stages.

Subject field	Stage 1	Stage 2	Stage 3	Stage 4	Stage 5 +
Operational health and safety (HSE, 2012) UK	Look for hazards	Decide what can be harmed	Evaluate the risk from the hazards/decide if precautions are adequate	Record your findings	Review
Sport and leisure safety (CISMPA, 2014) UK	Identify the hazards	Decide who might be harmed and how and decide on precautions	Evaluate the risks and decide on them	Record your findings and implement them	Review your assessment and update if necessary
Sport and recreational, general (Vicsport, 2012) Australia	Make a commitment	Identify general risk areas	Identify specific risks	Evaluate the risks	
Project Management Institute (Heldman, 2005: 13)	Risk identification: collecting and reviewing data	Qualitative risk analysis: focusing on the consequences of risks	Quantitative risk analysis: focusing on the probability assessment side	Risk response planning	Risk monitoring and control
Business/insurance (Rejda, 2010)	Identify loss exposure	Analyse the loss exposure	Select appropriate techniques for loss exposure/risk controls (avoidance, prevention, reduction) and risk financing	Implement and monitor the risk management programme	

(Continued)

Table 2.2. Continued.

Subject field	Stage 1	Stage 2	Stage 3	Stage 4	Stage 5 +
Business management (Turnbull Report, 1999)	Setting objectives	Identifying significant risks	Ranking and prioritizing	Manage risks and control strategies	5. Monitor 6. Improve
Adventure (Brown, 1999: 277)	Risk awareness	Risk evaluation (frequency and severity)	Risk adjustment or control (retain, reduce, transfer or avoid)	Risk management plan	Plan evaluation and update
Event project management (Getz, 1997: 241)	Identification, hazard assessment	Comparative analysis of the risks	Predicting possible hazards	Evaluate probability of occurrence	5 .Categorize the risks (e.g. high/low/ medium) 6. Opportunities and threats of the risks 7. Formulate strategies (take, transfer, terminate, reduce)
	Identification of the risks				

encompasses *all* of the risk process stages, which is in line with how various international standards may use the term.

- Some of the examples give a useful *context* stage, which can: (i) clarify the purpose of the activity, project or strategy; (ii) involve consultation of the key stakeholders; and (iii) even clarify the commitment to risk management by managers.

- A *monitoring* stage is essential, whereby it can often be represented as a constant part of the process, running alongside the other stages at the same time.

2.6 DEVELOPING A SYNTHESIZED RISK PROCESS

The previous comparisons help to identify a number of critical process stages that must be conducted, represented in Fig. 2.2. Although it was highlighted that different terminology may be applied to describe a process stage, the critical point is that certain key actions must be engaged with at some point in the risk management process. It should also be appreciated that the headings in Fig. 2.2 are broad, designed to encapsulate many subsidiary actions or *nested processes* that need to be done, examples of which appear in Table 2.3. The model and table are relevant for all levels of management, ranging from conducting a workplace health and safety risk assessment, to developing an event project plan or conducting a strategic review. Each of these stages is explained in more detail in the subsequent discussion.

Stage 1 focuses on attempting to understand the nature of the organization, its purpose, what the activity is being done for (or its objectives) and beginning to identify the key risk exposure areas (the *who*, *what* and *how* dimensions of risk exposure discussed in the Section 2.3.4). In Table 2.3 a checklist of questions is given of some of the key points that can be considered at this stage. The checklist shows that there are many types of questions which can be asked and ways of collecting information. For example, the notion of key stakeholders can be considered beyond those who are not directly involved in the activity, such as the local community, sponsors and shareholders, where it can be just as important to consider which groups may be

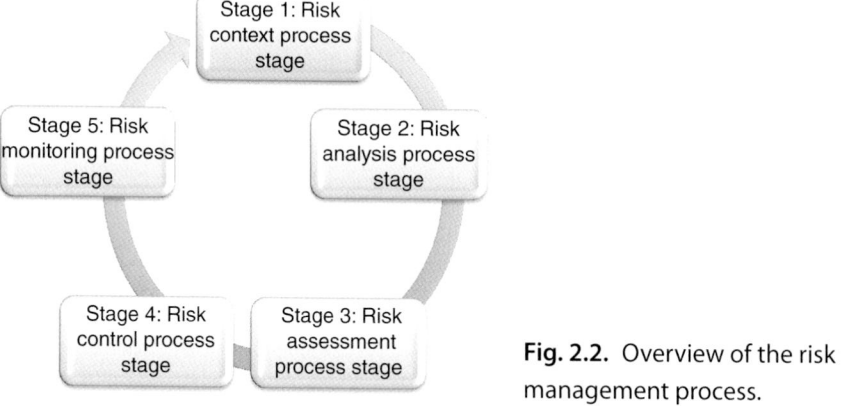

Fig. 2.2. Overview of the risk management process.

Table 2.3. Checklist of actions for each process stage.

	What needs to be considered
Stage 1: Context	What is the nature of the organization? • Is it a commercial profit-oriented organization, or a public or voluntary organization with social objectives? Any interest or concerns over issues of sustainability and ethical behaviour?
	Who is at risk? (stakeholder analysis) • Staff and customers involved with the activity (essential for health and safety regulatory compliance). Consider physical, psychological and social well-being • Are there other stakeholders to consider? Can consider managers, trustees, sponsors, local community, fans, investors, shareholders, etc. (more for strategic assessments as part of good governance and planning)
	What is at risk and how? • Physical objects (e.g. equipment and buildings); reputation (e.g. brand and associations, credibility); finances (e.g. losses and gains); competition (e.g. rankings); ethical considerations; operational time scales, etc.
	Degree of risk exposure? • How much has been invested? Degree of captive investment, etc.
Stage 2: Analysis	Identifying key risks • Builds on stage 1 in relation to who and what is at risk
	Identifying key hazards • Surfaces, equipment, people, buildings, natural environment, etc. For more complex project/strategic assessments, PESTLE factors can be considered
	Job hazard analysis (JHA), if needed • Used more in America for analysing manual jobs, such as operating a machine in a factory, where people are exposed to hazards and risks (Swartz, 2001)
	Identifying key causation factors • Equipment, organizational culture, people, communications, external environmental conditions
	Identifying any triggers • Sudden changes in environmental conditions such as change in weather, government action, etc.
	Analysing the relationships of factors (use different tools and techniques, such as scenario writing)
	Identifying and analysing suitable indicators of causation

(Continued)

Table 2.3. Continued.

	What needs to be considered
Stage 3: Assessment	Assessing type of impacts and severity
	Assessing likelihood
	Applying assessment scales to represent or categorize the risk (e.g. high, low, medium)
Stage 4: Control	Prioritizing resources (use of assessment scales?)
	Reviewing points where control measures can be put in place (review previous analysis)
	Type of control measure (e.g. new systems/cultural practices, new equipment)
	Measures to remove or reduce negative risk events occurring
	Measures to reduce severity of impact
	Summarizing information on a risk form or checklist
	• Producing action checklists and communicating to key stakeholders
Stage 5: Monitor	Review checklists, forms, assessments and analysis
	• Set dates for reviewing data/activities, performance indicators, or as conditions change
	Amend control measures

adversely affected by the activity as those who benefit (JISC, 2012). The various ways information can be collected is explained in Chapters 3 and 4.

The questions relating to the organization and activity purpose represent a particularly important area to consider, as it can have significant effects on the nature of the risk exposure. For example, companies that set themselves up as being ethically responsible can experience more damage to their brand if they are found to be complicit in activities which undermine human rights or damage the environment. This damage to reputation, in turn, can have many profound financial repercussions. Other areas to consider can be to reflect on the type of clients and how the risk exposure can vary, such as the differences between having adults compared with children as the key users of a service.

Stage 2 relates to the *analysis* of the hazards and risks. Of all the stages, this can be the most complex and difficult stage to implement effectively, which is illustrated by the range of checklist tasks and questions given in Table 2.3. While the identification of risks and hazards is not always that difficult, trying to understand how the different anatomy of risk elements (see Fig. 2.1) interact with each other can be challenging to say the least; hence it is returned to in Chapter 4.

Stage 3 relates to *assessing* risk and is based on the analysis already conducted. This stage is designed to give an assessment, measure or value to the identified risks, such as in relation to their likelihood and the type of impact. Just how this assessment is presented varies considerably. For example, one can find instances where risk is given a simple descriptor of high, medium or low; alternatively, more complex scales are used, such as using a percentage scale where both the probability and outcome are given a rating. This is another complex area and it is returned to in Chapter 3, where the theory of frequency profiling is looked at, and in Chapter 6, where different scales are examined in relation to designing forms.

Stage 4 considers how risks are controlled. Ultimately, this is what the whole purpose of risk management is about. In essence, *control* measures look to reduce or remove the likelihood of occurrence, or deal with the severity of consequences. Information gathered from the earlier analysis stage (stage 2) should give an indication of where the control measures should be put in place, such as how to remove trigger events, dealing with certain causation factors or how hazards should be managed. The assessment scales can help focus and prioritize resources.

Finally, *stage 5* involves *monitoring* and reviewing what has taken place and the impact any control measures has made. Although the monitoring and review stage is presented as a separate stage, it is important to appreciate that the aspect of monitoring and reviewing should be considered as something which constantly takes place. It is the reason why in some examples of risk process stages, monitoring is not presented as a separate stage, but as running alongside all the stages. In essence, monitoring and reviewing will be done in response to changing operating or environmental conditions, such as a change in the weather or political situation, or on set time periods for review, such as an annual review and update of any risk registers, or when key performance indicators (discussed in Chapter 3) are reviewed.

Although the process stages are presented in a sequential fashion, in practice the application of these process stages should be viewed in a cyclical, dynamic manner, where the work done at each of the process stages can often overlap. But what it does show is that at times, particularly for more complex projects and risk assessments, a more considered and deeper analysis is needed where a variety of analytical tools (see Chapter 4) can be employed, which then allows for a more thoughtful assessment to take place to help decide on the control measures.

2.7   CONTEXTUALIZATION TO THE INDUSTRY SECTORS

In this section, the anatomy of risk concepts and some of the key process stages are applied to the different industry sectors. They are derived from mind maps which have helped distil or identify a range of possible hazards, risks and risk factors that can be considered when initially engaging with the process stages 1 and 2. In terms of the risk culture, the approach is framed by the fourth-age risk paradigm, so that the possible benefits of undertaking the activity are considered (upside and downside risks) together with considering how the risks may be embedded in a complex network of causation factors.

2.7.1   Adventure contextualization

The following examples of the anatomy of risk concepts and some of the process stage elements can be considered in relation to a variety of non-specific outdoor adventure-related activities.

- *Context*: consideration given to the nature of the organization, such as if it is committed to sustainable policies or fair trading. Is it a profit-based organization or a charity? Key stakeholders can relate to target markets, company owners, the local community and those responsible for the natural environment. Exposure can also change depending on the country operated in, the client attributes and the type of activity. For example, the risk exposure for a trekking expedition in the Himalayas will be much higher for an organization conducting a school expedition, compared with doing a tour for a group of experienced, highly skilled mountaineers. In turn, this understanding of the different dimensions of exposure influences the risk tolerance levels, so in the case of the experienced mountaineers, the tolerance for taking risks will be much higher.
- *Examples of hazards*: weather (hot weather, cold weather, storms, rain, etc.); natural environment (mountains, rivers, the sea, etc.); activity equipment (canoes, climbing gear, surf boards, bikes, etc.); people (behaviour, attitudes, conduct, etc.); political conditions (e.g. terrorism, riots, wars, taxation, etc.).
- *Examples of benefits/upsides*: positive emotional experiences from which to relate learning experiences; satisfaction of doing challenging activities; satisfaction and repeat business.
- *Examples of downside risks*: groups become lost; physical injuries to group members; sunstroke; hypothermia; death; kidnapping and attacks; animal bites/attacks; reputational damage to the business; equipment loss and damage; financial losses, etc.
- *Examples of underpinning causation factors*: level of challenge; changing environmental conditions; level of skill of participants; level of expertise and qualifications of the leaders or instructors; quality of incident protocols; methods of communication, etc.
- *Examples of triggers*: equipment failures (e.g. rope snapping); sudden environmental changes (e.g. freak gust of wind, lightning); political turmoil (e.g. elections, arrests).

2.7.2   Project event contextualization

Risk is an inherent part of all parts of project management as highlighted in Chapter 1. The following factors focus on a generic range of hazards and risks for a sport or music event that may take place in a stadium.

- *Context*: is the event for profit, raising brand awareness or promoting a city/country? Key stakeholders can relate to players, fans/spectators, sponsors, local community, local businesses, police, stadium owners, etc. The exposure elements will be affected by the scale of the event, its project time scales and the size of the stake or the investment. In the earlier stages there can be more uncertainty, but less to lose; however, as the event date nears more time, money and reputation has been invested, so in theory while the uncertainty may be less, there could be more to lose.

- *Examples of hazards*: weather; stadium structures; players and officials; traffic and transport; thieves; protestors; competitors; physical barriers and stairwells; terrorists, political tensions and controversies; wars and conflicts; environmental disasters; outside contractor failures (e.g. failure to supply service or deliver equipment); spectators (e.g. pitch invasions, throwing objects).
- *Examples of benefits/upsides*: enjoyment of a shared experience; opportunities for advertisement and brand awareness; seeing the best performers; economic activity and job creation; city, region or country promotion.
- *Examples of downside risks*: people being crushed; physical injuries; litter and environmental damage; equipment failures; event delays or cancellations; project schedule time delays; theft; physical attacks on players; brand and reputational damage; disruptions by protestors; sponsor logos covered up (by accident, such as fans draping their flags on advertising hoardings, or by design which can be an example of ambush marketing); bribery or corruption allegations damaging the brand and attractiveness to sponsorship; direct terrorist attack on the event (e.g. Munich 1972); indirect terrorist attack (e.g. the 2001 terrorist attacks on New York resulted in many sport events being cancelled); racism damaging sport or country reputation.
- *Examples of underpinning causation factors*: numbers of people; mood of the crowd; uniqueness of the event; demand for the event; what's at stake (e.g. cup final place); effectiveness of communication systems; quality of the built environment, such as the stadiums; business environmental conditions (e.g. PESTLE) that can affect the viability of staging the event; management culture.
- *Examples of triggers*: equipment failures; death or injury of an individual; failure of communication systems; external environmental triggers can relate to economic collapses or the death of key political figures.

2.7.3 Sport and leisure contextualization

The following examples of the anatomy of risk concepts and some of the process stage elements can be considered in relation to a variety of small-scale sport and leisure activities.

- *Context*: is the activity for profit, or to achieve wider social objectives such as health, or for skill development? Key stakeholders can include participants, coaches, teachers, governing bodies, parents, facility owners, etc. An important part of sport is the uncertainty of outcome, which can affect the risk exposure.
- *Examples of hazards*: equipment (e.g. balls, sticks or bats); players; spectators and fans; seating and fencing; nets and barriers. Note also differences between indoor and outdoor sports, or invasion (e.g. football, rugby and hockey) and non-invasion (e.g. athletics) sports, or land- and water-based activities.

- *Examples of benefits/upsides*: physical, social and mental health and well-being; key source of stimulation; enjoyment; building sport foundations for future elite athletes; welfare impacts and gains; facilities with leisure features can attract more families, etc.
- *Examples downside risks*: injuries such grazes, broken/dislocated limbs, spinal injuries, etc.; damage or loss of property; games abandoned or postponed; violent attacks on participants; sexual, emotional or physical abuse by coaches; reputational damage to the sport and governing body; drug taking impacting on health of the individual and reputation for the sport.
- *Examples of underpinning causation factors*: communications failures; poor risk cultures; entrenched coaching practices that may be prejudiced or dangerous; referee control; design of play/pool spaces; lapses in supervision; history of previous encounters or animosity; financial pressures prioritized over safety ones; fitness levels of participants; use of safety equipment; risk homeostasis (discussed in Chapter 6); ignoring medical evidence or good practice.
- *Examples of triggers*: game incident; poor tackle; sudden change in weather; referee decisions; abuse by spectators; equipment failures; media investigations, etc.

2.7.4 Tourism contextualization

Tourism is a complex, diverse industry covering many different areas of operation. It is still, however, possible to identify some common generic type of hazards and risks as illustrated here.

- *Context*: the type of organization and its operational ethos can be important, such as whether it is an organization that has made a commitment for responsible tourism; is it a commercial or charitable enterprise? Key stakeholders can relate to: tour operators, customers, local community, support services, etc. What type of assessment is it for (e.g. seeking new markets in developing countries or a safety tour assessment)? The exposure areas can be affected by the type of tourism product or service, such as the degree of captive investment, the type of country operated in or the client attributes. The nature of the clients and the stake invested in a holiday (i.e. if it is a significant part of the disposable income) may mean that many clients may be more risk averse.
- *Examples of hazards*: weather, the natural environment and terrain; water, ranging from pools to the sea; transport used; wildlife and diseases; terrorists and criminal gangs; government policies; war and political instability; natural disasters; other group members.
- *Examples of benefits/upsides*: physical, social and mental well-being; excitement from the discovery of unfamiliar environments; stimulation; job creation; social community projects helping others, etc.
- *Examples of downside risks*: personal injury or death; financial loss for individuals or organizations; cancellations of holidays; food poisoning; kidnapping; bribery; reputational or brand damage; local communities exploited; transport accidents; damage or loss of building or equipment.
- *Examples of underpinning causation factors*: poor safety regulations; natural environmental operating conditions changing; contracting out to third parties; poor communication of risks; political turmoil and demonstrations; government policies, etc.

- *Examples of triggers*: political unrest in response to an event, such as someone dying, being murdered or arrested; tensions between countries; contamination of food or water.

2.8   CONCLUSION

So risk is everywhere, in many forms, and continues to grow as a management practice. It is both a concept used to explain our world and a practical management activity to deal with it. Yet despite this ubiquity in usage and regulatory requirement, this does not mean there is one single practical process and language of risk. And here lies the problem. One could pick up a variety of books that have the word 'risk' in the title and find that they will define risk clearly and with authority; yet when compared with other definitions, they can in fact use different descriptions or terms for certain key concepts relating to risk management. It is a difference that does not always have clear logic to it, as variations can be time bound, or simply following past practices, rather than a vital necessity to define and approach risk in a particular way.

The preference in this work is to define risk symmetrically, as part of the fourth-age risk paradigm, whereby risk can be both opportunistic and threatening, rather than the simplistic definition that focuses on danger, harm and loss. Furthermore, this paradigm also embeds the analysis of risk as part of a complex system. As part of the representation and understanding of risk, it is considered to have two key attributes: likelihood and consequence. Risk is also considered in relation to how it interacts with hazards. Although the concept of hazard is commonly used in operational health and safety assessments, it is less frequently referred to in project and strategic assessments. There is, however, no reason why the concept cannot be used in project and strategic risk assessments. Using the concept of a hazard helps to focus on sources of risk and causation factors (the recipe of chaos), which can be extended to consider a range of hazards generated by the political, economic or natural environment (i.e. the external business environment).

What this chapter ultimately illustrates is that it is possible to develop more coherent approaches to a variety of risk management activities, ranging from operational safety, project and strategic risk assessments. The approaches are also adaptable for any sector in any country, where they can be refined depending on any specific country regulations or standards of best practice.

DISCUSSION QUESTIONS AND TASKS

1. Write down what you understand about risk, or reflect on how your views and understanding of risk may have changed after reading this chapter.
2. Conduct a simple Internet search looking for risk definitions. What emerges in relation to how they are defined and how do they compare with the approaches used in this book?

3. For an activity of your choice, try and identify as many hazards as you can, along with how people or the organization may interact with them to generate opportunistic or threatening risks.

4. Scan the news for an incident relating to a chosen industry sector and apply the anatomy of risk concepts. Ensure you try and analyse causation in relation to a complex interaction of factors.

REFERENCES

AS/NZS (2009) *AS/NZS ISO 31000:2009 Risk Management – Principles and guideline.* Joint Australia/New Zealand Committee OB-007.

Aven, T. and Renn, O. (2009) On risk defined as an event where the outcome is uncertain. *Journal of Risk Research* 12, 1–11.

Brown, T.J. (1999) Adventure risk management. In: Miles, J.C. and Priest, S. (eds) *Adventure Programming.* Venture Publishing, State College, Pennsylvania, pp. 273–284.

Cloutier, R. (2002) The business of adventure tourism. In: Hudson, S. (ed.) *Sport and Adventure Tourism.* Haworth Hospitality Press, New York, pp. 241–272.

CIMSPA (2014) *Risk Assessment Manual 5th Edition (IMSPARAM).* Chartered Institute for the Management of Sport and Physical Activity, Loughborough, UK.

Fitzgerald, P. (2003) *Risk Management Guide for Tourism Operators.* Canadian Tourism Commission, Ottawa.

Frosdick, S. (1997a) Risk as blame. In: Frosdick, S. and Walley, L. (eds) *Sport and Safety Management.* Butterworth-Heinemann, London, pp. 33–66.

Frosdick, S. (1997b) Managing risk in public assembly facilities. In: Frosdick, S. and Walley, L. (eds) *Sport and Safety Management.* Butterworth-Heinemann, London, pp. 273–291.

Gardiner, P.D. (2005) *Project Management: A Strategic Planning Approach.* Palgrave Macmillan, Basingstoke, UK.

Getz, D. (1997) *Event Management & Event Tourism.* Cognizant Communication, New York.

Heldman, K. (2005) *Project Manager's Spotlight on Risk Management.* Harbor Light Press, Alameda, California.

HSE (2001) Reducing Risks, Protecting People, HSE's Decision-Making Process. Available at: http://www.hse.gov.uk/risk/theory/r2p2.pdf (accessed 12 July 2013).

HSE (2012) Frequently asked questions. Available at: http://www.hse.gov.uk/risk/faq.htm#q7 (accessed 5 May 2013).

Irwin, W.T. (1998) Political risk: a realistic view toward assessment, quantification, and mitigation. In: Moran, T.H. (ed.) *Managing International Political Risk.* Blackwell Publishers, Oxford, pp. 57–69.

Jablonowski, M. (2001) Thinking in numbers. *Risk Management Magazine* 48(2), 30–36.

JISC (2012) A 5 step risk management model. Available at: http://www.jiscinfonet.ac.uk/infokits/risk-management/five-step-model/ (accessed 12 July 2013).

Klinke, A. and Renn, O. (2001) Precautionary principles and discursive strategies; classifying and managing risks. *Journal of Risk Research* 4, 159–173.

Knight, F.H. (1921) *Risk, Uncertainty and Profit.* Houghton Mifflin Co., Boston, Massachusetts.

Lupton, D. (1999) *Risk.* Routledge, London.

ISO (2009) *Risk Management – Principles and Guidelines.* International Organization for Standardization, Geneva, Switzerland.

McKerlvey, B. and Andriani, P. (2010) Avoiding extreme risk before it occurs: a complexity science approach to incubation. *Risk Management* 12, 54–82.

Piekarz, M.J. (2009) Tourism in an unstable and complex world? Searching for a relevant risk paradigm and model for tourism organisations. PhD thesis, Cranfield University, Cranfield, UK.

PMI (2000) *A Guide to the Project Management Body of Knowledge*. Project Management Institute, Newtown Square, Pennsylvania.

Rejda, G.E. (2010) *Principles of Risk Management and Insurance*. Pearson Education, London.

Sadgrove, K. (1997) *The Complete Guide to Business Risk Management*. Gower, Aldershot, UK.

SPARC (2004) Risk management of events. Available at: http://www.sportnz.org.nz/managing-sport/guides/risk-management-for-events (accessed 20 August 2014).

Swartz, G. (2001) *Job Hazard Analysis: A Guide to Identifying Risks in the Workplace*. Government Institutes, Rockville, Maryland.

Tarlow, P.E. (2002) *Event Risk Management and Safety*. Wiley, New York.

Turnball Report (1999) *Internal Control: Guidance for Directors on the Combined Code*. Financial Reporting Council, London.

Vicsport (2012) Sport and injury risk management. Available at: http://www.vicsport.asn.au/Risk-Management/Sport-Injury-Risk-Management/ (accessed 3 May 2012).

FURTHER READING

Frosdick (1997b: 275) provides some really useful discussion and insights into stadium hazards, risk, stakeholders and understanding the deeper roots for previous UK stadium disasters

'The Green Guide' (5th edition) relating to stadium event safety, available via the SGSA website at: http://www.safetyatsportsgrounds.org.uk/publications/green-guide

The International Organization for Standardization (ISO) has a variety of useful publications, available at: http://www.iso.org/iso/home.html

Responsible tourism gives some interesting information about the awards it gives, available at: http://www.responsibletravel.com/awards/

Sport New Zealand has many invaluable materials relating to risk management. For example, the publications on risk and event risk management give many practical tips, available at: http://www.sportnz.org.nz/

Standards New Zealand (2004) New Zealand Handbook: Guidelines for Risk Management in Sport and Recreation. SNZ HB8669:2004. Available at: http://www.sportnz.org.nz/assets/Uploads/attachments/managing-sport/strong-organisations/Risk-Management-Toolkit.pdf (accessed 20 August 2014)

US Department of Homeland Securityy (2008) Evacuation Planning Guide for Stadiums, available at: http://www.dhs.gov/sites/default/files/publications/Evacuation%20Planning%20Guide%20for%20Stadiums.pdf

chapter 3

Key Theories Underpinning Risk Management

CHAPTER OBJECTIVES

- To understand the key scientific theories which have underpinned risk definitions, processes and practices.
- To explain the theory of probability and how it can be used by practitioners.
- To explain how chaos and complexity theory have influenced more recent theoretical understanding of risk management.
- To contextualize and relate the theories to the industry sectors.

Key concepts

Interpretivism and positivism; laws of probability; frequency versus probability; chaos and complexity theory; edge of chaos; social construction of risk; Heinrich's incident triangle; evidence-based arguments.

3.1   INTRODUCTION

Does risk exist? After all that has been discussed, this may seem a strange question to pose at the beginning of this chapter. The reason it is done so is in recognition that risk is a contested subject, where some writers question the extent that risk can be truly measured in a rational, scientific manner.

This chapter therefore explores these differences in the scientific communities and how they have influenced risk management. It then moves on to discuss a number of key theoretical constructs that are important to understand, not only to try and help improve risk management processes, but also to gain an insight into why certain risk practices are used. An important part of this discussion is the critical review of some of the common practices used in risk management, which are grounded in a traditional scientific approach. This is not done to undermine some of the prevailing methods used in risk management, but to explain why certain concepts, theories and practices are utilized, together with giving managers an appreciation of the strengths and weaknesses of these approaches.

3.2   THE CONTESTED NATURE OF RISK

Simply put, there are two contrasting scientific approaches that influence how risk is studied and understood. Bernstein, in his invaluable book on the historical development of risk theory and practice, tries to encapsulate the differences between these two positions, saying:

> The story I have to tell is marked all the way through by persistent tension between those who assert that the best decisions are based on quantification and numbers, determined by patterns of the past, and those who base their decisions on more subjective degrees of belief about the uncertain future ... The issue boils down to one's view about the extent to which the past determines the future. We cannot quantify the future because it is unknown, but we have learned to use numbers to scrutinize the past. But to what degree should we rely on the patterns to tell us what the future will be like? Which matters more when facing risk, the facts as we see them or our subjective belief in what lies hidden in the void of time? (Bernstein, 1998: 6)

Broadly speaking, these two scientific traditions identified by Bernstein can be described as the *positivist* scientific school and the *interpretivist* scientific school. The positivist position relates to Bernstein's group who believes that decisions should be made on the basis of collecting past data and studying the patterns to help quantify risks. This position is still best encapsulated by Lord Kelvin's (the 19th century British mathematician and physicist) argument that if anything exists, then it exists in some quantity and can therefore be measured and so verified (Adams, 1995: 10; citing Beers, 1967). This scientific approach tends to be associated with the natural sciences, such as physics, chemistry and biology, and forms a key scientific underpinning for areas such as engineering and medicine which have always strived to try and quantify risk (Frosdick, 1997: 34). A crucial part of this position is the belief that it is possible to identify, observe and measure the world in an objective or unbiased manner, which can allow for better analysis to underpin management decisions, sometimes described as *evidence-based arguments*. As part of this tradition the distinction is sometimes made between:

- *Objective risk*. This is defined as the experts' or scientists' assessment of risk, who make probability risk assessments in an unbiased, emotionally free manner, usually based on statistical evidence. There can be a belief that this type of risk assessment is one which is more accurate (Pedersen, 1997: 756) and therefore more trusted, although as will be discussed later others are more sceptical about how unbiased they actually are.

- *Subjective/perceived risk.* This is defined as the lay person's or non-expert assessment, which can be biased or distorted by the person's preconceived views, emotions, experiences or a lack of information. Where subjective risk assessments contest the scientific objective assessments, Adams (2011: 90) describes this as *virtual risks*, which represent areas that are contested between scientific research and people's direct experiences, or even perceptions of fear.

- *Inherent/real risks.* This is defined as the risks closely associated with the activity, but which cannot be removed without destroying the essence of the activity. Geary (1996), adapting these concepts for adventure activities, uses the term *real risk* to refer to two types of risk: (i) *subjective real risks*, referring to risks that can be controlled through skill, judgement and equipment; and (ii) *objective real risks*, referring to risks that cannot be controlled, such as a rock fall.

The interpretivist scientific position relates to the social sciences, particularly sociology and anthropology. This position contests and disputes a number of the underpinning principles of positivism, arguing that the world is socially constructed, complex and the idea of objectivity difficult to attain. They are sceptical about the extent that risks can actually be identified and objectively measured, as it can be near impossible to remove all emotions, experiences and preconceptions when analysing and assessing risks (Frosdick, 1997: 34).

Cahn (1994) gives a variety of examples of how, at the turn of the 20th century, conservative forces who opposed women participating in sport would draw on evidence from 'experts' and the science of biology and medicine to construct arguments based around the risks women who played sport could be exposed to. These encompassed such things as: the dangers to the female body, such as reproductive damage and the loss of sexual control; strenuous sport leading to depression and the lessening of inhibitions and physiological control during the fluctuations of puberty and menstruation; and the emotional and sexual dangers of the 'over-enthusiastic' athlete (Cahn, 1994: 45). These examples Cahn offers are striking and are now seen as ludicrous, but because they were presented by some doctors or scientists at the time, they were sometimes given the status of an objective assessment or truth, and so carried greater weight and credibility. The reality was that such arguments were simply based on subjective prejudices, not research, but dressed up in the language of science. Use of such arguments of the various risks to women to justify exclusion has steadily been deconstructed, but not eradicated in some countries, as witnessed by the controversy surrounding Saudi Arabia and Saudi women being allowed to participate in the 2012 Olympics for the first time. In Saudi Arabia, the Ministry of Education (who in theory could present itself in its country as a holder of the objective assessment) has consistently banned women from physical education based on various risk rationales, such as it can lead to 'corruption of morals, lesbianism, making them masculine and damaging female health' (Nafjan, 2012).

Most practitioners in adventure, sport, tourism and events will be blissfully unaware of these two scientific positions, with such discussions appearing sterile and divorced from the actualities of managing businesses. There are, however, a number of reasons why understanding these differences are important, which can be summarized as:

- *Explaining certain practices.* The positivist tradition has tended to dominate many risk management practices, which gives an insight into why there is a belief that hazards and risks can be identified and measured.
- *Explaining why accidents are recorded.* In many countries, safety-related legislation can require any accidents or near misses in workplaces to be recorded. This again reflects the positivist tradition whereby there is a belief that by recording and analysing past events, patterns can be seen which can then help inform future actions to remove or reduce risks.
- *Creating awareness of the limitations of risk management.* While the positivist school has dominated risk theory and practices, the critiques offered by the interpretivists act as a vital counter weight, reminding managers that their decisions can always be prone to error and bias and that scientific or expert opinion about risks can change over time, sometimes because of more research, or sometimes because social attitudes change.

3.3 HOW CAN WE MAKE AN ASSESSMENT OF PROBABILITY OR LIKELIHOOD?

3.3.1. Underpinning concepts

Kaplan and Garrick (1981) distilled the essence of risk analysis based around three simple questions: What can happen? How likely is it to happen? If it does happen, what are the consequences? While it is an approach grounded in the positivist tradition and may not fully convey just how complicated the answers to these questions can be, it does provide a good starting point for beginning any practical risk process.

In Chapter 2 it was noted that the notion of chance, probability or likelihood is an important part of many definitions of risk. Which term is used can depend on the type of assessment; *probability* is often used as the more precise statement of chance, which can be given a percentage value derived from mathematical modelling, while *likelihood* is the less precise term and is often expressed by qualitative statements, such as the high, medium and low risk types of categorization.

In order to make probability or likelihood assessments, data is needed, the amount and quality of which can affect the accuracy of the assessment. This is the research process, where practitioners need information to make evidence-based arguments that inform decisions and actions. Adapting and expanding Boyne's (2003: 3) work, four ways of constructing probability assessments can be identified, with the degree of scientific rigor diminishing as one goes down the list. The methods are:

- *Identification of frequency of past events.* This is the classic method, grounded in positivist scientific methods. Here it can be a process of looking at the frequency of past incidents to try and (i) identify all the key risks, then (ii) build up an assessment of the likelihood of these risk events occurring in the future. It should also be noted that while *frequency* and *probability* are sometimes used interchangeably, these are in fact different concepts, as observing frequency is a means to build up probability estimates. That is to say, by looking at how frequently certain past events have occurred, such as sport injuries, natural disasters, acts of terrorism, etc., data can then be used to estimate or quantify (Stutely, 2002: 224) future likelihood and event severity. The importance of this theory is further illustrated in Boxes 3.1 and 3.2.

Box 3.1. Lloyds of London, the growth of the insurance industry and the impact on risk practices

Lloyds of London began in 1688 when Edward Lloyd, owner of a coffee house, encouraged ship captains and owners to visit his establishment to share shipping news, later published in a paper updated three times a week. It was on the foundation of the information which was shared that the early forms of insurance were developed, whereby the premium paid would be calculated based on such things as the previous safe sailings, along with losses at different times of the year and in different parts of the world. One of the factors explaining Lloyd's early success was that, previously, collecting information about sailing was variable, less accessible and sometimes unreliable. The people meeting at his coffee house could directly share their experiences and give updates, so it provided an environment to get some of the most up-to-date sailing information at the time, which in turn could be used in the (then new) science of statistical mathematical modelling of probability.

The insurance industry has continued to grow and now forms the vital bedrock for modern economies, allowing businesses and people to take risks and so drive economic development. This growth has also given impetus for numerous risk practices, which are underpinned by positivist scientific methods, whereby the statistical estimation of risks (performed by people known as *actuaries*) forms a key part for working out insurance premiums based on the statistical likelihood of risk events occurring and their impacts. In relation to probability analysis for the insurance industry, Rejda (2010: 69) focuses on the probability of an adverse event occurring, which he defines as:

Probability (p) = number of events likely to occur (based on past frequency) × number of units.

He gives the example of a car hire company having 500 vehicles with, on average, 100 suffering physical damage. Therefore the probability is:

P (physical damage) = 100/500 = 0.20 or 20%.

These simple ratios are easy to adapt to a variety of risk situations for adventure, sport, tourism and events provided that one has the relevant data.

Box 3.2. The identification and construction of the risks of concussion in sport

In their book, *League of Denial*, Fainaru-Wada and Fainaru (2013) examine how the American National Football League (NFL), one of the richest bodies in sport, sought to consistently cover up or deny the risk of brain disease that could result from playing the game. The book shows an organization failing in its duty of care to its employees, where commercial interests override the health and safety of the players.

The medical evidence had been building up about the dangers of concussion, particularly from the sport of boxing. The case of a former NFL player, Mike Webster, helped to encapsulate the risks to players and the failures in risk management by the NFL. Mike Webster played football from 1974 to 1990, dying in 2002 at the age of 50. He had been suffering various mental health problems, such as amnesia, dementia and depression, with the post-mortem confirming that he had chronic traumatic encephalopathy (CTE), which is a disease to the brain caused by multiple traumas or knocks. Subsequent post-mortems on other former players confirmed similar findings, building up a case of statistical evidence of the risks. Even the post-mortem of the young professional player, Chris Henry, who died in a car crash aged 26, revealed that he was already exhibiting the early signs of CTE on his brain. The NFL, however, continued to deny the link, even issuing its own medical evidence to counter these claims.

As the medical evidence was built, along with a growing number of individual cases of former players experiencing mental health problems and who were taking the NFL to court, the NFL finally conceded that there was in fact a risk. In 2013 the NFL reached a financial compensation settlement of US$765 million for 4500 former players suffering from various brain-related injuries.

The whole management of the issue has been profoundly damaging for the NFL. The paradox is that while the NFL was motivated to avoid the damaging headlines, all it did was delay the story, with the damage far worse, particularly as it turns out that NFL was aware of the issue for many years before the case of Mike Webster. While in the short term this reputational damage has affected the NFL financially, others have highlighted the long-term strategic risk implications, where the sport is experiencing shrinking participation levels in young people. That reputation has been further eroded in relation to how the NFL has dealt with the issue of players who have committed acts of domestic violence, where once again commercial pressures seemed to override issues of morality and safety.

The issue of concussion is being played out in other sports, such as soccer. For example in the UK, the case of the footballer Jeff Astle, who died in 2002 aged 59, has focused attention on the risks of concussion in football. Astle had suffered from early-onset dementia which, after the post-mortem, the coroner confirmed beyond reasonable doubt had been caused by the damaging effects on his brain of repeatedly heading a

(Continued)

Box 3.2. Continued.

ball during his football career and could be classed as an industry-related disease. The response by the English Football Association (FA) also bears similarities with the NFL, where after issuing assurances to investigate the matter in 2002, little was actually done.

The legal action taken by parents and players in the USA against FIFA (the international governing body of association football), demanding rule changes to reduce the risk of head trauma, primarily around heading the ball, illustrates that this is still very much a live issue – one which the governing bodies of all sports around the world must deal with, particularly when one considers that concussion can be a common injury in many other sports such as rugby and hockey.

- *Identifying frequency of similar events.* For some activities that are new, or have little precedent, looking at the frequency of past events may not be an option, such as tour operators developing services in a new destination, or sports or adventure activities taking place in less familiar environments. Here, what can be done is *comparative analysis*, where data is drawn from other areas to allow inferences to be made about future possible risks. For example, a tour operator looking at a country recovering from war could look at the pattern of tourism development for other countries that have recovered from conflict. Alternatively, a manager of a new sport facility could look at the pattern and frequency of incidents in other sport facilities to try and identify the key hazards and risks for his/her facility.
- *Analysis of specific case studies.* While the previous two examples involve the process of collecting data on many events and incidents, an alternative is to focus on one or two case studies in more detail, which can reveal insights into the factors of causation, the failures in systems and the critical paths that lead to the outcomes of the event. Case studies can also be added (aggregation) for focused comparisons to try and build up statistical profiles, identify patterns of causation and make comparison of the effectiveness of control measures (Boyne, 2003: 11).
- *Professional judgements, heuristics or the guesstimate.* This method is not necessarily any less accurate or useful than the other methods, as it can be based on a great deal of past experience and knowledge (known as *heuristics* and explored in Chapter 7). For example, a sport coach, tour guide or adventure instructor preparing for an activity session may complete a risk assessment form without necessarily having done any research, making a judgement about the key hazards and risks based on his/her own experiences and having done the activity many times before.

It is important to note that in reality practitioners will most likely use a mixture of the above methods in order to help analyse risks and make decisions, whereby the first category represents the ideal and a key foundation for making proper evidence-based decisions, while the last category, which relies more on professional judgement, perhaps best describes what actually occurs in practice. Which method is used will most likely be governed by the degree that the system is closed (all possible outcomes are known), or open and complex (all outcomes cannot be known), together with the resources (e.g. time and money) and the expertise available. Finally, if the opportunity for conducting more detailed statistical data collection arises, then the greater use of statistical tools and concepts (such as exploring probability distributions, the laws of large numbers, bell curves and regression analysis) can add depth to the analysis and accuracy to the assessments. Areas all well served by literature, but which cannot be examined here in this book.

3.4 THE USE OF HEINRICH'S RATIO IN PROBABILITY ANALYSIS

Intimately tied in with all these theories about probability is the development of Heinrich's ratio triangle or incident pyramid. Herbert Heinrich was an American who investigated industrial accidents, publishing a book called *Industrial Accident Prevention, A Scientific Approach* in 1931. One of the key findings related to the idea that for every serious accident, there can be a number of less serious incidents and numerous near misses.

Over the years, this theory and the ratios of serious incidents, minor incidents and near misses have been adapted, one of which can be seen in Fig. 3.1. Brown (1999: 274–275), for example, discusses the benefits of the theory in relation to adventure and the need to collect 'hard facts of incidents and accidents' and writes of the value of recording near misses. The purpose of collecting these 'hard facts', he argues, is to develop confidence intervals based on *empirical distributions*, or data-rich simulations (Klinke and Renn, 2001: 167). That is to say, the patterns observed from past data (i.e. the distributions) can give a sense of what could occur in the future, with the richer the data, in theory, the greater the confidence one can have in

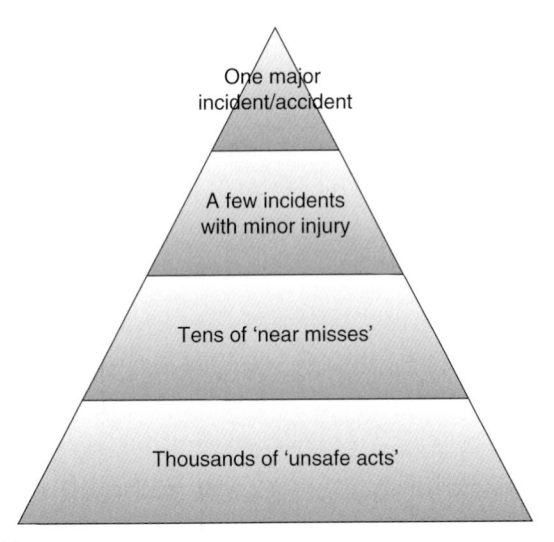

One major
incident/accident

A few incidents
with minor injury

Tens of 'near misses'

Thousands of 'unsafe acts'

Fig. 3.1. Example of a generic incident triangle. (From Parry, 2004; citing Davies and Teasdale, 1994.)

the conclusions. Hence it could be the adventure operator looking at past accidents and incidents on treks in certain destinations; it could be the sport coach who investigates the variety of injuries taking place during a training session; it could be the tour operator investigating patterns of transport incidents in a country; or it could be the event organizer looking at incidents of congestion, falls and crushing.

Practitioners investigating such incidents can use the triangle to develop a likelihood rating for a serious accident, whereby if a serious accident has not taken place, but a number of minor incidents or near misses have, then asking if it is only a question of time before something more serious takes place if practices are not altered. Aspects of this can be explored in Boxes 3.2 and 3.3.

Box 3.3. The risk of death in sport, adventure and recreation

The Bandolier (2014), reviewing a variety of journal articles from around the world, produced the following statistical calculations of the likelihood of death from doing certain recreational activities. While it has many gaps, it gives an insight into how a likelihood assessment could be developed.

Cause of death	Country	Year	Number of deaths	Odds of dying (1 in …)
Base jumping	Norway (Kjerag Massif)	1995–2005	9	2,317 jumps
Swimming	Germany	1997–2006	31	56,587
Cycling	Germany	1997–2006	19	92,325
Running	Germany	1997–2006	18	97,455
Skydiving	USA	2006	21	101,083 jumps
	Sweden	1994–2003	9	125,189
Football	Germany	1997–2006	17	103,187
Hang-gliding	UK			116,000 flights
Tennis	Germany	1997–2006	15	116,945
Sudden cardiac death in a marathon	USA	1975–2005	26	126,626 runners
Horse riding	Germany	1997–2006	10	175,418

(Continued)

Box 3.3. Continued.

Cause of death	Country	Year	Number of deaths	Odds of dying (1 in …)
American football	USA	1994–1999 (average annual figures)	6	182,184
Scuba diving	UK			200,000 dives
Rock climbing	UK			320,000 climbs
Canoeing	UK			750,000 outings
Skiing	USA	2002/2003	37	1,556,757 visits

This approach of calculating odds is easy to adapt using other research. For example, in their investigation into diving accidents Wilks and Davis (2000) produced the following incident data: Queensland Australia, 430,000 dives to one fatality; rest of Australia, 120,000 dives to one fatality; USA, 100,000 dives to one fatality. The point of all the data should be to raise questions in the practitioner's mind during the analysis process stage, such as: what can be deemed an acceptable and tolerable level of risk? Why are there such variations in the ratios? Is it because of the control safety measures in place, or is it because of the different diving conditions? How many minor accidents were there? Can this be mapped out on an incident triangle? Are there examples of good practice that can be learnt and adopted to improve the ratios?

Another interesting observation Wilks and Davis made was that the disappearance of two American divers in 1998 (it was two days before it was realized that they had not got back on board the boat) received a great deal of media attention, focusing on the dive operators and their failings in their duty of care, the results of which had far more impact than any of the statistics (it was also used as the basis for the 2003 film, *Open Water*).

Although the validity of Heinrich's early ratios have been questioned, the underlying principle of a ratio of near misses to actual incidents and serious accidents has been very influential in risk practices, such as the need to record workplace accidents and near-miss incidents to comply with health and safety work or occupation regulations. This practice of recording near misses has also long been adopted in the aviation industry, whereby any incidents the pilot feels could have resulted in a midair collision, or the plane crashing, must be reported to a relevant regulatory authority, dependent on the country in which the airline is based.

The recording of near misses is important because it provides data to analyse, which, over time, can reveal patterns whereby appropriate control mechanisms can be put in place to avoid more serious incidents.

The difficulty with the incident triangle is that while it can initially appear a precise and measurable instrument, in practice it can be difficult to collect the relevant data. Adams (1995: 20) highlights this problem in relation to road accidents, which in theory are a well-documented area of risk, but notes the ambiguity and variations as to what can be deemed a minor accident or a near miss. The many possible variations in answers, Adams argues, mean it can be difficult to develop a precise formula that can answer the question of how many minor accidents may equate to a fatality. The same is true for adventure, sport, tourism and event activities, where just what a *near miss* is can be difficult to identify and record. One could also add that while recording all incidents is attractive in theory, the practicalities of doing this may not be liked by staff, where it may be seen as more paperwork and bureaucracy.

Perhaps the incident triangle's real use is not as an accurate model for identifying risk, but as a cultural mindset to help reflect on incidents. This can be particularly useful in dynamic risk assessments of live situations, whereby coaches, tour leaders, teachers, etc., can draw on their own experiences to help them analyse a current situation. For example, an activity leader for a group of children doing a hill walk may have noticed that a certain part of the route has resulted in slips and minor falls, so that when this area is approached again an adjustment can be made, such as avoiding the area or slowing the group down, in order to avoid the potentially more serious injury that could occur. Similarly, tour or event operators may observe instances of criminality and may take precautionary measures to avoid more serious incidents, such as kidnapping, physical assault or terrorist attack.

3.5   THE PROBLEMS WITH PROBABILITY ESTIMATION

The process of collecting data on past events, to measure and observe patterns in order to help make decisions, is an important foundation for risk management. It is, however, one that should not be accepted without criticism. It is therefore important for practitioners and students of risk management to gain an appreciation of some of the problems, which can be summarized as:

- *Problems of the unexpected 'black swan event'.* Taleb (2007: 117) uses the old philosophical analogy of the black swan to explain a fundamental problem with many systems of risk analysis. The analogy goes that through the counting and observation of swans in Europe, one could collect a huge amount of historical statistical data (the empirical distributions mentioned earlier) which could be used to develop a conclusion that all swans are white. It would, however, need just one example of a black swan to nullify this conclusion (as in fact happened when black swans were in found in Australia). Today, the term *black swan event* is often referred to in relation to the unexpected event that does not fit with any observed patterns and frequency of events; hence accounting for the ease with which one can find examples of organizations, governments and people being caught out by an event that may have no precedent, or is so extreme it does not enter into people's mindset as a possibility of occurrence.

- *Limitations of using previous events*. While looking at past incidents is no doubt invaluable in risk management, relying solely on past data can mean new hazards and risks can be missed. Adams (2011: 99) provides a great deal of useful discussion in this area, using the example of the drunk who searched for his keys in the light of a lamp post where he can see, not in the dark where he last had them. The relevancy of this can be seen in numerous cases, where many of the decisions and actions are simply framed in the light of previous experiences, not in relation to what is possible. Risk, he therefore argues, refers to the future, having no objective existence (Adams, 2011: 99).

- *Problems of a complex system*. While probability can work well in closed, simple management systems, the management of adventure, sport, tourism and event activities is marked by its complexity and difficulty to know all the possible outcomes. It is of interest that despite the large numbers of very sophisticated probability models developed for the financial industry, many of these failed to anticipate the global banking crisis in 2008 which nearly precipitated a global depression. If this is true for finance and banking, then it is certainly true for other industry sectors. Indeed, some writers such as Beck (1998) argue that there are some realms of our world, such as the development of new technologies, which are so complex that they are beyond the realms of realistic probability calculations.

- *Creeping crisis*. Parry (2004: 222) uses Handy's (1990) analogy of frogs, which apparently will jump out of hot water, but will not do so if they are in water that is slowly brought to the boil, because their skin is designed to spot sudden changes in temperatures, not gradual ones. The inference is that a crisis can creep up slowly on an organization and therefore not be spotted. McKerlvey and Andriani (2010) illustrate these ideas differently, with their discussion about 'incubation events', which refers to the idea that various tiny initiating events (TIES) can appear at random and can seem at the time meaningless, or give off a weak warning signal, and so are ignored. The result is a smouldering crisis that just needs a triggering event to lead to an actual crisis event.

- *Decisions are not made just on the basis of probability*. Probability assessments are guides to management actions. As will be examined in Chapter 7, various factors influence our decisions to take or avoid risks. Aven and Renn (2009: 6) note that a probability may be assigned a value of 0.00000001, but it could still be regarded as intolerable. Aven and Renn (2009: 7) use the example of a terrorist attack to explore different facets of their discussion on risk, describing that despite how fragmentary the data can be on terrorism to make accurate probability assessments that does not mean no actions are taken. This is certainly true in relation to the huge and escalating cost of security for large sporting events, where the amounts are justified because of the very low tolerance threshold of a terrorist attack by the public and politicians.

- *Dangers of certainty, false positives and hindsight bias*. Watts (2003) gives an overview of the problems of risk and some of the difficulties with statistical theory. He comments that if one was to toss a coin and, for example, get seven heads on the trot, it would not change the likelihood of obtaining heads or tails as being 50/50. The point of using this old statisticians' question is to remind one that chance has no memory and no matter how many times heads or tails comes up, this does not change the probability; the problem is that people have the capacity to see patterns that are not in fact there, then use this to try and anticipate the future. This is described by Taleb (2007) as being *fooled by randomness*, whereby he argues humans have an amazing capacity to see patterns which do not really exist, so care should be taken about relying on models based on the past to make decisions about the future.

- *Rubbish in, rubbish out.* This refers to the idea that if the data collected are of variable quality, then how can one trust the quality of the conclusions? Boyne (2003: 5) notes this problem, arguing that any estimation of the future is only as good as the quality of the work or data used. In theory, the fewer the cases, the more difficult it is to project or assess probability.

- *Assessments made to legitimize decisions.* In theory risk assessments are done to help make decisions, but what can in fact happen is that data is collected to justify and legitimize decisions that have already been made. This also relates to the earlier point about creating false certainties and seeing patterns and links which do not in fact exist.

These problems do not mean that consideration of probability or likelihood based on an analysis of the frequency of past events should not be done. Far from it. They are highlighted to show some of the inherent weaknesses in many risk theories and models which need to be understood and worked with. Examining past frequency of events to help gauge the likelihood and outcomes is a vital part of the risk process, where numbers can sometimes help with the assessment of risk, but sometimes the analysis of a single case study can give critical insights into the causation and what control measures should be put in place in the future.

3.6   COMPLEXITY THEORY

The lead-up to a crisis event is sometimes represented in a simple linear manner, or a domino effect, where one event precipitates another. When a deeper analysis of various crisis or disaster situations is undertaken, one soon discovers a complex interaction of factors which have often incubated for years. It is because of the importance of trying to understand the dynamic interplay of forces that new risk paradigms have been developed, such as the fourth-age risk paradigm, explained in Chapter 2.

To help understand the value of this approach, it is worthwhile exploring chaos and complexity theory. To deal with chaos theory first, this was initially developed to understand natural systems, such as weather, but it has since been adapted and utilized for many other areas of business, politics and economics. In essence it refers to the idea that systems are interconnected, where small changes can reverberate through the system, eventually leading to more profound changes or even to an extreme unexpected event. This is often encapsulated by the analogy of the butterfly flapping its wings, with the small changes in air currents leading to a hurricane on the other side of the world.

While chaos theory is intimately related to complexity theory, they are not the same things. Simply put, while the world is complex, it is not always chaotic. Furthermore, complexity theory looks to understand aspects of the world as part of a wider system, where many different elements connect and can influence each other. It has been used to try and understand ecosystems, the complex interaction of life forms and natural environmental conditions and how they support and interact with each other. It has been an attractive theory to try and adapt to the world of business and risk.

The relationship is clarified when one considers the idea of businesses operating at the *edge of chaos* (Johnson, 2006: 237), which refers to the theory that business companies try and run their operations so they can adapt, or are agile enough to change practices, as the external business environmental conditions change (such as economic downturns or political changes), meaning they can deal with the downside risks and seize the upside risks. It is a process where change is embraced and which can nurture innovation, with such systems being described as a *complex adaptive system*, because they change as the environmental conditions change. Failure to adapt can mean going out of business, with the example of the dodo used as a metaphor to illustrate this problem: a bird which had become so specialized to its ecosystem that it was unable to adapt when the equilibrium of its environment was disturbed (i.e. humans arriving) and so became extinct.

Writing in the context of tourism, Baggio (2008) argues that most 'real systems' operate on the edge of chaos, which he describes as existing between complexity and chaos, where the systems are always in a condition of 'fragile equilibrium' and on the 'threshold of collapsing into a rapidly changing state'. It is this state, he argues, that limits so many forecasting tourism models which approach the system in a linear, deterministic way.

Complexity and chaos in systems can often be illustrated by what is sometimes described as the *boomerang effect* or the law of unintended consequences. This means that when one brings in a control measure to deal with a risk, it can in fact create a new set of risks. For example, safety equipment brought into sport and adventure activities to reduce the likelihood of injuries, or the severity of impacts, can in fact mean more accidents happen, as people take more risks because they feel emboldened by the safety equipment. See Chapter 7, Box 7.2, for more examples of this effect.

The terms *open* and *closed* systems have been used a number of times already, with the argument developed that management decisions tend to be made in open complex systems, whereby it is impossible to know all the possible outcomes. Baggio (2008: 4) says a system is considered complex if its parts react in non-linear ways, in that there is not a simple pattern of cause and effect. He also makes the distinction between *complex* and *complicated*. A modern car engine he says is complicated, but it can be taken apart and studied and there is a linear composition to it. Complex systems, however, have an adaptive element to them, responding to the environment around them, which perhaps also can help explain why the past is not always the best predictor of the future.

Adams (1995) writes about risk as a general concept applicable to all industries and managers, and is a writer who attempts to place risk within more complex systems. He is critical of the constant attempt to quantify risk in relation to probability, arguing this can often mean that risk is not recognized as operating in complex systems. To illustrate this, he develops the idea of the *risk thermostat* (Adams, 1995, 2011) whereby he embeds risks in a complex web of factors that can interact with each other, going on to argue that decisions about risk should not simply focus on risk avoidance, but also on how taking risks can bring rewards or benefits. He says:

> Overhanging everything are the forces of nature – floods, earthquakes, hurricanes, plagues – that even governments cannot control, although they sometimes try to build defences against them. And fluttering about the dance floor are the Beijing Butterflies beloved of chaos theorists; they ensure that the best laid plans of mice, men and governments gand aft agley (a reference of the Robbie Burns poem, of things going awry or wrong). (Adams, 1995: 23)

While the use of complexity theory has clearly been influential in risk and management literature, the problem is how to turn this theoretical paradigm into something more practical. This turning theory into practical risk management practices is therefore explored in more detail in Chapters 4 and 5.

3.7 CONTEXTUALIZATION TO THE INDUSTRY SECTORS

In this section, a number of the key concepts discussed in this chapter are explored in relation to the different industry sectors and more specific examples. Both the strengths and the weaknesses of the more traditional scientific position are examined which focus on: looking at past events; the social construction of risk; consideration of the more complex interaction of factors; and how systems operate on the edge of chaos.

3.7.1 Adventure incidents

In relation to adventure tourism, a more specific example is focused on an adventure tour that took place in Ethiopia. The people planning the trip wanted to identify some of the hazards and risks, along with gaining an insight into the likelihood of some of these risks. From the preliminary meetings of the expedition members, a variety of hazards and risks were identified which were further informed by other research conducted, such as consulting the UK Foreign and Commonwealth Office, the US Department of State and the Australian Department of Foreign Affairs (see additional links at the end of this chapter).

- *The value of looking at the past and frequency profiling.* Some of the hazards identified early on related to terrorists and criminal gangs, with the risk of kidnapping, being shot at or caught up in a bomb explosion identified as key risks. Table 3.1 presents a sample of the sort of data they collected, which enabled them to assess the risks. What the expedition members quickly noted was how the likelihood varied considerably depending on the different regions of the country, such as the border areas with Somalia, where the risk of kidnapping, stepping on a landmine or being shot at was far higher in comparison with other parts of the country.

Table 3.1. Terrorism incidents in Ethiopia.

Year	Date/month	Type of incident	Injuries	Fatalities	Location	Target	Group	Source
2007	6 Aug	Bomb	8	1	City of Jijiga, Eastern Ogaden (Somali region)	Christians	Mujahideen Youth Movement	MIPT DFAT UK FCO
2007	Sept	Bomb	7	1	Jijiga	Business	Unknown	MIPT
2007	28 May	Not known	Not known	Not known	Jijiga Stadium	Civilians	Not cited	DFAT UK FCO
2007	24 April	Firearms and kidnapping	Unclear	74	Obele, Ogaden region	Business	OLF	DFAT UK FCO USDS
2007	1 March	Kidnapping	0	0	Danakil desert area/Afar region	Tourists	Not known	DFAT UK FCO
2006	20 Sept	Kidnapping	0	0	Gode	NGOs	Unclear	UK FCO
2006	11 June	Bomb	Unclear	Unclear	Gambella	Transport	Not specified	UK FCO

NGO, non-governmental organization; OLF, Oromo Liberation Front; MIPT, Memorial Institute for the Prevention of Terrorism; DFAT, Australian Department of Foreign Affairs and Trade; UK FCO, UK Foreign and Commonwealth Office; USDS, US Department of State.

- *Risk as a social construct.* As the expedition members planned the project, their greater awareness of the country meant they constructed many more risks which for them did not exist at the beginning, or at least did not exist in their consciousness. For example, the risk of kidnapping was not fully appreciated, but became a key risk for which they put in control measures, particularly after the high-profile kidnapping of some UK foreign office staff in 2007.

- *Using complexity theory to develop a deeper analysis.* Here, one of the factors that could affect the ability to travel out to the country was the dependence on the political conditions, particularly as there was a risk of war and more political instability, which could mean the trip to the destination would have to be cancelled.

3.7.2   Stadium and event disasters

A key risk in any large-scale event is the chance that people can be crushed and injured. For anyone involved with staging events of any sort, examining a variety of past cases from around the world can be very revealing, helping to reflect on current practices and the likelihood and impact of a future incident. In this instance, a key focus is given to UK stadium disasters that have taken place over the past hundred years.

- *Looking at the past and frequency profiling.* Examining various stadium disasters, deaths and injuries, a notable feature was how failures from the past were not learnt from or cases from other countries not scrutinized. This is particularly true when one examines the UK and the 1989 Hillsborough football disaster, where 97 Liverpool football fans lost their lives, being crushed to death against an iron fence designed to stop pitch invasions. Looking back at the history of stadium disasters in the UK, by no means could the Hillsborough disaster be considered a black swan event: hundreds of people had died and thousands had been injured because of collapsing stands and walls, or being crushed in stairwells. There was clearly a failure to look at the past and analyse the cases in order to gain a true assessment of the risks, how such events occurred and how they could be prevented in the future. To state it bluntly, people had to die before more radical changes in risk practices were done. While large-scale events in the UK are now far safer, unfortunately in other parts of the world there can still be failures to learn from such disasters in their own and other countries.

- *Risk as a social construct.* The management of sport events in the UK has gone through some fundamental changes. Before Hillsborough, the key risk to be managed was hooliganism: hence the immovable barriers put in place to keep fans in the stands, stop pitch invasions and segregate fans to prevent fighting. The risk of people being crushed was known, but it was not a coherent construct in the minds of the event organizers and so it did not significantly influence their practices and approaches. After Hillsborough, while this risk of hooliganism was not deconstructed, the construct of spectator safety received far more priority, whereby the risk was more clearly defined and represented when managing sport events.

- *Using complexity theory to develop a deeper analysis.* Elliot *et al.* (1997) are particularly critical of the key agencies involved with football in the UK, such as the FA, club owners and the police, and the weakness of their analysis of past events. Indeed, it is difficult not to concur with their criticisms about the breathtaking failures in imagination of the possibility of people being crushed to death when attending a football match at the time. The response by legislators to previous events had always been to focus only on the immediate causes of previous accidents, rather than the more significant underlying causation factors. The result was that the solutions to deal with crowd safety only dealt with the problem in a superficial way, whereby the pressure to deal with other risks, such as hooliganism, led to policies that increased the likelihood of a stadium disaster (e.g. the erection of a solid, immovable barrier). Looking back on the many factors that underpinned Hillsborough, it is clear that football in the UK was operating on the edge of chaos for decades, having a complex interaction of slowly incubating factors (politics, stadium design, lack of investment, dynamics of group behaviour, etc.), which just needed the catalyst event on the day (the gates being opened) to be tipped over into tragedy.

3.7.3   Sporting injuries and concussion

Playing and watching sport can bring many physical, social and mental health benefits, with the challenge being to try and maintain these benefits while controlling the risk of injuries. In many risk assessments the focus may be on the more immediate playing of the game, but as some of the cases relating to head injuries illustrate, there can be long-term health implications long after people have stopped playing the sport, as illustrated in Box 3.2 on the risks of concussion.

- *Looking at the past and frequency profiling.* In sports such as boxing, there has been a long list of incidents where the dangers of repeated knocks to the head have been shown, where people have died, become disabled or suffered from brain-related diseases later in life (i.e. punch-drunk syndrome). The other key sport where this issue has had a profound impact has been the NFL, where it was likened to a black swan event. While perhaps it can be considered as this type of event in terms of its impact, this is however wrong in the sense of it being unexpected or without precedence. The approach of the NFL was to simply ignore and deny the issue, even suppressing stories about the risks. The data were there, not only in their own sport, but from all sorts of other areas, ranging from domestic violence to car accidents and sports. The truth is that the NFL did not want to know about it. As the frequency data built up and the medical evidence grew, denial of the issue became impossible. Other sports are now also looking at the data. These cases should be studied not only for the circumstances of their injuries, but also for the poor response by the relevant governing bodies. In some sports, such as rugby, the English Rugby Football Union now publishes a regular audit of injuries in the top-flight professional game (which incidentally also has a high incidence of concussions), allowing for a build-up of rich statistical data on injuries.
- *Risk as a social construct.* The risks from head injury have been known for a long while, but a proper, consistent objective risks assessment about concussion is still being constructed.

As the amount of research grows, an objective assessment is made more attainable, but seems most likely to exist in the realms of virtual, contested risk. The term concussion may for many people conjure up an image of someone losing consciousness. In fact concussion relates to a trauma to the brain, where consciousness may or may not be lost, occurring not just from a direct impact, such as hitting the ground or another player, but also from a sudden deceleration. When looking at how different sports are dealing with the risk of concussion, one does not see consistency in approach by governing bodies, such as: variations in the amount of time a sport person has to remain out of play, ranging from 3 to 10 min; and differences as to who controls the return, from the medical expert to the player or coach.

- *Using complexity theory to develop a deeper analysis.* The science of understanding how repeated blows to the head can lead to brain damage and disease is complex. While the full science about brain injuries is beyond the scope of most practitioners, many of the causation factors in the different cases are not so difficult to understand and analyse. It is possible to examine the key findings of the research to develop appropriate control mechanisms. For example, in boxing, why some boxers survived relatively unscathed while others could die after a few fights, or suffer more serious health problems later, was sometimes thought to be simply a matter of chance. In fact, as the research has developed, what appears important is the biomechanics of the injury, where it is not necessarily the direct blunt force, but the rapid rotation of the skull (i.e. more of the whiplash-type injury people can get in a car accident) that causes the damage, and this goes some way to explaining why there can be a higher number of deaths in lower weight divisions. Recognizing this reveals that protective headgear may in fact not necessarily reduce the risks of concussion. Other factors to consider relate to the different organization cultures and the commercial pressures to deal with the issues. The damage to the NFL and its reputation for trying to ignore, repress and deny the issue is a case in point. The variations in approaches in different sports can also relate to other issues, such the rugby union 'bloodgate scandal' (rugby players in England would fake injuries, by biting on a blood capsule, to allow them to come off and a fresh player to be brought on) and concerns that it could be used as a mechanism for cheating.

3.7.4 Tourism incidents

Collecting statistical information from government departments that deal with foreign affairs is both essential and useful in building up risk assessments. It is essential in the sense that before an organization conducts any foreign travel, it must consult the relevant government travel advice site, which will inform of some of the hazards and risks of travel. Any guidance or advisory notes to avoid travel to all or parts of the country should be considered carefully, particularly as most insurance companies would not cover such travel. The information given is useful as such government departments can provide both statistical and more specific case study data to help identify and analyse risks.

- *The value of looking at the past and frequency profiling.* The US state department has an interactive database where the time parameters and country can be selected to find the number of US citizens who have died overseas. For example, looking at this database between 2012 and 2013, 43 American citizens died in Afghanistan, primarily as a result of terrorist actions (24) or air accidents (US Department of State, 2014). In the same year, the number of US citizens who died in the UK was 19, five of whom were suicides, four car accidents and one homicide. For Thailand, there were 52 deaths, with six drowning, ten suicides and 20 car/motorbike-related deaths. The data begins to identify the type of risks that travellers can be exposed to, which, if put into a ratio in relation to the number of travellers, can be given a better sense of perspective in terms of the likelihood per thousands of visitors.

The UK Foreign and Commonwealth Office (UK FCO) also has a useful database where there is an interactive map highlighting the number of incidents where people have required assistance. In the 2013 report, for example, the Office gave assistance to 19,000 British people abroad, with incidents ranging from arrests, sexual assault, detentions to hospital treatment, with most incidents taking place in Spain, Turkey and Greece (UK FCO, 2014). A summary of the incidents, for a number of selected countries, appears in Table 3.2.

Looking at other sites for Canada, Australia and New Zealand one can get similar data, all presented in different ways. For any organization, in terms of collecting data, it should be encouraged to look at statistics for citizens not only of its own country, but also other countries, as this can help create awareness of risks. Because a particular incident might not have happened to its own citizens, this is not to say it could not do so in the future (the principle of the incident triangle).

- *Risk as a social construct*. In many ways, the government advice sites can be seen as offering the closest to the objective truth, but the subjective element, particularly in relation to the influence of politics, cannot be ignored. This is why variations can be found in travel advice between the different government sites, such as if one compares the advice offered by the US Department of State for Cuba, compared with the travel advice offered by the UK, Canada or Australia.

Table 3.2. Top five countries where British nationals required the most Consular assistance from 1 April 2012 to 31 March 2013. (From UK FCO, 2014.)

Country	Number of visitors	Number of residents	Drugs	Total arrests	Deaths	Rape	Hospital
Spain	13,653,846	795,784	103	1,599	1,492	31	899
USA	3,800,000	829,000	159	1,120	153	5	140
Thailand	870,164	50,000	36	188	389	9	285
Australia	592,400	1,101,021	2	106	87	2	69
China	1,187,706	284,600	10	119	72	4	46

- *Causation factors.* Looking at the data, some interesting patterns emerge, helping to identify risks and gain a sense of their likelihood. What the data does not do is give much insight into the causation factors. For example, looking at the incident data from the UK FCO (2014), 1599 British citizens died in Spain and 1120 died in the USA in the period considered. Does this give a true sense of the risk? They are certainly striking statistics, but they need more careful analysis. Turning them into ratios can help put them into perspective. In this sense, for Spain there is approximately one death for every 9000 visits, while in the USA it is approximately one in 3000. More investigation is needed and one of the points to consider relates to the high numbers of residents in the countries, which suggest people both living and working in the countries. Spain has become a popular area for retirement, so part of the deaths will reflect this. Another causation factor to consider may be in relation to the large numbers of young people who visit these destinations for partying and drinking.

3.8 CONCLUSION

There is no denying that looking at past events is an invaluable part of the risk management process of analysing and assessing current and future risks. The process of researching past events allows for hazards and risks to be initially identified, which, if built into frequency profiles, can help make judgements about how likely such risks are in the future. This is at the heart of the positivist scientific tradition, where evidence can be collected, weighed up and then judgements made based on weight of evidence.

While this approach is invaluable, it is also essential that the limitations of the positivist method are understood. The analysis of past events can be prone to become distorted by personal biases, external influences or simply that the information collected is not complete. Having this sensitivity to its limitations can help maintain an open mind and humility as to the accuracy of judgements and the fallibility of decisions. Furthermore, it was shown why it is always important to explore in more depth the potential factors of causation during the analysis process stage, as these are often bound in complex systems. Here the detailed case study analysis can be invaluable, as insights can be gained into some of the factors that can contribute to the risks manifesting themselves, for good or bad. This analysis and assessment can then be used to develop the control measures, to deal with causation factors or to try and reduce the severity of outcomes.

DISCUSSION QUESTIONS AND TASKS

1. In Box 3.1, Rejda (2010: 69) gives the following formula for calculating probability:

   Probability (p) = number of events likely to occur (based on past frequency) × number of units.

For an activity of your choice, see if a probability can be estimated based on data that have been collected.

2. Search for examples of an injury, such as concussion or spinal injuries, in a number of sports and compare the incident rates and the control measures the sport has to deal with the injury.

3. Conduct research into the most common incidents that are likely to occur while travelling, using a variety of databases.

4. Choose a country that has a challenging environment, such as a desert, rainforest or mountains, then go to the relevant government travel advice sites and:

- build up a table which identifies the key hazards and risks;
- build up a frequency table of incidents; and
- consider how these data could be used to inform an adventure expedition to the selected destination.

5. For a large sport event of your choice, such as the Olympics, look for articles that discuss the amount of money spent on security and consider what factors are driving these costs. Is the money justified based on the probability of occurrence?

REFERENCES

Adams, J. (1995) *Risk*. UCL Press, London.

Adams, J. (2011) Not a 100% sure? The 'public' understanding of risk. In: Bennett, D.J. and Jennings, R.C. (eds) *Successful Science Communication: Telling It Like It Is*. Cambridge University Press, Cambridge, pp. 90–100.

Aven, T. and Renn, O. (2009) On risk defined as an event where the outcome is uncertain. *Journal of Risk Research* 12, 1–11.

Baggio, R. (2008) Symptoms of complexity in a tourism system. *Tourism Analysis* 13, 1–20.

Bandolier (2014) Risk of dying and sporting activities. Available at: http://www.medicine.ox.ac.uk/bandolier/booth/risk/sports.html (accessed 11 October 2014).

Beck, U. (1998) *World Risk Society*. Polity Press, Cambridge.

Beers, S. (1967) *Management Science*. Aldus, London.

Bernstein, P. (1998) *Against the Gods: The Remarkable Story of Risk*. Wiley, Chichester, UK.

Boyne, R. (2003) *Risk*. Open University Press, Buckingham, UK.

Brown, T.J. (1999) Adventure risk management. In: Miles, J.C. and Priest, S. (eds) *Adventure Programming*. Venture Publishing, State College, Pennsylvania, pp. 273–284.

Cahn, S.K. (1994) *Coming on Strong: Gender and Sexuality in Twentieth-century Women's Sport*. Harvard University Press, Cambridge, Massachusetts.

Davies, N. and Teasdale, P. (1994) *The Costs to the British Economy of Work Accidents and Work-related Ill Health*. HSE Books, London.

Elliot, D., Frosdick, S. and Smith, D. (1997) The failure of 'legislation by crisis'. In: Frosdick, S. and Walley, L. (eds) *Sport & Safety Management*. Butterworth-Heinemann, London, pp. 83–107.

Fainaru-Wada, M. and Fainaru, S. (2013) *League of Denial*. Three Rivers Press, New York.

Frosdick, S. (1997) Risk as blame. In: Frosdick, S. and Walley, L. (eds) *Sport and Safety Management*. Butterworth-Heinemann, London, pp. 33–66.

Geary, R. (1996) The Lyme Bay sea kayaking tragedy and the criminal law. *Canoeist Newsletter* 65, 4–6.

Handy, C. (1990) *The Age of Unreason*. Harvard University Business Press, Cambridge, Massachusetts.

Heinrich, H. (1931) *Industrial Accident Prevention, A Scientific Approach*. McGraw-Hill, New York.

Johnson, J. (2006) Can complexity help us better understand risk? *Risk Management* 8, 227–267.

Kaplan, S. and Garrick, J.B. (1981) On the quantitative definition of risk. *Risk Analysis* 1, 11–27.

Klinke, A. and Renn, O. (2001) Precautionary principles and discursive strategies; classifying and managing risks. *Journal of Risk Research* 4, 159–173.

McKerlvey, B. and Andriani, P. (2010) Avoiding extreme risk before it occurs: a complexity science approach to incubation. *Risk Management* 12, 54–82.

Nafjan, E. (2012) The Olympic triumph of Saudi Arabian women. *The Guardian,* Tuesday 31 July. Available at: http://www.theguardian.com/commentisfree/2012/jul/31/olympic-triumph-saudi-arabian-women (accessed 2 August 2013).

Parry, B. (2004) Risk management. In: McMahon-Beattie, U. and Yoeman, I. (eds) *Sport and Leisure Operations Management.* Thomson, London.

Pedersen, D.M. (1997) Perceptions of high risk sports. *Perceptual Motor Skills* 85, 756–758.

Rejda, G.E. (2010) *Principles of Risk Management and Insurance.* Pearson Education, London.

Stutely, R. (2002) *The Definitive Business Plan,* 2nd edn. Pearson Education Ltd, Edinburgh.

Taleb, N. (2007) *Fooled by Randomness: The Hidden Role of Chance in Life and in the Markets,* 2nd edn. Penguin, London.

UK FCO (2014) Britons in trouble abroad. Available at: http://fco-bba-2013.s3-website-eu-west-1.amazonaws.com/ (accessed 20 October 2014).

US Department of State (2014) US citizen deaths overseas. Available at: http://travel.state.gov/content/travel/english/statistics/deaths.html (accessed 10 October 2014).

Watts G. (2003) The trouble with risk. EurekAlert. Available at: http://www.eurekalert.org/pub_releases/2003-07/bpl-tco070203.php (accessed 20 October 2014).

Wilks, J. and Davis, J. (2000) Risk management for scuba diving operators on Australia's great barrier reef. *Tourism Management* 21, 591–599.

FURTHER READING

Books and journal articles

Allen, P.M., Varga, L. and Strathern, M. (2010) The evolutionary complexity of social and economic systems: the inevitability of uncertainty and surprise. *Risk Management* 12, 9–30.

Aven, T. (2009) *Risk Analysis: Assessing Uncertainties Beyond Expected Values and Probabilities.* Wiley, London.

Oates, W. and Barlow, C. (2011) An Injury Prevention Curriculum for Coaches. Available at: http://www.stopsportsinjuries.org/files/coaches_curriculum_toolkit/AOS-103%20Coaches%20Curriculum%20Toolkit%20(nm)%202.8[1].pdf (accessed 18 January 2015).

Websites that can give information on accidents and incidents

Bandolier is an online healthcare journal that has useful information about accidents, injuries and research, available at: http://www.medicine.ox.ac.uk/bandolier/index.html

Headway is a charity that deals with brain injuries and has a range of useful information to help practitioners, available at: https://www.headway.org.uk/home.aspx

National Center for Catastrophic Sport Injury Research (NCCSIR) has a variety of useful case studies and statistical information, available at: http://nccsir.unc.edu/

National Safety Council has a useful database to find statistics and incidents, available at: http://www.nsc.org/about_us/Pages/Home.aspx

Stop Sport Injuries is a US-based charity and has a range of useful resources to help understand causation, track incidents and control measures, available at: http://www.stopsportsinjuries.org/

Travel advice and incident data

Australian Department of Foreign Affairs and Trade, available at: http://www.dfat.gov.au/
Intelligent Life, a consultancy that has all sorts of useful information, available at: http://intelligent-travel.com.au/
New Zealand Ministry of Foreign Affairs and Trade, available at: http://www.mfat.govt.nz/
UK Foreign and Commonwealth Office, available at: https://www.gov.uk/government/organisations/foreign-commonwealth-office
US Department of State (foreign travel), available at: http://travel.state.gov

chapter 4

Risk Management Research, Models and Tool Application

CHAPTER OBJECTIVES

- To explain the difference between theories, tools and models.
- To provide an overview of the many different tools that can be used to identify, analyse and assess risks.
- To provide a variety of examples to illustrate how the tools can be used for the different sectors.
- To explain the basic principles of the research process and where data can be accessed from.

Key concepts

Theories and tools; scenario analysis; fault and event tree analysis; mind mapping; complexity theory; causal loops and spatial analysis.

4.1 INTRODUCTION

Analysing the risk an individual or business is exposed to is perhaps the most complex part of any practical risk process. As explained in Chapter 2, this analysis stage involves not only the identification of risks and hazards, but also a need to identify and understand how multiple causation factors or variables can combine to generate risk events. The question raised here is: just how should this analysis actually be done?

This chapter explores some of the practical techniques and tools that can help with this analysis. A distinction is made between theories and tools, which, although intimately related, have some important differences. While theories give the reasons *why* certain approaches should be used, such as using probability theory which requires researching past events, they still give only a broad indication of *what* should be done; what tools do is go into the specific details of just *how* the theory should be put into actual practice.

This chapter therefore examines a variety of analytical tools that turn theories into practical analytical activities. Particular attention is given to tools that help to 'fire-up' a practitioner's imagination as to what risks are possible and how they may manifest themselves; a process that is of crucial importance when imagining crisis scenarios, no matter how improbable they may seem. To help illustrate the application of the tools, they will be applied to the different industry sectors throughout this chapter.

4.2 CLARIFYING THE KEY TERMS AND USING A MIXED THEORY APPROACH

When reading the literature on risk management, one can find variations in how the terms tools, theories and models are defined. In relation to this discussion, the terms model, tool, theory, data and information, while all intimately related, are used in particular ways, which are:

- *Theory* (discussed in Chapter 3) gives an insight, understanding or explanations about the world, or, in this instance, how and why risks manifest themselves in particular ways. The use of theories is a vital foundation for any process of risk analysis, but may not be always be sufficiently practical or detailed enough to help practitioners.
- *Tools* are specific techniques that put theory into practice, generating information which can help in decision making. Tools are used at various stages in the risk process, from helping to identify hazards and risks in the early context phase to giving more depth to the analysis stage, informing assessments and deciding on control measures.
- *Models* are a way to represent the world, usually by simplifying it, in order to make it more understandable and tangible. The anatomy of risk model (Chapter 2) and the factors influencing perceptions model (Chapter 7) are two examples used in this work. At times the differences between models and tools can be blurred.
- *Data*, or facts, make tools and models work. Brink (2004: 37), citing Pidd (1996), also makes the observation that *data* plus *interpretation* equals *information*, while intelligence is information that has been collated, corroborated, analysed and applied.

An illustration can be given for how all these concepts can work. A practitioner knowing the *theoretical* benefits of researching the frequency of past events, or finding more detailed case studies, undertakes more research to find data on past incidents. Using the anatomy of risk model (Fig. 2.1) helps the practitioner initially organize some of the *data*, identifying the key risks, hazards, triggers and potential causation factors. Next, using the data collected and continuing to use theoretical constructs such as *complexity theory*, various *tools* are used, such as mind mapping, which try to identify and connect how various causation factors interact to generate certain outcomes.

In this chapter, a mixed theory approach will be used in the sense that encouragement is given to use many traditional theories relating to probability frequency analysis, blended in with using complexity theory to help underpin the analysis. This is in keeping with the encouragement for students and practitioners to adopt the fourth-age risk paradigm discussed in Chapter 2, whereby risk is often embedded in complex systems, operating on the edge of chaos, but can be both opportunistic and threatening. While some may not like this mixed use of theories, it does reflect an operational reality of working in the adventure, sport, tourism and events industries. Practitioners and students must draw on any theories that ultimately help them try and make a good decision about how to deal with risks.

4.3 THE RISK PROCESS, TOOLS AND RESEARCH METHODS: AN OVERVIEW

How does one progress from general probability theories that require researching past events or embed the analysis of risks within a complex system? Modelling, where the world is reduced or simplified, can be part of this process, but one still needs to have practical, more mechanical if you like, procedural steps for collecting and using the data.

When reading literature on risk there can be a bewildering number of tools and techniques that can be used by practitioners to try and identify, analyse and assess risks. Works such as APM (2004), Merna and Faisal (2005) and Standards New Zealand (2004) give useful overviews of the rich number of techniques that are available, many of which are presented in Table 4.1. When looking at this long list, it should be appreciated that many of these tools are not necessarily just for use in risk management, but are more generic management tools designed to help analyse past, present and future business conditions. To put it another way: because risk or risk management is not referred to in a management tool or activity, this does not mean that risks are not being dealt with, as risks are often an implicit not an explicit part of these tools. Whether something is described as risk management does not really matter; what does matter is that the tools are used in an effective manner to help make better decisions.

Table 4.1 gives a list of possible tools and research techniques, showing how they can fit into the different process stages based on the more detailed Table 2.3, discussed in Chapter 2. The tools used not only relate to the process stage focused on, but also the type of risk analysis and assessment being done, such as the variations between operational health and safety assessments compared with project or strategic risk assessments.

There is not the scope to fully explain all of the tools and methods presented in Table 4.1, many of which are well served by other literature. Table 4.1 is designed to show the breadth of activities and how risk management can blend with everyday management activities.

Table 4.1. Process stages, tools and examples of research methods.

	What needs to be considered (see Table 2.3 for a more detailed question checklist)	**Examples of tools and research techniques**
Stage 1: Context	• What is the nature of the organization? • Who is at risk? • What is at risk? • How are they at risk? • Factors affecting degree of exposure	Tools • Mind mapping • SWOT (leading into PESTLE and process stage 2) useful for project and strategic assessments Research • Draw on own/team experience and knowledge, individual meetings and interviews • Review organizational objectives; audit of resources; review strategic plans; organization history • Meet with key stakeholders • Delphi techniques
Stage 2: Analysis	• Identifying key risks • Identifying key hazards • Identifying key causation factors • Identifying any triggers • Analysing the relationships of factors • Identifying and analysing suitable indicators of causation	Tools • SWOT and PESTLE (expanded from the previous stage) • Mind mapping (see Section 4.6.1) • Fishbone analysis (see Section 4.6.2) • Causal loops (see Section 4.6.3) • Event and fault tree analysis (see Section 4.6.4) • Spatial analysis (see Section 4.6.5) • Checklists (see also Chapter 6) • Financial tools, such as costs of capital returns, cash flow forecasts or payback period, etc. • Other (e.g. Monte Carlo statistical analysis, trend analysis) Research • Frequency profiling (see Chapter 3) • Scanning of news events • Interviewing and focus group discussions • Observational analysis of practices/physical inspection of locations and equipment • Research past case studies (see Chapter 11) • Case study hindsight analysis • Secondary data on accidents, reports, incidents, etc. • Trade and journal publications

(Continued)

Table 4.1. Continued.

	What needs to be considered (see Table 2.3 for a more detailed question checklist)	Examples of tools and research techniques
Stage 3: Assessment	<ul><li>Assessing type of impacts and severity</li><li>Assessing likelihood</li><li>Applying assessment scales to represent or categorize the risk (e.g. high, low, medium)</li></ul>	Tools<ul><li>Statistical analysis of frequency profiles, impact matrices, spatial analysis (see Chapter 3)</li><li>Risk mapping on grids</li><li>Monte Carlo method</li><li>Trend extrapolation</li></ul>Research<ul><li>Frequency of past events, statistical reports, journal articles (see Chapter 3)</li><li>Risk registers, accident books, etc.</li></ul>
Stage 4: Control	<ul><li>Prioritizing resources</li><li>Reviewing points where control measures can be put in place</li><li>Type of control measure</li><li>Measures to remove or reduce negative risk events occurring</li><li>Measures to reduce severity of impact</li><li>Summarizing information on a risk form</li><li>Producing action checklists and communicating to key stakeholders</li></ul>	Tools<ul><li>Review critical paths, scenarios and assessments</li><li>Scenario training</li><li>Checklists of actions (see Chapter 6)</li><li>Decision tree scenario analysis</li></ul>Research<ul><li>Case study analysis to review robustness of measures (see Chapter 11)</li><li>Testing of procedures, such as via scenario training</li></ul>
Stage 5: Monitor	<ul><li>Review checklists, forms, assessments and analysis</li><li>Amend control measures</li></ul>	Tools<ul><li>Reviewing key performance indicators (see Section 4.7)</li><li>Responding to events</li></ul>Research<ul><li>Staff meetings, reviews, data monitored, scanning news and incident events</li></ul>

SWOT, Strengths, Weaknesses, Opportunities and Threats; PESTLE, Political, Economic, Social, Technological, Legal and Environmental.

4.4   RESEARCH METHODS

It was explained in Chapters 2 and 3 that despite the theoretical benefits of collecting data in a systematic and logical way, a great deal of risk analysis, assessment and decision making can still be based on personal experiences and judgements, which are called *heuristics* (discussed in more detail in Chapter 7). While heuristics are adequate for many quick assessments of risks, when activities or projects become more complex, such a limited approach will not be good enough. It would not be good enough to ensure that a proper and robust analysis is done of all the potential risks and how they may manifest themselves; it would not be good enough to identify the most appropriate methods to control risks; and it would not be good enough to ensure an individual or organization is protected from litigation, which may lead to large financial pay-outs, even a prison sentence.

What is therefore needed is more consideration for how students and practitioners actually go about collecting information and data that can be used in different models and tools. Aspects of the research process were discussed in Chapter 3, where it was explained how one can collect a mixture of statistical or case study data to help analyse and assess risks, but this needs further elaboration in relation to some of the key terms and methods used in research, which are:

- *Primary data* relates to data that is collected first hand by the individual or organization. These data can be collected via questionnaires, interviews, observation studies, collation of incident data and other statistics found within the organization, such as financial performance or usage figures.
- *Secondary data* relates to data that someone else has collected, such as statistics on sport or adventure injuries, or on the various tourism-related incidents, such as transport accidents or disease outbreaks.
- Data can be classified as *quantitative*, which refers to data that is expressed numerically, such as when looking at accident data, or *qualitative*, which can be more descriptive of an event or situation, such as reviewing a case study looking at how an accident occured. In some risk processes (examples given in Chapter 2) quantitative and qualitative data analysis are presented as separate stages, but Gardiner (2005: 165) notes that in practice many organizations do not have such a distinction, as they believe it can be distracting and does not necessarily improve the quality of decisions, particularly if too much focus is given to 'number crunching' (i.e. just analysing the numbers and not considering the wider management implications).
- *Interviews*, *team meetings* or *risk clinics* (Gardiner, 2005: 165) are a vital part of the early stages of the data collection process, whereby people's experiences are pooled to help identify hazards, risks and what may cause them. A Delphi technique, which uses a variety of experts to comment on future issues and trends, can further refine this process.
- *Observations* and direct inspection of equipment, facilities, locations, or even countries (the latter is sometimes known as the grand tour approach).

- Interviews and meetings can have a *formal* structure, with a set of predesigned questions, or be *informal*, where ideas are encouraged to develop freely, or even a mix of the two, such as with focus groups (broad parameters are set, but free-flowing discussion is encouraged within these bounds).
- The identification of key risk factors as part of the anatomy of risk model can be given more scientific refinement and rigour by classifying them as *variables* (Bryman and Bell, 2003: 34), where distinctions can be made between *independent* (the variable that can theoretically cause the independent variable to change and measure the effects on the dependent), the *dependent* (this is the variable affected) and the *intervening* (what modifies any changes).

It should be appreciated that research methods have whole books written about them, so all that is offered here is the merest of snapshots into what is involved. For those who are interested in doing more formal research into risk, they would have to think about this research process in terms of a *methodology*. In essence, this refers to explicitly stating the guiding principles that shape how data is collected and analysed, which can depend on the scientific position adopted, such as the differences between positivism or interpretivism discussed in Chapter 3. The methods used can also be described in relation to the extent that they rely on primary or secondary data, qualitative or quantitative data, and any of the theories and analytical tools they may use. Two examples of student risk-related research projects are given in Box 4.1.

4.5   COLLECTING DATA

A great deal has been said about *why* it is important to collect data, with the previous section giving some indication of *how* data can be collected. The next point to consider is just *where* data can be collected from.

If primary data is being collected, then careful and more detailed consideration can be given for formal techniques of data collection, such as the many ways that questionnaires can be designed (such as having open or closed questions) or administered (such as being contacted by e-mail, online surveys, post or conducted by an interviewer). Other useful techniques include observational analysis, interviews and focus group discussions, which are all well served by literature. There is also the obvious starting point of scrutinizing organization data, such as examining accident and incident books, to build up incident frequency tables.

Researching incidents is a vital part of the risk process as it helps to initially identify potential hazards and risks, providing a platform for deeper analysis and assessment. At times, using primary research is not appropriate, possible or perhaps even relevant, such as when activities are new or the organization is too small to generate enough incident data. In this instance, accessing secondary data is vital, whereby both incident data and more complex case study

Box 4.1. Examples of student research topics relating to risk

Example 1: Investigating rugby injuries for a club

A student wanted to research sport injuries in rugby as part of an undergraduate research topic. The student's interest was sparked by playing rugby and having been injured. While being taught the theory of risk homeostasis, the student thought about their own injuries and how wearing some light shoulder padding made them over-confident and went into tackles harder. This experience and theory, together with some high-profile incidents and questions being asked about the safety of the sport, gave a context for investigating the issue in more detail. As a student, resources were limited, so the decision taken was to do a more in-depth analysis of a local club with which they had links. A mixed methods approach was taken whereby the student could review the incident data relating to accidents and injuries for the club going back a number of years. This *quantitative* data would be complemented by *focus group interviews* with the players giving more *qualitative data* about their experience of injuries. When analysing some of the cases, the student used the concept of variables, so in one case the player who suffered the spinal injury was labelled as the *dependent* variable, the scrum collapsing the *independent*, while the experience of the players, or the referee, the *intervening* variable. This data was also compared with *secondary quantitative data*, such as the RFU reports on injuries for elite players. Evidence for homeostasis was found, along with feedback given to the club as to how it could refine some practices to reduce the likelihood of some injuries.

Example 2: Adventure tourism and future markets for a backpacker hostel in Cambodia

A student who had backpacked around the world and had used hostels became interested in the potential to develop a backpackers' hostel in Cambodia, which at the time of the study was still emerging from a long period of conflict. These personal experiences helped give the project an initial context, further refined and defined by the growing number of articles in travel literature and magazines of the increasing interest in the country, which were contrasted with an older article that reported on the kidnapping and murder of some tourists. Reviewing the literature helped to identify more relevant theories to help guide the study, such as how destinations move through a life cycle, where more adventurous travellers with limited financial means open up a destination in the beginning. Having an interest in potentially setting up a hostel in the country, the student decided to investigate the risks of not only the financial investment of building a new hostel, but also the safety of travellers. The methods employed related primarily to the use of *secondary quantitative* and *qualitative* data and a variety of analytical tools, such as *fault tree analysis* and *payback methods*. Accessing a variety of databases the student was able analyse and assess the political risk of investing in the country and travelling out there, concluding that the overall underlying trend, while far from risk free, was an improving situation.

analysis can be done. Depending on the activity and sector, the following examples illustrate the range of incidents that can be researched to build up a frequency table:

- accidents in a sport which resulted in death or disability;
- event or stadium accidents from around the world;
- transport accidents in different countries and regions;
- acts of criminality or terrorism;
- incidents of natural disasters such as earthquakes, tsunamis and hurricanes;
- disease outbreaks; and
- incidents of political instability such as riots, demonstrations and strikes.

What can help in this process is to carefully collect and organize both quantifiable and qualitative data, such as creating a frequency table that can consider some of the following headings for the columns (see Chapter 3, Table 3.1 for an example of a layout):

- date and time of incident;
- place or location (site, region and country if appropriate);
- incident description/categorization (who was involved, what happened, etc.);
- type of incident and outcome categorization (e.g. injury, death, financial impacts, equipment damage);
- location;
- indication of any causation factors/description; and
- source of data.

In addition to secondary incident data, there can be numerous databases and websites that can give deeper insights into the risks, such as looking at research journal articles or databases offering advice and information about risks and their management. Table 4.2 gives examples to illustrate the breadth of databases that can be accessed to: (i) obtain incident data (e.g. news databases); (ii) gain advice information (e.g. government travel advice, governing bodies who offer guidelines on best safe practice); or (iii) utilize ready-made analysis and assessments (e.g. journal articles) or statistical data.

4.6 APPLICATION OF THE TOOLS

What is done in the following sections is to give some examples of how the data that may have been collected can be utilized in a variety of tools and models identified in Table 4.1. It should be appreciated that many of these tools can be used for both analysing past incidents and mapping out future possible scenarios.

An important part of some of the tools selected for discussion here relates to the broader-based management tool of scenario writing. The tools focused on are designed to give possible insight into what the future may hold, depending on what factors, events or variables combine, or how different actions or strategies taken affect the outcomes. Even with basic

Table 4.2. Examples of secondary data sources.

Category	Examples
News databases	BBC News, Sky News, Reuters, Global Post, France 24, Al Jazeera, NBC News, Spiegel Online
	UK newspapers: *The Times, Daily Mail, Financial Times, The Guardian, The Independent*, etc.
	US and Canadian newspapers: *USA Today, National Post, The Washington Post, The New York Times*, etc.
	Australian and New Zealand newspapers: *The Australian, The New Zealand Herald, The Canberra Times, The Sydney Morning Herald*, etc.
International agencies	World Tourism Organization, International Tourism Partnership, World Bank, United Nations
Governing bodies	International Olympic Committee (IOC); Fédération Internationale de Football Association (FIFA) and regional and country governing bodies; International Rugby Board (IRB) and subsidiary country boards (e.g. English RFU, Australian Rugby Union (ARU)); International Federation of American Football (IFAF); etc.
Government departments and related agencies	UK: Department of Culture, Media and Sport, UK Foreign and Commonwealth Office (travel advice), UK Sport, Sport England/Wales/Scotland
	USA: Department of State (foreign travel)
	New Zealand: Ministry of Sport and Recreation New Zealand (SPARC), Ministry of Foreign Affairs and Trade (travel advice), Sport New Zealand
	Australia: Department of Foreign Affairs and Trade (travel advice), Department of Health, National Integrity of Sport Unit
	Canada: Department of Foreign Affairs, Trade and Development (travel advice), Department of Canadian Heritage, Sport Canada
Charities	Tourism, adventure and events: Christian Aid, Amnesty International, Freedom House, etc.
	Sport and leisure: Sport Charitable Trust, Aspire, Headway, etc.
Strategic business environment	Coface International, Uppsala Conflict Database, World Trade Organization, United Nations, World Bank, etc.

(Continued)

Table 4.2. Continued.

Category	Examples
Accident data	Royal Society for the Prevention of Accidents (RoSPA), European Home and Leisure Accident Surveillance System (EHLASS), Centers for Disease Control and Prevention (CDC)
Research journals and trade magazines	Tourism: *Tourism Management; Annals of Tourism Research; International Journal of Hospitality and Tourism Research; Journal of Hospitality and Tourism Management; Journal of Sustainable Tourism; Journal of Tourism Studies; International Journal of Culture; Tourism Hospitality Research; Tourism Geographies;* etc.
	Adventure: *Outdoor Education Research; Wilderness Therapy*
	Sport and leisure: *Journal of Sport and Health Research; Journal of Strength and Conditioning Research; Journal of Sports Science and Medicine; Medicine and Science in Sports and Exercise; Exercise and Sports Sciences Reviews; Graduate Journal of Sport, Exercise and Physical Education; Journal of Science and Medicine in Sport; Sport and Leisure Studies; International Journal of the History of Sport; Managing Leisure; International Journal of Sport Policy; European Sport Management Quarterly; Journal of Sport and Tourism*
	Events: *International Journal of Event Management Research; International Journal of Event and Festival Management; International Journal of Hospitality and Event Management*

mind mapping, future scenarios can be played out, such as what are the key risks, what causes them and what are the implications of these risks? The answers can mean a variety of pictures can be created of what the future may look like, helping managers to make decisions about what they should do to manage these potential upside or downside risks.

4.6.1 Mind mapping and creative thinking

An obvious starting point for any risk assessment is for staff and managers to draw on their collective experiences to initially identify a variety of possible hazards and risks. It is a process relevant for safety, project or strategic risk management, whereby people's different experiences, knowledge and background can be used to start the risk management process. It is a process sometimes encapsulated by such clichés as 'thinking outside the box' or 'blue sky thinking', whereby in the early stages nothing is ruled in or out. Indeed, for many simple risk assessments this can be as far as the research process goes, as all the necessary information is felt to have been gathered. An example of a mind map is presented in Fig. 4.1, which results

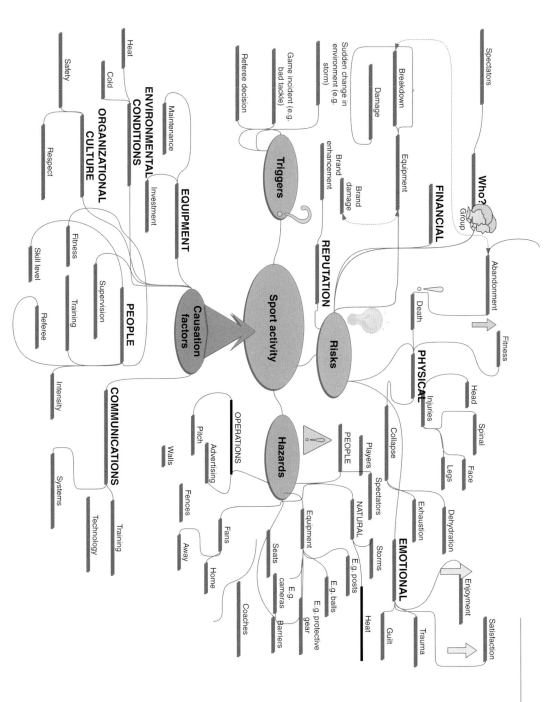

Fig. 4.1. An example of a mind map using the anatomy of risk concepts.

from applying the anatomy of risk concepts to a sport activity to help initially identify a range of hazards, risks, triggers and potential causation factors.

Mind mapping, brainstorming and developing spidergrams are likely to be familiar techniques for many. Although each term can have its own subtle variations, what they share is a focus on creativity and trying to unlock ideas, along with representing them in a visual manner. This familiarity and superficial simplicity may blind people to their value and how, through adaptation and refinement, they can actually become quite sophisticated tools to use. In essence, when considering mind maps, the following points should be considered:

- The focus on being relaxed and open, which in the early stages should rule nothing in or out, no matter how farfetched or outlandish.
- Focus on key words, then let ideas and associated words flow from these.
- It begins with a central word or idea, then has branches flowing from this (sometimes the subsidiary branches are called twigs).
- If using a defined approach, such as the Buzan method (see links at the end of this chapter), it recommends using single words, lots of colour and if possible pictures.
- It represents ideas in a radial format (hence why they are sometimes known as spidergrams).
- In the early stages, go for quantity rather than quality.
- It draws on ideas of lateral thinking, a term coined by Edward de Bono (2009). In essence it involves approaching problems in a creative, non-linear fashion which can relate to wishful thinking, exaggeration, being provocative, challenging or questioning existing assumptions.
- If doing mind mapping as part of a group, avoid criticizing ideas and draw on different people's knowledge and experiences.
- Use it to both understand the breadth and variety of risks, then later develop solutions and control measures.

Referring back to Table 4.1, many of the checklist questions asked in relation to the process stages can all be used to begin a mind map. Figure 4.2 offers two (a and b) generic examples which have some of the initial key starting branches begun, such as using SWOT and PESTLE, or using the six classic questions of management (Who is at risk? What is at risk? Why are these things at risk? Where are they at risk? When are they at risk? How are they at risk?). It should be noted that SWOT and PESTLE are combined because it is a way to generate more ideas by considering how the PESTLE hazards can create a variety of upsides/opportunities or downsides/threats.

While mind maps may initially be used in the early stages, it should be appreciated that they can continue to be used at all stages or adapted into more sophisticated formats. Whereas in the early stages they may be used to generate lots of ideas and possibilities, in later applications they can delve into complexity theory, such as looking at what the key causation factors may be, how they connect and how certain outcomes and events may occur.

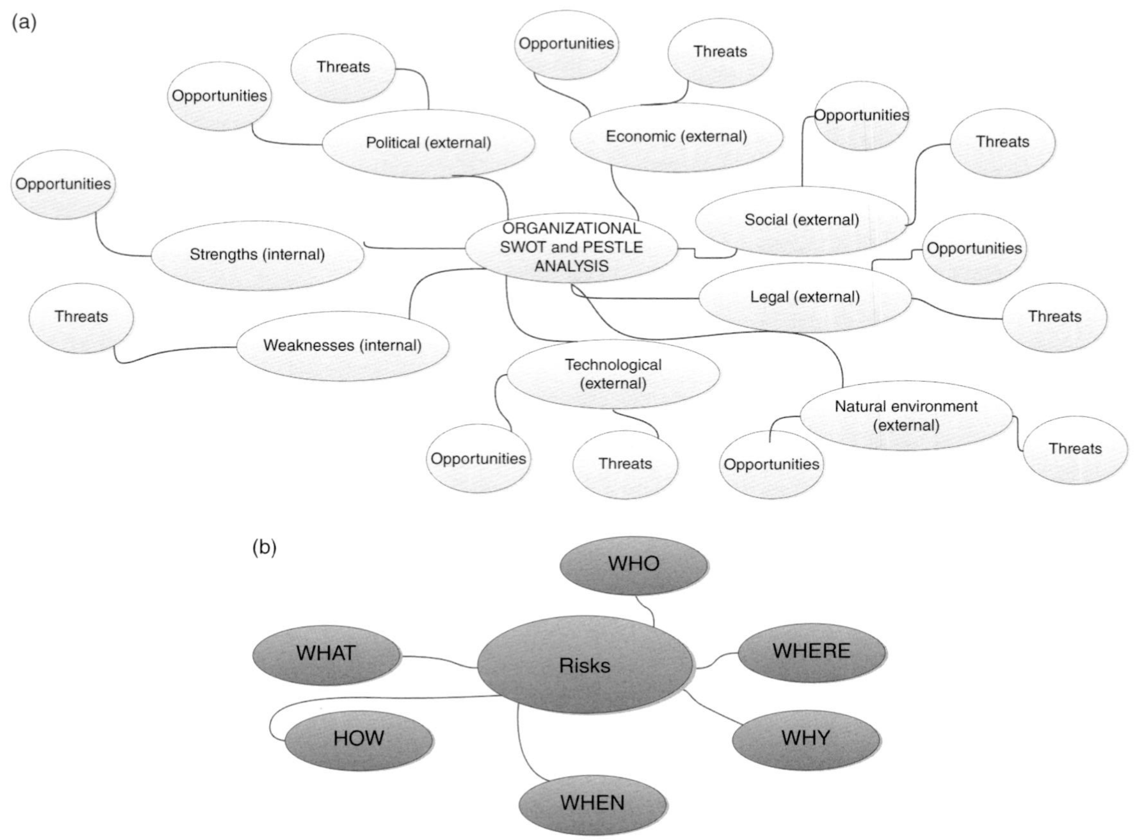

Fig. 4.2. Examples of mind map branches: (a) using PESTLE and SWOT; (b) using classic management questions (PESTLE, Political, Economic, Social, Technological, Legal and Environmental; SWOT, Strengths, Weaknesses, Opportunities and Threats).

4.6.2 Fishbone analysis and diagram

The fishbone diagram is a visual tool to help identify and analyse *cause* and *effect*. It has had a wide variety of applications in the areas of business, engineering and medicine where an understanding of causation is sought, and has some useful potential applications in risk management. While there are a number of variations, the classic fishbone diagram will be the main area of focus in relation to how it can be adapted to analyse risks.

The fishbone diagram can help to explore and analyse any risks and hazards that may have been identified via the initial mind mapping creative thinking exercises, or from further research. It is a way of identifying factors and how they may be linked to generate risk events, which can relate to operational health and safety risks, project event schedules or strategic risks generated in the business environment. The fishbone diagram should consider the following points:

- the head of the fish encapsulates the problem, or as it is considered here, the risk;
- from the head, one works backwards to create the diagram;
- the bones represent the key factors that can contribute to causation;
- the key, broad causation factors spur from the main spine (e.g. causation factors based around people, equipment, communications, organizational culture, using PESTLE, etc.);
- some of the checklist questions in the process stages (Table 4.1) can be used to generate ideas for the main spurs;
- from the main spurs, further causation factors are developed which give more detail; and
- it can be drawn with Post-it® notes used in the beginning, so that primary and secondary causation factors can be moved.

An example of a fishbone diagram for a sport injury is presented in Fig. 4.3. Parts of the data which informed the diagram came from a mixture of the initial mind maps and reviewing a variety of case studies and some journal articles. What it helps to illustrate is some of the key causation factors that need to be considered, such as using some of the broader generic hazard categories of people or the natural environment. These broader areas can then have a cluster of subsidiary factors, such as the different weather conditions for the natural environment. Any area where a cluster of factors appears can be an area for closer scrutiny. For example, using this for rugby: a scrum can be a key hazard, where the risk of a spinal injury can be increased in poor weather conditions, inexperienced players, mismatches in strength and the intensity of the game, all of which the referee could consider during the game to try and reduce the likelihood of a serious injury occurring.

The fishbone does have its limitations in that it is not quite as useful as other approaches to convey the full complexity of an issue. While it may not encapsulate complexity, it does at least show system connectivity with the visual format being easy to scrutinize.

Fig. 4.3. Fishbone analysis for sport injuries.

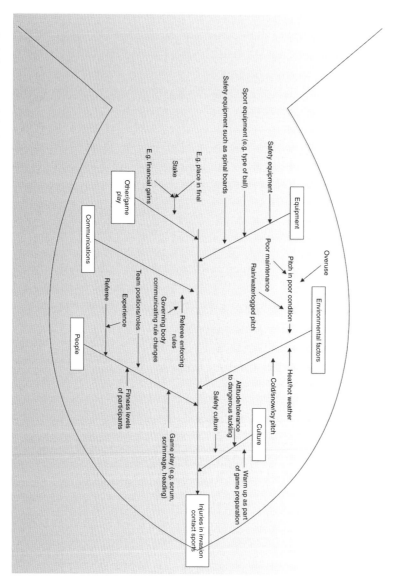

4.6.3   Causation loops

Causation loop diagrams are a way to try and represent complexity and how multiple factors can contribute to an outcome, rather than considering a problem in a simplistic, linear way. Sherwood (2002: 3) emphasizes the importance of showing the connectedness in systems and the key component parts. He argues that if you wish to understand a system, and so be in a position to predict its behaviour, it is necessary to study the system as a whole, whereby simplifying too much or cutting factors out can destroy the system connectedness. He uses the term 'complexity driven by connectedness' (Sherwood, 2002: 4), which refers to the idea that complex systems have many different parts that can shape outcomes. The following are some of the key elements when considering causation loops:

- there are different types of loops, such as reinforcing loops (it will see an increase or improved effect, indicated by a + sign) and balancing loops (as something is put in, something leaves, or has a negative effect, indicated by a − sign);
- systems have feedback, where events lead to other events, such as a stock market crisis where panic in one group of sellers can cause panic in another group;
- systems can also stabilize themselves (the theory of homeostasis);
- you need to identify the key dynamics, then try and consider the relationships;
- it can be useful to identify key stakeholders and relationships;
- it can be particularly useful in project risk management analysis; and
- it can consider how one factor can affect another factor or identify which factors are related.

An example of a system loop is presented in Fig. 4.4, which looks at the variety of factors that can affect the future success or problems of a professional soccer or football club. A number of these factors were identified from an initial SWOT and PESTLE analysis, as Fig. 4.4 illustrates a range of internal and external environmental factors that may create upside or downside risks. It is an analysis designed to show how the more immediate operational challenges can have more long-term strategic implications, such as how a run of poor results can mean reduced attendance, leading to reduced revenue from gate receipts and merchandise sales. This can be accentuated by potentially lost revenues from sponsors, advertising and corporate hospitality. Both are examples of negative causation loops. What Fig. 4.4 also illustrates are the potential impacts and risks of other factors in the system, which can have the potential to make things better or worse. For example, paradoxically, clubs that after a run of poor results find themselves in a relegation battle can actually sometimes be rejuvenated and see the excitement and fans return as they become embroiled in the fight to avoid relegation. Another example is the potential risk of how a club that becomes more successful and attracts more corporate sponsors can end up alienating the more loyal, die-hard fans. The final point to highlight is that a number of other external environmental hazards and risks are represented floating around in the system, such as the potential for new government regulations, or the impacts of international sport events and global economic recessions, which are waiting to be mapped out and joined up with the system. What this representation is particularly useful for

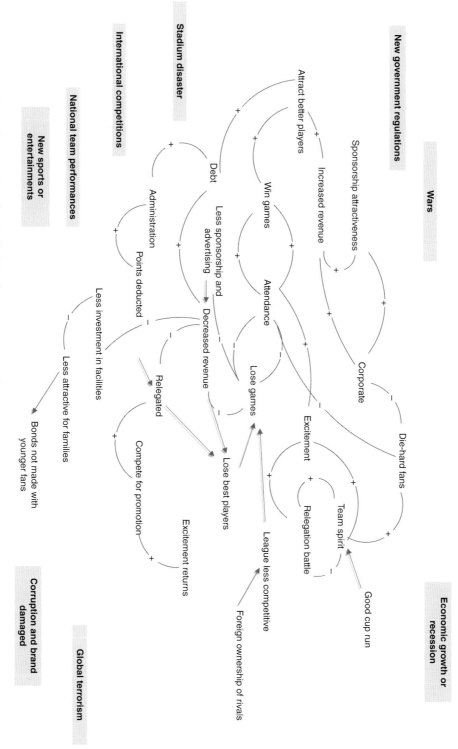

Fig. 4.4. Causation loop diagram for a football club's future success or failings.

illustrating is the complexity, or the potential recipe for chaos, which organizations always operate in (the edge of chaos theory).

4.6.4 Event and fault tree analysis and scenarios

Fault tree and event tree analysis encourage creativity to help identify the key hazards, risks and how key factors connect to determine certain outcomes, presented in a visual format that maps out the critical paths (Gardiner, 2005: 175). Event tree analysis traces out some of the outcomes if a specified risk event was to occur, while a fault tree analysis looks at the possible factors that can lead to a specified event. Frosdick (1997) illustrates the differences by using the analogy of a house fire. In relation to event tree analysis, the house fire is the failure node, where one can map out the consequences of various events, together with (very importantly) the consequences of various control mechanisms or safety devices, such as whether there are smoke alarms in the house. In relation to fault tree analysis, this looks at the conditions which create a fire, working backwards in relation to what can go wrong (a form of hindsight review), such as a fire needing a triggering event like an electrical fault or a dropped cigarette.

Fault tree analysis is also known as HAZOP (HAZard and OPerability analysis) and has its roots in the military, engineering and chemical industries, but it has the potential to be applied to a variety of risk situations. This approach has some of the following key characteristics which need to be considered:

- It can begin with mind mapping to identify some the potential failure points or risks, which can be done individually or as a team.
- It is a useful tool to use in the analysis stage to review causation factors and how *likely* an event may be. A selected failure node needs to be selected, such as an accident or incident, which could be labelled as the risk event.
- Consideration then needs to be given to the key elements or ingredients which can lead to that event (e.g. the house fire needs oxygen, fuel and a source of ignition).
- Causal factors are linked to the incident by 'OR' or 'AND' gates. An 'OR' gate indicates that only one of the causes needs be present to cause the event, while the 'AND' gate indicates that all of the causation factors are needed (e.g. for a fire to occur it would have the 'AND' gates of oxygen, fuel and ignition as all must be present; while ignition could have a number of possible 'OR' gates, such as an electrical failure or a dropped cigarette).
- It should form a tree like flow chart, where the critical paths that lead to the event should be seen and where a variety of standard symbols can be used, such as for the 'AND' and 'OR' gates.
- The different pathways are called 'nodes'.
- As part of the analysis, it can use some of the following terms to convey a sense of probability: 'none', 'more of', 'less of', 'reverse', 'other than', 'part of' and 'more than'.
- The method can also be used for analysing past events. For example, Haddock (1999) used it to examine adventure-related incidents and how participants on an activity became

exposed to hypothermia; while Salmon *et al.* (2009) use fault tree analysis to analyse the Hillsborough tragedy.

- It can also be used for future scenario speculative analysis, as the following examples illustrate.

Two examples are mapped out. The first relates to a sudden death scenario of someone playing sport or doing an adventure activity, which can be easily adapted to a variety of adventure, sport or event activities, and is represented in Fig. 4.5. From a mixture of mind mapping and additional research of medical databases, a variety of causation factors can be identified. In the first instance, a number of common causation factors can be identified, ranging from cardiac arrest, diabetes, concussion, asthma or over-exertion. Each of these key nodes can generate further pathways, such as the factors that can lead to cardiac arrest. This simple analysis begins to build an assessment of how likely the risk event is, together with potential areas that can be targeted for control measures, or the factors that can lend themselves for monitoring.

The second example, presented in Fig. 4.6, relates to a terrorist attack on a group of tourists travelling to Ethiopia, and is presented a little differently in terms of orientation compared with the previous example. This is done simply to illustrate that there is not necessarily a set approach to how fault tree diagrams have to be presented. This analysis also has more relevance for project- and strategic-related risk assessments. Reflecting on a variety of journalistic news articles, books and journal articles, a number of factors can be identified that can lead to terrorism and the risk of a terrorist attack. For example, the building up of resentment factor and frustrations are highlighted, such as the high levels of youth unemployment and religious differences, but have no legitimate outlet for any frustrations to be expressed because it is an authoritarian political system. This critical path also gives some useful factors which could be monitored to give a sense of some of the underlying factors in the political environment, such as the foreign policy of other governments.

In relation to event tree analysis, this can follow a similar pattern as the fault tree but maps out the potential critical paths after the event has taken place, with consideration given to the impacts certain control measures may have. It can be useful to let the event tree analysis continue to flow from fault tree analysis, as it looks at some of the future possible consequences or scenarios. This in essence is related to what is sometimes described as the bow tie model, where the causation factors taper to a centre, while the events taper away from it. In relation to using event tree analysis, the following points should be noted:

- research and identify previous incidents to help map consequences;
- identify the control mechanisms and the consequences if they are used or if they fail; and
- map out the event tree, attempting to identify the probability of each event stage occurring if possible.

While fault tree analysis is useful for gauging the likelihood of a risk, event tree analysis is invaluable for assessing the impacts or severity. It can also be useful to identify key checklists of actions and control measures.

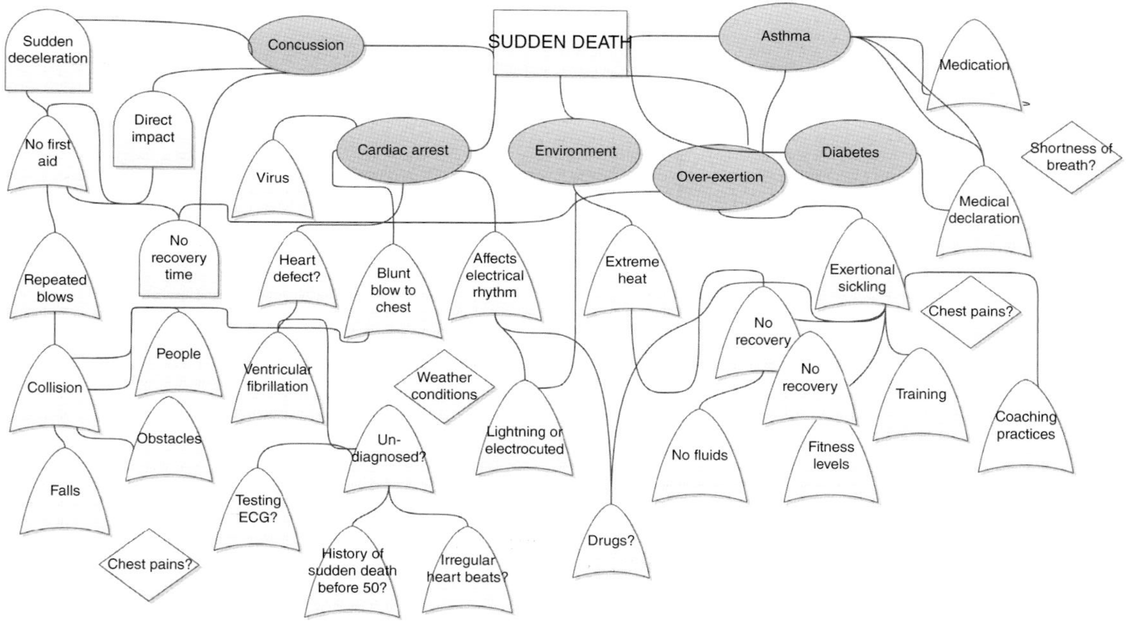

Fig. 4.5. Fault tree diagram for sudden death of a sport or adventure activity participant (ECG, electrocardiogram).

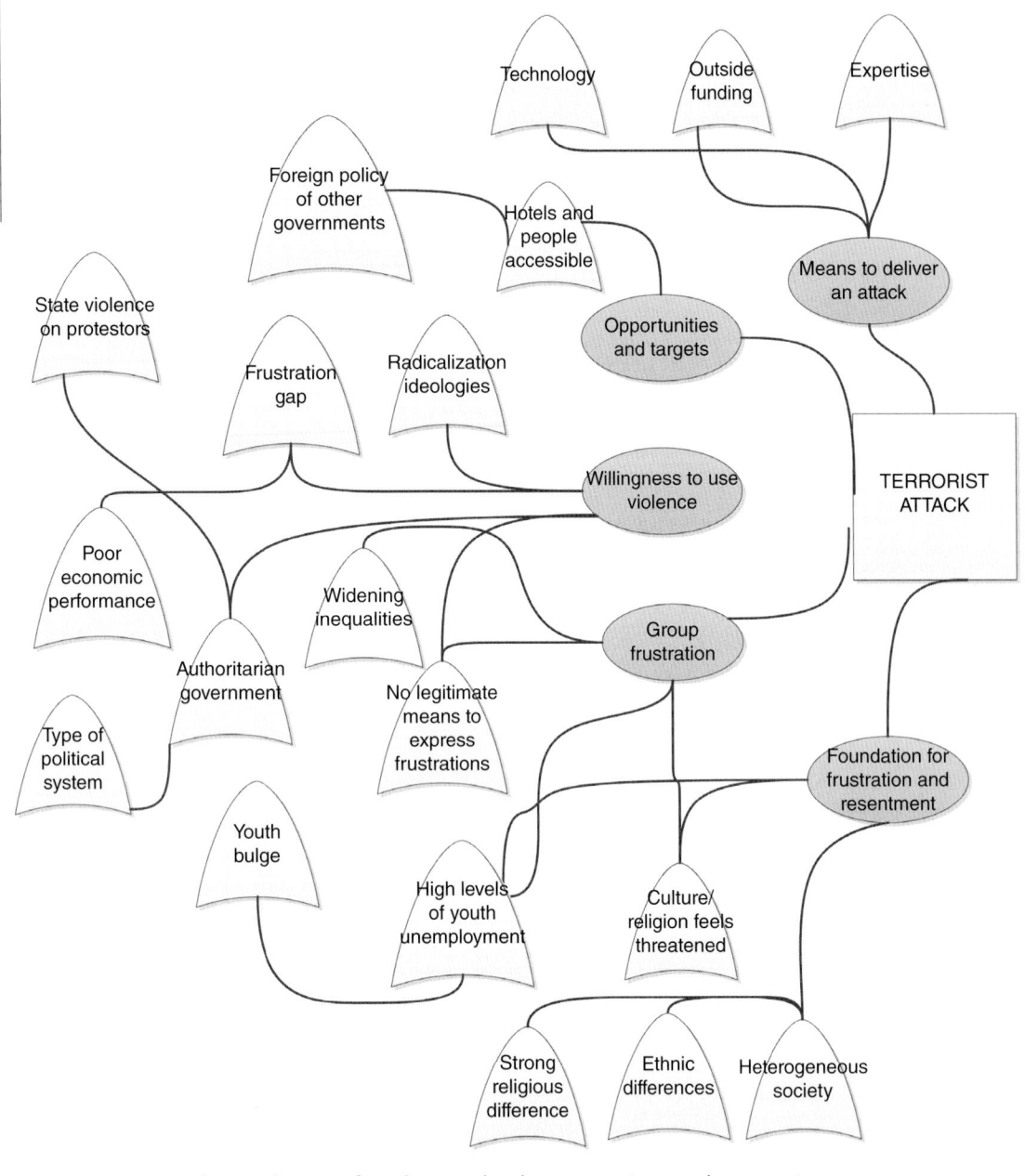

Fig. 4.6. Fault tree diagram for what can lead to a terrorist attack on tourists.

In Fig. 4.7 the scenario of sudden death of a participant in the sport context is elaborated upon. In terms of materials, examining different case studies can be particularly useful, such as the case of Fabrice Muamba, a Bolton Wanderers soccer player, who suddenly collapsed during a game suffering a cardiac arrest. Despite his heart having stopped for over an hour, his survival and recovery provides an excellent case study to draw on and map out. Figure 4.7 shows how a

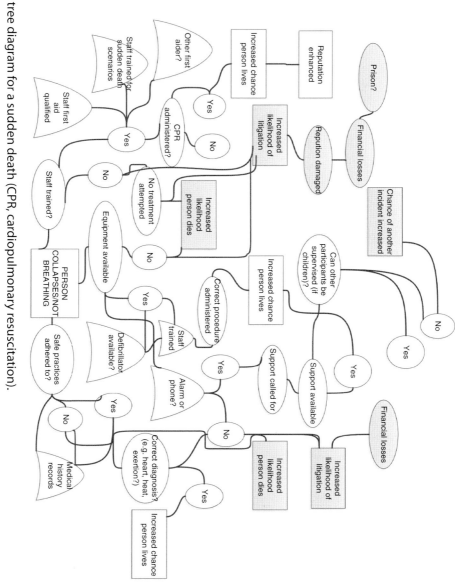

Fig. 4.7. Event tree diagram for a sudden death (CPR, cardiopulmonary resuscitation).

diagnosis needs to be given quickly, such as whether the collapse relates to heart failure or other conditions. It also looks at whether certain control mechanisms are in place, such as people who are trained in first aid and the availability of a defibrillator. Parts of the analysis also explore the consequences if certain control measures are lacking, such as not having trained first aiders, and the subsequent damage to reputation, even the risk of litigation and imprisonment.

The example presented in Fig. 4.8 relates to a scenario exercise for an expedition group travelling to Ethiopia and exploring the worst-case scenario of a terrorist bomb attack. It is slightly different in format in that it explores some of the critical paths that could occur if a group member is killed or injured. It uses a number of critical 'alarm bell' images to help focus attention on some key points to be aware of, such as checking the UK FCO travel advice and insurance cover.

4.6.5   Spatial analysis

Spatial analysis can be an invaluable tool for analysing operational and project-related risks. At its simplest, it is about looking at maps and plans where activities take place and identifying potential hazards and risks. It can also represent data collected as part of a frequency table in a different way. In this instance, it can work on the same sort of lines as a police hotspot map, whereby acts of criminality are highlighted. In the past these would be done with pins on a map, but now they are done electronically, as Box 4.2 illustrates, whereby acts of criminality can be examined around a sport stadium. The visual representation of hazards and risks can be particularly useful for instances such as:

- an outdoor adventure activity, where key hazards and risks are marked on a map which then gives guidance on points to avoid, or where to put in some precautions;
- an event organizer could look at a site plan for potential hazards, congestion points or locations where any previous incidents have taken place; and
- a tour operator doing guided tours could look at a hotspot map related to crime, or mark out any incidents he/she has identified from an incident frequency table, to identify any potential problems.

4.6.6   Other techniques

As was highlighted earlier, it simply is not possible to explain all of the operational, project and strategic management techniques that have the potential to be used to help in risk analysis and assessment. Some additional tools that can be useful relate to:

- Utilizing *techniques of statistical analysis*, such as regression analysis, scattergrams and many others.
- The *Monte Carlo* tool is a quantitative simulation tool that allows a variety of future speculative scenarios to be considered. It is used in a wide range of engineering and scientific projects, where a more intimate analysis can be done of probability and what may happen if certain outcomes or schedules are not met (e.g. due to periods of good or bad weather, or changing costs arising from fluctuations in energy or fuel costs). It has a

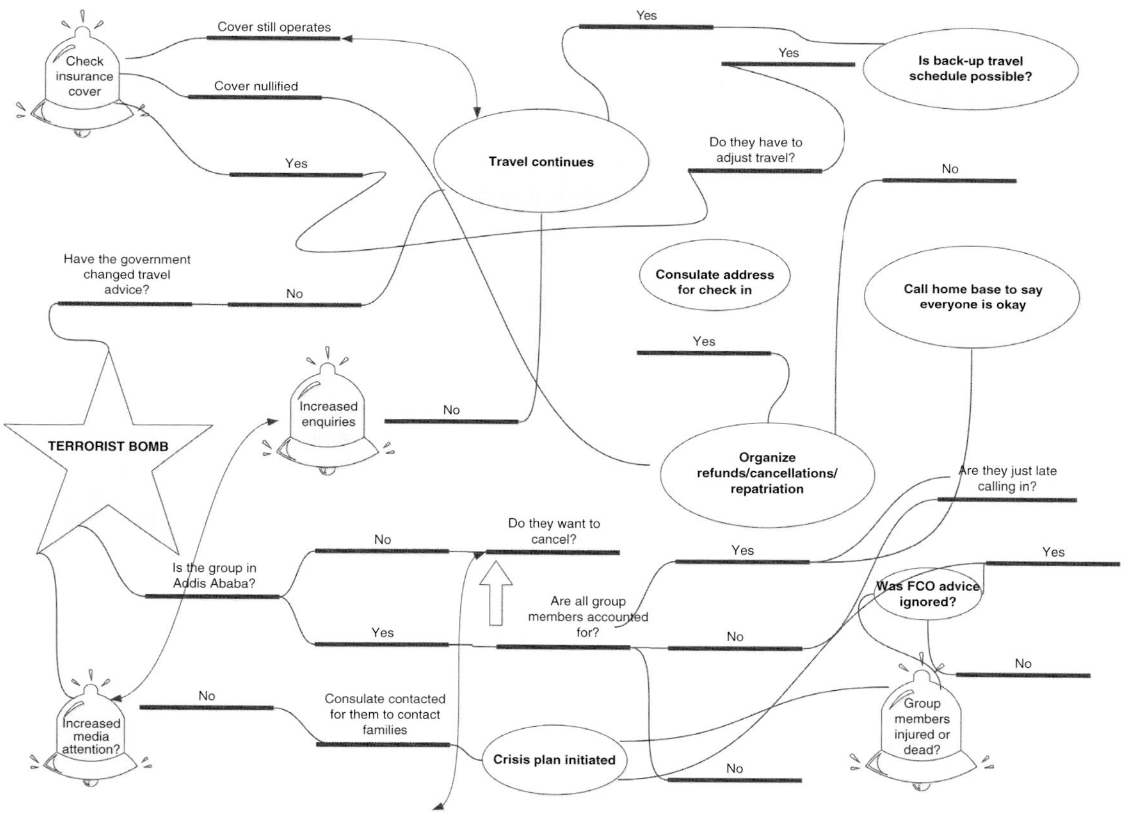

Fig. 4.8. Critical path event tree diagram for a terrorist bomb attack (FCO, Foreign and Commonwealth Office). (From Piekarz, 2009.)

Box 4.2. Example of spatial analysis: incidents of crime around the Olympic Park. (From Police.UK, 2014.)

Shown in (a) below is a map of the Olympic Park area in London, where the 2012 Olympic Games took place. The numbers highlighted give a snapshot of the crimes that took place in August 2014 and show the total number of incidents recorded, with the map in (b) giving a more detailed breakdown of the crimes that took place near the stadium. This spatial analysis quickly and easily helps to identify hazards (e.g. thieves), risks (e.g. loss of property) and where resources can be placed to deal with the risk of theft, such as placing more stewards in certain locations.

(a)

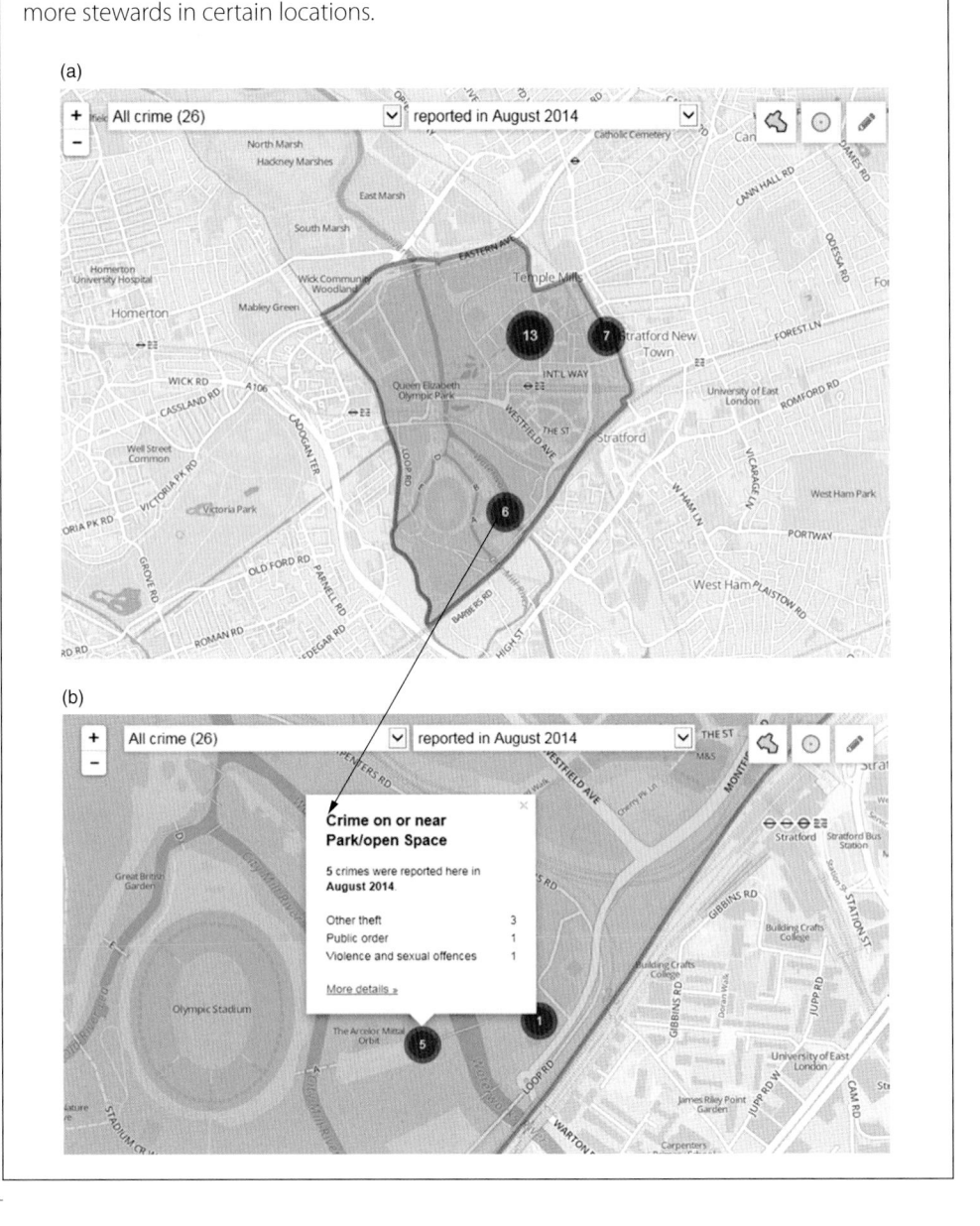

(b)

variety of uses; in the aviation industry, for example, it is used to examine aircraft component failures.

- *Carrying capacity* models examine and calculate how many people can move through a space safely, how quickly they can be evacuated and what the capacity is for watching an event. The calculation of carrying capacity is crucial because when carrying capacity is exceeded, the results can be tragic, as the Hillsborough case study illustrates.

4.7   INDICATORS AND MONITORING

One of the benefits of mapping out risk scenarios is that they can help to identify factors, or pieces of information, which can be monitored and help alert a manager or practitioner that a risk has a potential of occurrence. Bryman and Bell (2003: 73) distinguish between an *indicator* and a *measure*, with the latter being relatively unambiguous and usually quantifiable, while indicators are ways to tap into concepts that are less quantifiable and so are used to stand in for a concept; in practice, the difference can be more ambiguous. The reality is that one is often looking for indicators rather than true measures, as these can be hard to find.

The simple analogy is to think of an oil warning light on a car, which if it comes on warns that there may be a more serious problem in the car engine, and to continue to drive can lead to a bigger and costlier problem. The oil light does not cause the problems, simply indicates that there could be a problem. In terms of risk management, it is always important to try and find the pieces of information that can act as the oil light warning indicator.

An example of potential indicators is given in Box 4.3, whereby it is illustrated how one can use indicators which help alert the organization or practitioner of potential risks even though

---

Box 4.3. You don't need to understand the science of causation to monitor

The science behind what causes an avalanche can be complex; but that does not mean it is not possible to identify some key factors of potential causation which can act as indicators of the hazard and the risks posed to people on the mountainside. There can be many different types of avalanche caused by different weather conditions, which may relate to rain, sudden changes in temperature and even types of snow. Monitoring some of these conditions, along with knowing that a key trigger for an avalanche can be an explosion or someone skiing or snowboarding off-piste, means the risks can be evaluated. In theory, it is possible to make one's own judgement of the risks based on the weather conditions or use someone else's assessment of the risks. Additional dynamic assessment can be taken while doing the activity, such as monitoring for cracks in the snow. Reflection back to some of the heuristic traps, such as familiarity or scarcity of opportunity, can also be considered to try and make a better judgement.

a full understanding of causation is not had. In relation to this discussion on risk and the use of tools, examples of risk indicators could relate to some of the following:

- Monitoring of natural environment conditions, such how hot or cold it is, reflecting back as to how it can change the likelihood of certain risks.
- A review of financial performance or usage figures.
- A review of an accident or near miss incidents, to prompt a fuller review of control measures within the organization.
- A review of an accident or near miss incidents for other organizations, sectors or countries.
- Monitoring statistical country data to help look at general trends in economic and social development. For example, one indicator the CIA (Central Intelligence Agency) uses for predicting state failure or political instability relates to infant mortality rates, available from the United Nations or the World Bank.
- Review of tolerability thresholds, such as the levels of accident rates that can be considered tolerable and acceptable.
- Court rulings and government regulations which may have reverberations across all areas of work.
- Dynamic operational indicators, such as group dynamics, crowd behaviour and environmental conditions.
- Access to advisory sites, which can be as mundane as weather forecasts to advice issued by governments or relevant agencies, such as governing bodies of sport.

4.8   CONCLUSION

How much data is collected and the need to apply analytical tools will vary considerably, depending on the level of complexity of the activity, environment or project being risk assessed. For the simple activity, it is perfectly possible for a risk assessment to take place whereby a form is filled in directly based on visual observations and the person's own experience. The need (or desire) to conduct more detailed research, or apply more complex models and tools in order to analyse and assess the risks, can be felt to be unimportant and so ignored. While this can work for assessments based on simple activities, the failure to apply additional tools and models for more complex work, such as a sport event or assessing new tourist destinations, can result in weak analysis, misjudged assessments and poor control measures and decisions.

One point worth emphasizing is that some of the techniques can be applied to a variety of problem-solving situations. While at times the risk management process has to be carefully distilled and separated to ensure regulatory compliance, at other times many risk management practices should blend in with everyday working and planning practices. The various tools described in this chapter are not purely risk management techniques. This is emphasized because they illustrate that risk management should blend with everyday management practices, whereby risk management is not seen as an onerous, additional activity. Although the tools may seem initially complex, once one or two are mastered, it is surprising how often they are drawn upon to help in a variety of working problems.

Finally, the adoption of certain theoretical principles can help shape the organizational risk culture, which in turn influences the practical risk process; for example, the use of complexity theory should create a desire to try and understand more about why things may happen, always questioning and never being fully satisfied that a definitive analysis has been arrived at.

DISCUSSION QUESTIONS AND TASKS

1. For an organization or activity of your choice, produce a mind map for each of the checklist process questions:

- What is the purpose of the organization?
- Conduct a preliminary SWOT, with the 'OT' combined with PESTLE.
- Use the anatomy of risk model to branch off some of the risks.
- Use the six classic questions of: Who is at risk? What is at risk? Why are these things at risk? Where are they at risk? When are they at risk? How are they at risk?

2. Identify some of the most extreme risks/worst-case scenarios that may occur (e.g. death of a participant), then select two of the techniques to try and understand what may cause the event and what the consequences may be.

3. For an activity of your choice, identify an incident or accident and conduct a fault and event tree analysis to map out what led to the event and what the consequences were.

4. For a sector of your choice, research a range of secondary databases in order to construct an incident table and analyze the results.

REFERENCES

APM (2004) *Project Risk Analysis and Management Guide*. APM Publishing, Biggleswade, UK.

Brink, C.H. (2004) *Measuring Political Risk*. Ashgate Publishing Limited, Aldershot, UK.

Bryman, A. and Bell, E. (2003) *Business Research Methods*. Oxford University Press, Oxford.

de Bono, E. (2009) *Lateral Thinking: A Textbook of Creativity*. Penguin, London.

Frosdick, S. (1997) Managing risk in public assembly facilities. In: Frosdick, S. and Walley, L. (eds) *Sport and Safety Management*. Butterworth-Heinemann, London, pp. 273–291.

Gardiner, P.D. (2005) *Project Management: A Strategic Planning Approach*. Palgrave Macmillan, Basingstoke, UK.

Haddock, C. (1999) High potential incidents – determining their significance. Tools for our trade and a tale or two. Wilderness Risk Management Conference Proceedings. Available at: http://www.nols.edu/nolspro/pdf/wrmc_proceedings_99_high_potential_haddock.pdf (accessed 18 January 2015).

Merna, T. and Faisal, F.A. (2005) *Corporate Risk Management: An Organisational Perspective*. Wiley, Chichester, UK.

Piekarz, M.J. (2009) Tourism in an unstable and complex world? Searching for a relevant risk paradigm and model for tourism organisations. PhD thesis, Cranfield University, Cranfield, UK.

Pidd, M. (1996) *Tools for Thinking: Modelling in Management Science*. Wiley, Chichester, UK.

Police.UK (2014) Crime map. Available at: http://www.police.uk/ (accessed 20 September 2014).

Salmon, P., Stanton, N.A., Gibbon, A., Jenkins, D. and Walker, G.H. (2009) *Human Factors Methods and Sports Science: A Practical Guide*. CRC Press, Boca Raton, Florida.

Sherwood, D. (2002) *Seeing the Forest for the Trees: A Manager's Guide to Applying Systems Thinking*. Nicholas Brealey, Yarmouth, UK.

Standards New Zealand (2004) New Zealand Handbook: Guidelines for Risk Management in Sport and Recreation. SNZ HB8669:2004. Available at: http://www.sportnz.org.nz/assets/Uploads/attachments/managing-sport/strong-organisations/Risk-Management-Toolkit.pdf (accessed 20 August 2014).

FURTHER READING

Books and journal articles

Cagno, E., Caron, F. and Mancini, M. (2007) A multi-dimensional analysis of major risks in complex projects. *Risk Management* 9, 1–18.

Fuller, C.W. (2007) Catastrophic injuries in rugby union: an assessment of the risk (final draft). Available at: http://irbplayerwelfare.com/pdfs/CI_Risk_Assessment_EN.pdf (accessed 12 May 2013).

JISC (2014) Cause and effect. Available at: http://www.jiscinfonet.ac.uk/infokits/risk-management/identifying-risk/cause-and-effect/ (accessed 12 July 2013).

Johnson, J. (2006) Can complexity help us better understand risk? *Risk Management* 8, 227–267.

Kletz, T. (2001) *Learning from Accidents*, 3rd edn. Gulf Professional Publishing, Oxford.

Kwak, Y.H. and Ingnall, L. (2007) Exploring Monte Carlo simulation applications for project management. *Risk Management* 9, 44–57.

Salmon, P., Stanton, N.A., Gibbon, A., Jenkins, D. and Walker, G.H. (2009) *Human Factors Methods and Sports Science: A Practical Guide*. CRC Press, Boca Raton, Florida (provides some excellent examples of different tools used to analyse individual case studies).

Databases

Centers for Disease Control and Prevention (CDC) has a great deal of useful US accident data, available at: http://www.cdc.gov/nchs/fastats/accidental-injury.htm

Department for Culture, Media and Sport (DCMS) produces 'The Green Guide' which has invaluable information on how to model carrying capacities in stadiums, available at: http://www.safetyatsportsgrounds.org.uk/sites/default/files/publications/green-guide.pdf

European Agency for Safety at Work (EASW) gives a useful overview of some of the additional techniques that can be used and accident data, available at: https://osha.europa.eu/en

ExamTime provides various techniques and mind mapping templates, available at: https://www.examtime.com/mind-maps/

International Safety News Institute (INSI) can be a useful database to track accidents and incidents around the world, available at: http://www.newssafety.org/home/

JISC has an excellent overview of numerous analytical tools, available at: http://www.jiscinfonet.ac.uk/infokits/

Mindmapping.com provides various techniques and templates, available at: http://www.mindmapping.com/

MoreSteam.com has examples of various tools, with an example of a fishbone diagram for a basketball coach and missed throws, available at: https://www.moresteam.com/toolbox/fishbone-diagram.cfm

ThinkBuzan provides various advice, examples and mind mapping templates, available at: http://thinkbuzan.com/how-to-mind-map/

chapter 5

Management and Control of Risks

CHAPTER OBJECTIVES

- To provide an overview of the key types of control measures that practitioners can use.
- To explain how the decisions taken to control risks will be based around utilizing a mixture of resources.
- To explain why the controls should be viewed as dynamic, where adjustments should always be considered as operational and external business environmental conditions change.

Key concepts

Risk management; hazard management; management of risks; risk controls; control categories; hazard management; ALARP and SFAIRP; jigsaw of management controls.

5.1 INTRODUCTION

The beginning of the risk process is the identification of risks and hazards. These should be analysed and assessed in terms of their likelihood and potential outcome. From this analysis and assessment comes perhaps the most critical part of the risk management process: making decisions and taking actions to control or treat risks. The implementation of suitable and sufficient controls is the practical outcome of the risk assessment process, whether this relates to safety, operations, projects or strategic planning.

This chapter focuses on the control stages of the risk process, which can also be described as *exposure reduction* (Wilks and Davis, 2000: 594), *exposure avoidance* (Cloutier, 2000: 98) or *treatments* (Fitzgerald, 2003: 7) or even *risk management*. The preference is to use the broader and more neutral term *risk control* or the actual *management of risks* (not risk management, as that is used as the overarching phrase to describe all the process stages). This fits in with the ISO (2009) definition of risk controls, which is used to refer to the actual 'measures, policies, devices, practices or other actions which modify the risk' (ISO, 2009: 6).

5.2 THE JIGSAW OF CONTROLS

After the risks and hazards have been identified, analysed and assessed, next comes the critical process of deciding just what should be done with these risks. Practitioners and managers have a range of options in terms of what they decide to do with risks, how they employ resources and how they implement control measures. These three broad dimensions can each be broken down into more specific choices, which can be represented as a jigsaw or mosaic of management options, presented in Fig. 5.1. The three key elements represented in Fig. 5.1 are:

- *key control categories*, represented as the dark shaded areas, based on transferring, taking, avoiding, reducing or monitoring the risks and hazards;
- *mix of resources employed*, represented as the lighter shaded areas, based on equipment, removing hazards, training staff, insurance, changing practices and managing expectations; and
- *implementing measures*, represented as the non-shaded elements, based on documentation, appointing staff, communications, team work, research and leadership.

It should be appreciated when deciding on the type of control measure, the resources employed and the ways they are implemented that it is not always a simple question of selecting just one of the elements from each category. There is a dynamic element to the selection process, whereby it often means a multiple selection is done between the controls, the resources employed and how they are implemented. For example, a hotel or sport centre with a swimming pool has a *hazard* of water, which means that when people *interact* with it, it can create *risks* of injuries, drowning or becoming ill if the water is not properly treated. It is impractical to remove all these risks if the benefits of having a pool are desired, so in the first instance the risks are *taken* but then certain measures are put in place to *reduce* either the *likelihood* of an incident or the *severity* of outcome. This is done by using the resource elements of *training* lifeguards, *hazard management* by having barriers to stop children accessing the pool unsupervised and providing safety *equipment* such as buoyancy aids or spinal boards. At the same time, liability *insurance* is taken out, which *transfers* some of the financial risks in case of any claims for compensation if an incident was to occur. This mix-and-match approach is why the different elements are presented as a jigsaw of selection pieces, with each of the three broad element categories noted earlier examined in more detail in the next three sections.

5.2.1   The jigsaw of controls: key control categories

When faced with hazards and risks, managers have a choice of control options. Health and safety publications often focus simply on either *avoiding* or *preventing* risk arising in the first

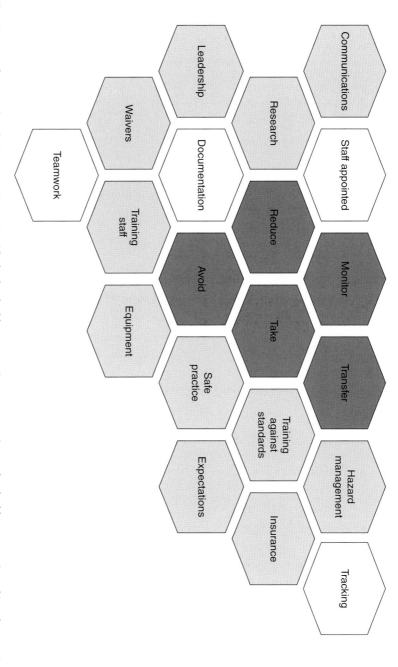

Fig. 5.1. The jigsaw of controls relating to categories (dark-shaded hexagons), resources (non-shaded hexagons) and implementing (light-shaded hexagons).

instance, or if this is not possible, *intervening* in some way to reduce the severity of outcomes. This is certainly evident in American-based literature, where writers such as Masteralixis *et al.* (2005) and Spengler *et al.* (2006) stress the importance of these two control options, with both emphasizing it is vital these things are done because of the potential threat of litigation if things go wrong. Spengler *et al.* (2006: 2) go on to argue that 'risk management entails reducing or eliminating the risk of injury and death and potential subsequent liability that comes about through involvement with sport and recreation programs and services.'

While this identifies two basic control options or categories, it has many limitations. This is because risk, or at least the perception of risk, is a critical factor in delivering enjoyable, sport, adventure and touristic activities (discussed in Chapter 1). It also relates to the essential quality of project and strategic risk management whereby projects and business activities without risks are not always considered worth undertaking. Finally, while the more cautious approach may be more appropriate for the USA, it may be less so for other countries, where there can be a higher tolerance for certain forms of risk taking.

When examining the literature on risk controls additional categories can be identified, such as those offered by Gardiner (2005: 167), in relation to project risk management, or the ISO (2009). Usually, the number of control options ranges from four to six. To deal with these variations, the preference here is to focus on the most commonly cited risk option categories available to managers when dealing with hazards and risks. The categories used here synthesize and embody many of the key control categories, with a 'monitor' categorization given more prominence. They are also appropriate for health and safety, project management or strategic planning. The five key control options available to managers relate to:

- *Risk reduction or modifying.* This can reduce the risk likelihood or the severity of its impact. Other related terms used can be *contingency* (UK Sport, 2005: 44), *substitutions* (Fitzgerald, 2003: 8) or *mitigation.*
- *Risk avoiding.* This involves avoiding the exposure to hazards that could be a source of risks, which can in turn avoid liability for accidents or financial losses from investment decisions. Other terms can be *eliminate* risks (e.g. Fitzgerald, 2003: 8; UK Sport, 2005: 44), *reject* risks (APM, 2004: 107) or *elimination.*
- *Risk taking.* This simply means the risks are taken as they are, perhaps because the risks are an integral part of the activities, or because they are assessed as so low in terms of probability or severity of outcome that the potential gains are considered worthwhile. Other related terms include *acceptance* (UK Sport, 2005: 45) and *exploit* (APM, 2004: 107).
- *Risk transferring and sharing.* This relates to transferring different aspects of risk to a third party. Insurance is the most commonly cited method here, whereby large financial losses or payments that may occur from, for example, storm damage to buildings or legal actions from injuries are taken by the insurers. Outsourcing activities such as security operations for events (UK Sport, 2005: 45) or transportation are other examples. *Sharing* risk can relate to people or organizations pooling resources to help spread the risk of any losses.

- *Monitoring*. Although this does not always appear in the control category lists, it reflects an operational reality whereby risks can be taken only under certain conditions, such as children learning to sail are taken out only in calm seas or not playing golf when rainy weather turns to a thunderstorm. Conditions will always need to be monitored to reflect the dynamic interplay of risk factors, whereby one can move from taking risks to avoiding them in short spaces of time.

The category of risk transference may be a less obvious option for some reading this book, so it is worthwhile to clarify some important points. Some may regard using a third party as a way to remove or absolve the risk exposure to an organization. It does not. For example, there is still a *duty to diligence* to appoint competent people to do contracted-out tasks, such as letting a community hall to a martial arts instructor where there is still an expectation that the instructor is checked for being qualified and suitably insured, as some *residual liability* still resides with the landlord/premises owner (i.e. who could be found liable in a legal action). Also, in terms of brand and reputation, if a problem occurs with a contractor, the business offering the service is still the one held accountable. This happened to British Airways (BA) in 2005, when baggage handlers who were not directly employed by BA went on strike, causing huge disruptions, frustrations and resentment: customers blamed BA for the problems, caring little that they related to an outside contractor.

5.2.2   The jigsaw of management controls: the mix of resources applied

The key control categories have been identified. The next point to consider is how a broad range of resources can be employed to help reduce, transfer, avoid or monitor the risks. These options, represented as the non-shaded areas in the Fig. 5.1, are explained in more detail here. They are:

- *Hazard management*. Removal of the hazard or avoiding exposure to the hazard all sounds very idealistic, but in reality this can often result in the elimination of the activity altogether. For example, if one was to remove the hazard of water in a swimming pool, then this removes the service itself! While some industry sectors, such as those relating to the chemical industry, tend to focus more on hazard management, for adventure, sport and leisure, this is an option only in certain circumstances, such as replacing a hazardous cleaning chemical with a non-hazardous one, or taking an alternative walking route that avoids a perilous drop. More realistic is to consider how hazards can be isolated to avoid damage, injury or loss. Physical prevention from access is easy to identify in a machinery context where, for example, a guard is fitted over a moving part. In leisure environments this can be more difficult to apply, but not impossible, such as a swimming pool area being secured or closed when the pool is not staffed, or preventing unaccompanied children accessing hotel pools, which do not always have lifeguards. In terms of safety, there can be preference to use *hard controls* (i.e. physically preventing hazard interaction, such as locking cleaning chemicals in safe storage areas) rather than *soft control* measures (i.e. having a policy or procedure, such as telling people not to use certain chemicals unless wearing protection), an example of which appears in Box 5.1.

Box 5.1. Hard and soft control measures in swimming pools

A *hard control* measure is guaranteed to protect unless removed, but a *soft control* measure relies on human compliance. In a swimming pool, a drowning detection system that alerts the lifeguard to a swimmer in difficulty is a hard control measure. It overcomes the failure of the human to spot a bather in difficulty. The drowning detection system cannot physically rescue the bather, but if the lifeguard doesn't see the bather due to glare, distraction or obstruction of sight lines by other bathers, then the rescue cannot commence. On the other hand, an underwater camera system that relies on the lifeguard to monitor the screen to see under the water for bathers in distress is still a soft control measure as it has a human element for control. As part of devising control systems, it is important to always look first for isolation of hazards and implementation of hard control measures, such as secure storage of hazardous equipment or chemicals, accessible only to authorized personnel.

- *Insurance.* Quite simply, no formal activity should take place without some proper form of liability insurance to cover for injury, damage or loss. It is essential this is in place and that the conditions which validate the insurance are built into control measure checklists.
- *Establishing effective and safe practices.* Devising working practices which may or may not be committed to paper provides the opportunity to achieve the service standard and manage risk. They should try to change behaviour, whereby certain key routines are established to either prevent certain risks occurring, or manage them more effectively if they do. In a strategic or planning setting, this can relate to set times that key performance indicators are monitored or audited. In relation to operational adventure, sport and touristic activities, establishing practices to ensure safe environments is of crucial importance, which can range from checking weather forecasts before activities or events are engaged with, to setting routines for inspecting equipment. This can relate not only to staff, but also customers, such as training users on the safe way of using gym equipment, or advising tourists how they should behave in other countries. This can also relate to referees and game officials implementing rules, such as in soccer penalizing dangerous tackles to try and change player behaviour.
- *Training against standards.* In order to achieve the service standards and implement the safe or effective working practices, training is fundamental. In terms of safety, effective training regimes require induction for new employees and a sound ongoing training system that is both realistic and proportionate to maintain competence. Competency does not always rely on the production of a certificate from an external training organization. Sound on-the-job training where the trainer and trainee can demonstrate competence is often sufficient in many instances, but it should be carefully checked according to the sector and area worked in.

- *Manage expectations*. Related to this area of safety are considerations of risk perceptions, whereby a balance is being struck between perceived risk and actual safety. Glass platforms that extend out over chasms or tall buildings, and roller coaster rides where people have open seats with their legs free, offer some interesting examples of how people can experience the excitement and thrill of looking down from a great height, even recreating the sensation of falling, while being remarkably safe.

- *Equipment provision*. Providing employees and users with the optimum equipment for the task are key control measures for both avoiding the likelihood of risks and reducing the severity of impact. Examples can range from giving protective gloves to employees, eye protection for junior squash players, shin pads worn in soccer, helmets in American football, and ropes and clips used in climbing. This can also relate to equipment designed to deal with incidents to try and reduce the severity of outcomes, such as the use of spinal boards to keep the head and neck immobile in suspected spinal injuries. For events, it can relate to such things as cameras, even heat spot cameras, to scan for congestion or potential crush zones. In tourism and adventure, equipment such as satellite phones can be invaluable in dealing with certain risk situations. One could even extend the notion of 'equipment' to include the use of computer software packages that can help analyse and assess risks.

5.2.3 The jigsaw of controls: implementing measures

Generally speaking we are better at planning than implementing. We are better at organizing than doing. For all the work involved in conducting risk assessments and devising control systems, this is often the 'easy bit'. The actual implementation of the control system will be the most challenging. Why? Well it relies on people to interpret and implement the requirements, which can be an issue, particularly if the process has not been defined with precision. It also often requires people to change the way they are working and what they do. Managing change to achieve the desired outcome of control measures is a significant challenge that should not be underestimated. In terms of the key mechanisms for implementing controls, represented in Fig. 5.1, these are:

- *Appoint appropriate and competent staff*. Before anything may be written down, the very first control measure that is put in place to deal with risk management is to identify the person responsible for conducting the initial risk analysis and assessment, often labelled the *risk assessor*. As the assessment exercise is done, further clarification is given of the people who are responsible for implementing the more specific control measures. It is important that clear lines of responsibilities are identified in all aspects of risk management (SPARC, 2004: 6). In terms of safety, it is of critical importance that the person appointed for both the assessments and the implementation of controls is deemed *competent*, discussed in more detail in Section 5.5. Ideally the risk assessor should be from within the organization as this provides the best chance of ownership of the process.

- *Do the research and apply the tools*. Along with the appointment of risk assessors, the engagement with the early risk process stages of context setting, analysis and assessment is vital. This refers to the research methods and tool applications discussed in Chapter 4. These early stages can involve team meetings and desk research focusing on existing safety documentation, accidents, then later extending the research to incidents and cases outside the organization, even in other sectors or countries. Awareness of current legislation and good practice documentation is also essential, which can be accessed via government or relevant agency websites.

- *Documentation*. Recording information is of vital importance, as discussed in Chapter 6. Documents do not in themselves provide a vehicle for ongoing improvement, but are crucial in setting standards and benchmarks, identifying responsibilities and detailing the checks that should be in place. While documents can be of critical importance if any incidents occur and an audit investigation is done to check the robustness of the risk and safety procedures, not everything has to be recorded down. For example, while there may be a document specifying the training for lifeguards and where they should be stationed around the pool, a qualified lifeguard will not have documented systems on how to perform a rescue, as he/she is trained and qualified to do so.

- *Training staff*. The common weakness in training is to ask employees to read new procedures and then assume they have understood them and will implement them. This in itself is not communication or training. In most cases internal training will be suitable and sufficient; however, the organization may also identify training and education of employees which requires formal certificated training, outside the organization. For example, virtually all pools in the UK use lifeguards trained against a nationally recognized external award; however, in theory there is no legal impediment for an organization devising its own internal training of lifeguards, although it would be a significant and time-consuming challenge.

- *Teamwork*. It is important that identified control procedures and systems of work are followed by the entire team. Where documented systems are in place, the team should be working to the same version of documentation and the latest issue. For example, over the years the advice for administering first aid has changed, so it is vital that old documents are removed and new ones put in place. Issues of new documentation should also highlight the changes from previous documentation, which can also provide an indication if any training is required.

- *Use of waivers*. Waivers refer to those notes and signs which attempt to adjudicate responsibility, whereby they attempt to transfer the risk back to the customer. They are ubiquitous in all activities, from buying goods, to parking a car or using a changing room. They usually refer to those signs stating such things as activities are done, or items are left, at the person's own risk. In reality, waivers cannot truly transfer risk. Their effectiveness is also country dependent, such as in the USA, where an act being voluntary does not necessarily transfer liability or reduce the risk of litigation. This is not to say that waivers have no value, as they can be useful mechanisms to communicate risks to people, helping them decide if they want to undertake the risk or put in measures to reduce the risk.

- *Leadership and cultures.* When the risk processes were compared in Chapter 2, it was noted that one of the first phases in some Australian models is that there needs to be a cultural acceptance of the risk process. This suggests that leadership by senior managers is important in ensuring the whole risk management process is taken seriously by everyone in the organization.
- *Communication.* Communication can be one of the most critical elements of risk management, whereby if there is a failure to communicate the risks and how they should be approached by both staff and customers, the whole risk management process can count for nothing. Communication is vital in all process stages, where there is encouragement for two-way flows, so managers can communicate with operational staff and operational staff can communicate with senior managers (Heldman, 2005: 22–25).

A few additional points need to be said about communication and leadership as they are such critical elements in the implementation of control measures. Part of the effective communication process is not only the articulation of risks, but can also be active listening whereby people clarify questions, paraphrase, show interest and refrain from interrupting. It also relates to working effectively in a team and communicating with other key stakeholders. For example, how different staff or organizational departments communicate (i.e. the notion of joined-up thinking) is important, because poor communication can mean that as one risk is dealt with, another is created. Poor communications can often be a critical factor in precipitating crisis events, whereby poor or no communication meant a disaster was not prevented or the outcomes made far worse. Finally, consideration can also be given to *prospect theory*, discussed in Chapter 7, which can have some interesting applications in relation to how one can communicate the potential gains and losses.

5.3 RISK CONTROLS, RATINGS AND PRIORITIZATION OF RESOURCES

There is a great deal of a debate as to how risks should be assessed and scored, a number of which are discussed in Chapter 6. The debates encompass whether it is better to have a qualitative, descriptive rating system, or a numeric-based system, such as using percentage values. Indeed, some writers even question the whole value of using an assessment scoring system because, despite claims that using scores helps make risk more objective, the score or value arrived at is always likely to be highly subjective. Regardless of these many limitations, using a scoring system remains both a common practice and something attractive in the attempt to convey quickly and easily some form of objective assessment. A much fuller discussion of the wide range of assessment systems is presented in Chapter 6, but for now a simple illustration is given to show how a risk assessment evaluation can be matched up with the risk control option categories. As a guide, the following observations can be made:

- *Reduction.* This is most often done for risks deemed as low in severity or consequence, but having a higher likelihood of occurrence. These can relate to risks that occur as part of the activity, such as collision injuries in sport, but their likelihood reduced by controlling behaviour, or the severity of their outcome reduced by wearing protective gear.
- *Avoiding.* This is done for the risks usually categorized under high-severity and high-likelihood ratings. This could relate to a group avoiding going up a mountain in extreme weather conditions, or an event cancelled because of security risks.
- *Taking.* Risks of low severity and low likelihood can be considered as acceptable and worth taking if there are potential benefits to be gained. These can relate to everyday slips, knocks or scratches that can occur from doing the activity.
- *Transferring/sharing.* These often relate to the low-likelihood and high-severity risks, such as taking insurance out to cover for expensive damage, delays or cancellations.
- *Monitoring.* This relates to any of the areas, as it acts as a reminder that the operational and business environment is dynamic, so awareness must be had for how to adjust risk management controls.

The key point to remember with scoring systems for risk assessment is that they are only a guide. They should not be taken as prescriptive as there are always likely to be variations between assessment scores given by different assessors. The scoring essentially provides a means to assist with the prioritization of resources. It is easy to find instances where decisions taken about risk may not follow the guidance points relating to the mix of likelihood and impact ratings, particularly when one is dealing with dread risks (discussed in Chapter 7), where the severity of outcome is so severe that it is not considered tolerable or acceptable. For example, the risk of a terrorist attack at a large event may have a relatively low likelihood, but the outcomes could be so severe in terms of injuries, reputation, delays and costs, that the huge amounts of money spent on security to avoid, or at the very least further reduce the risk of an attack are justified because of the low tolerance threshold. In some activities of sport, adventure and business, one can see situations where risks that could be deemed as high severity and high likelihood are still taken, such as:

- In sport, athletes can sometimes be encouraged to take high risks in order to try and finish first. For example, the coach David Brailsford has brought huge success to British cycling, in terms of helping to win many Olympic medals and being instrumental in Bradley Wiggins' and Chris Froome's Tour de France wins. As part of his coaching approach, he can encourage athletes to sometimes take the risk to try and finish first, even though this can also mean they fail to finish or come last, rather than simply always playing safe and finishing in the middle order.
- In an adventure context, a group attempting to climb Mount Everest for example would never be far from the high-severity, high-likelihood rating, but people still undertake these risks because of the personal value and gains to be had.
- In business, there are many examples where organizations gamble because of the chance of high financial returns (Sadgrove, 1997: 11).

When decisions are made to take high-likelihood/high-severity risks, then serious questions need to be asked if things do go wrong, because this can have profound reverberations on the credibility of individual leadership (Gifford, 1983), or the reputation of the organization.

5.4 CONTROL AND ALARP IN RELATION TO OPERATIONAL OCCUPATIONAL HEALTH AND SAFETY

Special attention has to be given to controls as they relate to safety, to ensure that risk in work and play environments is 'as low as is reasonably practical' (ALARP) or 'so far as is reasonably practicable' (SFAIRP) (HSE, 2001). The two terms mean essentially the same thing and at their core is the concept of 'reasonably practicable'; this involves weighing a risk against the trouble, time and money needed to control it. Thus, ALARP describes the level to which we expect to see workplace risks controlled. Using 'reasonably practicable' allows us to set goals for duty-holders, rather than being prescriptive. This flexibility is a great advantage but it has its drawbacks too. Deciding whether a risk is ALARP can be challenging because it requires duty-holders to exercise judgement. In the great majority of cases, we can decide by referring to existing 'good practice' that has been established by a process of discussion with stakeholders to achieve a consensus about what is ALARP. For high-severity risks, complex or novel situations, we build on good practice, using more formal decision-making techniques, including cost–benefit analysis, to inform our judgement. The concept of 'reasonably practicable' lies at the heart of many safety systems around the world.

In essence, making sure a risk has been reduced, ALARP, is about weighing the risk against the sacrifice needed to further reduce it. The decision in countries such as the UK and the USA is weighted in favour of health and safety because the presumption is that the duty-holder should implement the risk reduction measure. To avoid having to make this sacrifice, the duty-holder must be able to show that it would be grossly disproportionate to the benefits of risk reduction that would be achieved. Thus the process is not one of balancing the costs and benefits of measures, but rather of adopting measures, except where they are ruled out because they involve grossly disproportionate sacrifices. Extreme examples might be:

- to spend US$ 1 million to prevent five staff suffering bruised knees is obviously grossly disproportionate; but
- to spend US$ 1 million to prevent a major explosion capable of killing 150 people is obviously proportionate.

Of course, in reality many decisions about risk and controls that achieve ALARP are not so obvious. Factors come into play such as ongoing costs set against remote chances of one-off events; for example, daily expense and supervision time required to ensure that employees wear ear defenders set against a chance of developing hearing loss at some time in the future. It requires judgement. There is also no simple formula for computing what is ALARP. But what it does allow for is that there does not have to be an automatic presumption that the risk management process relating to safety is simply about avoiding or removing risk, because risks can be opportunistic and an integral part of the experience.

5.5   RISK MANAGEMENT COMPETENCY

An often asked question is: 'Am I competent to conduct a risk assessment or to devise the control measures?' There can be a fear that failure to provide a suitable and sufficient risk assessment will leave the individual exposed to criminal proceedings. The reality is that the risk management team should be composed of individuals who have a good understanding of the work involved and the environment they work in. If they use their best efforts in a diligent way, they are unlikely to suffer repercussions. For organizations or individuals to be competent, in the UK for example, the HSE (1999) says they must have:

- sufficient knowledge of the tasks to be undertaken and the risks involved; and
- the experience and ability to carry out their duties in relation to the project, to recognize their limitations and take appropriate action to prevent harm to those carrying out work or those affected by the work.

This competency does not, however, always have to relate to an actual qualification or skill, and can depend on the level of complexity of the risks being analysed and assessed. Competence can also develop over time, through a mix of initial training, on-the-job learning instruction, assessment and formal qualification. In the early stages of training, individuals should be closely supervised. As competence develops, the need for direct supervision should be reduced.

Any independent examination of the risk management approach should also consider whether the organization has provided the opportunity and environment for the correct personnel to do the work. For example, conducting a risk assessment in a swimming pool plant room should include the people involved in that plant room, even if the documentation is put together by their manager, who may not have a detailed understanding of the technical processes. The same principle could apply to a sport coach or adventure tour leader, where managers must involve those who are delivering and conducting the activities, to help ensure any control measures are relevant, understandable and that a sense of ownership is had by those who must implement them.

This though begs the question as whether an organization can identify all the hazards and risks within a workplace or an activity? As always, this can depend on the complexity of the activity, but it can still be possible to identify some broad hazard and risk categories that all sport, adventure, tourism and leisure services may be exposed to around the world. Use of some of the tools discussed in Chapter 4 can help the practitioner imagine the impossible, when looking into an uncertain future. In addition, various government bodies and professional institutions can play a key role in identifying the key hazards, risks and key control measures required, where key benchmarks of good practice can be recognized in well-established activities. For example, standards of operation, such as the publication *HSG179 Managing Health and Safety in Swimming Pools* produced by the HSE (2003) in the UK, is a shared production of knowledge from the sport and leisure industry for managing swimming pools safely. This is an excellent example of where consolidated wisdom over many years has been documented and formalized. Similar guidance notes can be found in other countries, such as the advice and publications produced by the Swimming Pool and Spa Alliance (SPASA) in Australia and the advice on competence provided by the International Institute of Recreation and Safety Management (IIRSM, 2014).

So standards for well-established activities can provide information on hazards and future possible risks. There will, however, always be potential situations related to how much future hazards and risks are foreseeable, as the case in Box 5.2 illustrates. Furthermore, there can be a problem with new activities, where a lack of precedents, incident data or even a governing body that offers guidance notes can mean that the risks will be based on personal judgements

---

Box 5.2. The role of precedent to inform actions

In a test case in the UK (*Regina versus Geoffrey Counsell*, 2013) the concept of foreseeability of risk was integral to the acquittal of the defendant. Seven people were killed and 51 were injured when the smoke from a fireworks display organized by Mr Counsell was alleged to have mixed with fog to cause a motorway accident. Seven people died in the massive motorway pile-up involving more than 30 cars when they were engulfed in a thick fog on the M5 near Taunton at around 8.20 pm on 4 November 2011.

Mr Justice Simon ruled that Mr Counsell had 'no case to answer'. The judge said the prosecution's case was based on 'hindsight' and there was not sufficient evidence to show that Mr Counsell ought to have foreseen that smoke from the display could have drifted and mixed with fog to create thick smog. Fireworks displays have taken place in the UK for centuries. The chemical composition of fireworks has not changed for hundreds of years. All fireworks produce smoke; however, nowhere in any training or guidance is it suggested that firework smoke presents an actual or potential danger of any kind. The current authoritative guidance from the HSE contains no reference to any risk posed by firework smoke, whether on its own or in combination with fog.

This is therefore reassuring for those responsible for conducting risk assessments: that they need to simply apply their experience, training and any guidance from lead bodies to prepare a suitable and sufficient risk assessment. But beware – if you conduct a fireworks display risk assessment now, following this test case, the above scenario is no longer hypothetical and should be considered.

---

of the providers or facility operators. Interesting examples to explore here can relate to such activities such as slacklining (this relates to various tightrope-walking activities which have grown in popularity), coasteering (climbing and swimming along coastal shorelines) or tough mudding events (an outdoor adventure obstacle or assault course), where the safety measures put in place are done by intuitive, heuristic assessments based on observations or comparisons with similar activities (such as putting crash mats down for people slacklining, or giving buoy-ancy aids for those doing coasteering).

In terms of risk management related to safety, the adequacy of the approach of an organiza-tion to its safety risk management systems can ultimately be tested in court. The enforcement agency will form an opinion in advance of taking out a prosecution whether the organization has ensured the safety of persons involved in the activity so far as is reasonably practicable. Reference to published guidance will be made, but ultimately the enforcement agency will take a view as to whether the approach of the organization was reasonable, notwithstanding the arrangements. For example, in one legal action in the UK, Leisure Connection plc was taken to court regarding the drowning of Michelle Gellard in 2008. The defendant (Leisure Connection) pleaded guilty even though it had devised excellent safety systems. Its docu-mented operating procedure for the pool clearly identified that the pool would be operated with four lifeguards for the session concerned, based on the design of the pool and the activity. At the time of the drowning, there were only two lifeguards on the pool. While no specific industry standard existed for this design of pool, it was identified that four lifeguards were deemed reasonable for this session and the failure of Leisure Connection to comply with its own procedures was a key part in leading to the conviction.

5.6   MONITORING AND REVIEWING CONTROL SYSTEMS

Risk assessment is not a one-off exercise. Monitoring is a vital dynamic of the risk process, whereby if one accepts the theory that risks and hazards can be embedded in complex sys-tems, often operating on the edge of chaos, then small changes in the operational or external environmental conditions can change the effectiveness of the control measures in place. In-deed, it should also be appreciated that very often measures brought in to deal with one set of risks can in fact end up generating another set of risks. Heng (2006: 54) describes this as the boomerang effect, which is linked in with the theory of homeostasis discussed in Chapter 7, such as how equipment designed to reduce risk can end up encouraging participants to take more risks.

The difficulty is striking a realistic balance between the time spent monitoring and the need to get on with a wide variety of other operational, planning or management activities. There is a hierarchy of monitoring and review that should be in place, known as MMR (monitoring, measurement and review). *Monitoring* is concerned with day-to-day inspections of health and safety issues and operations. *Measurement* is a planned and systematic process of auditing and inspection. *Review* is concerned with reviewing performance. What is usual practice is for a range of monitoring mechanisms to be used. The following examples illustrate the range of monitoring activities of MMR, which vary in complexity and the time taken:

- *Monitoring*. Examples can relate to simple daily routine inspections, such as checking the temperature or water quality of a swimming pool. Another example could be a half-hourly inspection of the sauna area by a recreation attendant passing through on patrol. These can be visual inspections and do not need to be recorded.
- *Measurement*. Examples can relate to set monthly reviews of key performance data or indicators, such as in relation to income, expenditure and usage, which can help alert managers of future risks.
- *Measuring and reviewing*. Examples can relate to formal internal auditing against compliance procedures which is conducted on a systematic basis, over a frequency between 6 months and 3 years, depending on the degree of risk of the process being audited. Setting of review meetings, such as those that may be set for event projects to give updates on progress is another example.
- *Monitoring and reviewing*. Examples can relate to bulletin alerts of incidents, such as those sent out by government departments that deal with foreign affairs, who can send automated e-mails about any change in advice or reporting of incidents. Scanning news and trade publications for any changes or trends can also be done here.

The precise range of monitoring, measuring and review will be determined by the organization and will be proportionate to the risk involved. Furthermore, the organization needs to confirm and be reassured that the control systems that have been put in place are actually working. One critical question is, how much of this basic monitoring of risks needs to be recorded to demonstrate due diligence? The temptation to over-document, to provide evidence that can be demonstrated by the employee standing up in court and saying, 'Yes I checked this and this is what I found', should be avoided.

5.7   DYNAMIC RISK ASSESSMENT

Dynamic risk assessment (DRA) is a continuous process of identifying risk, assessing and coming up with a way to reduce or eliminate such risks. It operates at a systematic, strategic and dynamic level and involves all employees at all levels in an organization. Once the fundamental controls have been put in place following a risk assessment and developing of control systems, the day-to-day decision making and observations by employees provide for a dynamic assessment of individual situations in the workplace.

Some may call it common sense. It is in fact a combination of experience, training and other attributes of employees who are competent in their work and can make sound decisions to ensure the safety of all staff and users of a service. A climbing instructor will assess the individual competencies and given the speed of development of different participants in a lesson will revise the activity and controls accordingly. A lifeguard will observe the bathers in his/her zone and make judgements on an ongoing basis. A maintenance engineer conducting work on a roof will make judgements of the weather conditions, the nature of the task and changes to the planned control measures. Continuous audience profiling and monitoring at a rock concert will inform decision making and alert managers to any changes in the operational environment. Fundamentally, a high degree of observational skills is needed as part of the application of dynamic risk assessment. Dynamic risk assessment is particularly important in the leisure industry because of the unpredictable behaviour of customers and users.

A common question is whether this dynamic risk assessment should be recorded in any way. At the micro daily level, it does not need to be. It will be impractical to do so and in terms of demonstrating due diligence, a competent employee/person can explain in court what he/she did and why. He/she does not necessarily need a piece of paper or a record to prove it.

5.8   EXAMPLES OF SECTOR CONTEXTUALIZATION

In this section, while a broad range of hazards may be identified, only sample ranges of risks and possible control measures are represented. They are presented in simplified tables to illustrate the jigsaw of controls, showing how there will always be a mix in the control categories selected, the resources employed and the ways to implement the controls. It should also be observed that when identifying hazards and risks, although they appear in a list, there is not always a simple link of one hazard, to one risk, to one control measure, as they tend to be messier or more jumbled, with many areas of overlap or duplication. Finally, the ranges of examples selected from the different sectors also mix up the type of assessment based on safety (the adventure, sport and events examples), operations (the adventure and sport examples), projects (the sport and event examples) and more strategic assessments (the tourism and event examples).

5.8.1   Adventure example of coasteering

Coasteering is a relatively new, but growing commercial adventure activity in many countries. It essentially involves swimming, climbing and scrambling in intertidal coastal zones. It is an interesting activity to consider as its newness means there can be relatively few case study accidents to review, and little statistical data to analyse either within an organization or in the sector as a whole. It is still possible however to produce proper risk assessments using instructors' experiences and judgements, along with consulting more general guidance notes from professional bodies and government agencies such as the UK HSE (which produces an information sheet on combined water and rock activities). Despite the many risks, the activity also offers many benefits, such as: excitement, team building, adventure racing or even the novelty of seeing the sea and land from a different perspective. Table 5.1 gives examples of the range of control measures that could be considered.

Table 5.1. Example of controls for a coasteering adventure activity.

Examples of hazards	Examples of risks	Examples of the control measures mix (the jigsaw)
Sea/water (consideration given to different sea conditions, such as size of surf, tidal range, high and low tide times, etc.)	Swept out to sea: *drowning* and *hypothermia*	*Avoid* activity in extreme weather conditions such as a winter storm, being trapped by high tides or when a large surf is forecast
	Hypothermia (note warning signals of shivering, chattering teeth, etc.)	*Avoid* long exposure in water in certain conditions
		Take risks provided that other control measures put in place, such as buoyancy aids are worn
External environmental conditions/weather (consideration given to heat, cold, wind and how they can affect probability and severity of outcomes)	Cold, miserable and unhappy clients	Create opportunities for participants to warm up/cool down, get dry, have warm/cold drinks
		Dust down/group reflection on what was learnt
Natural environment (e.g. rocks that people can fall on, rocks that fall on them)	*Slipping on rocks* (risk increases near areas with seaweed and algae growth), which can lead to: • head injuries • spinal injuries • cuts and grazes	*Reducing* risks by use of equipment (reduces likelihood and/or severity): • buoyancy aids • gloves/shoes • wetsuits that fit • helmets • rescue ropes carried by leader *Reducing* risks by modifying behaviour/practices: • no diving in shallow pools • no pushing people off rocks
Disease (sewage outlets?)	*Illness* – gastrointestinal (digestive tract) and respiratory infections to ear, nose and throat	*Reducing* risks via training: • leaders to be trained in first aid • other training, such as mountain leadership, beneficial because it deals with weather

(Continued)

Table 5.1. Continued.

Examples of hazards	Examples of risks	Examples of the control measures mix (the jigsaw)
Wildlife (country specific)	Algae in stagnant rock pools Jellyfish sting (shark attack in some locations)	*Monitoring* (may lead to reduction, transfer or avoiding): • check weather forecasts • time activity around tidal range if appropriate • check water/ air temperatures
People	Behaviour of group, such as pushing, splashing, over-excitement, daring each other, etc.	*Monitoring* (may lead to reduction, transfer or avoiding): • report departure and estimated arrival times back to transport, centre, etc. • check emergency phone, etc. • check swimming abilities/ competencies • ratio of staff to participants • checks on water quality *Transfer:* • insurance is adequate for activities • third parties used for transport checked

5.8.2　Sport and a cycling event

The example chosen here relates to an elite cycling road race where a stage begins in a city. In this instance, one of the points to observe is how numerous hazards can relate or contribute to a range of risks. It can also be of interest to explore the many different stakeholders, from sponsors to the athletes, the racing teams, the city government and the local community, all of which can have interests that can both overlap and conflict. For example, while many in the community may welcome the stage, others may become frustrated at the disruptions to their lives. This is a broad generic assessment which overlaps between the cycling teams, the city council and the governing body of sport. Examples of the range of control measures that could be considered are given in Table 5.2.

Table 5.2. Example of controls for a cycling event.

Examples of hazards	Examples of risks	Examples of the control measures mix (the jigsaw)
Street furniture/barriers	Collision with barriers, curbs or lamp posts, with spectators and between cyclists	*Take* risks; collisions and crashes are always a possibility in racing conditions
People (cyclists and spectators)	Collision/impact injuries: • head injuries • spinal injuries • grazes • dislocated shoulders	*Reduce* likelihood of collision by using stewards to close roads
Road traffic	Protest groups upset sponsors or disrupt event by creating delays	*Reduce* severity of outcome by wearing helmets
Protestors using event to promote cause	Delays in race	*Reduce* community frustration by closing roads for limited times, only for the short periods before and after the race passes by and during the race itself
External environmental conditions/weather	Race cancellation	*Avoid* having people flow through pinch points where crush injuries can occur
Natural environment/road surface conditions (variable road conditions such as potholes)	Death (heat, drugs, over-exertion, collision, heart defect)	Segregate spectators from cyclists
Drugs	Big names go out, reducing interest (commercial risks)	*Monitor*: • weather conditions and how they alters risks, such as if there are any downhill areas, sharp corners, drops • news stories, political tensions, opportunities for protest, stories about sponsors that may mean they are targeted for protest

(Continued)

Table 5.2. Continued.

Examples of hazards	Examples of risks	Examples of the control measures mix (the jigsaw)
Crime	Crushing of spectators	• health checks on athletes
	Cyclists taking wrong turns	• drug checks
	Collision with stewards	*Transfer:* • use medical professionals in support vehicles • car breakdown and recovery vehicles cover • use emergency services such as the police in key areas where control and authority are needed (e.g. police riders opening race) • insurance
	Reputational damage of athlete, team and sport	*Equipment:* • wear helmets • clear signage showing closures/direction of route • communications with riders and team cars • cars and spare parts • steward bibs to help organize flow of people, make them visible
	Theft/loss of bikes, belongings	*Practice:* • rules on overtaking/leaning in • clear rules on drug abuse and cheating to discourage abuse *Training:* • medical teams • stewards organizing crowds

5.8.3 Tourism in Burma (Myanmar)

Aung San Suu Kyi was a key opposition leader to the military regime in Burma, who had been kept under house arrest for years. She had called for tourists to boycott the country, with this message supported and promoted for many years by various pressure groups, such as Tourism Concern. Any tour operator wanting to organize tours to this country would not only have to deal with the risks that the authoritarian, military regime posed, but also the reputational damage to the tour operator for ignoring the calls to boycott the country. However, in 2011 there were some important changes in the political system, when elections were held for the first time, marking the tentative steps towards political reform. Other events, such as the release of political prisoners and the US presidential visit, showed that there were opportunistic risks created by the changing political environment, and Aung San Suu Kyi's announcement in 2011 that the tourism boycott should stop removed a key barrier to market entry. The size of the tourism market in Thailand and Cambodia is also shows the future market potential, as Burma has a wealth of attractions. Table 5.3 gives examples of the range of control measures that could be considered for tourism operations in Burma.

5.8.4 Events and the Qatar World Cup

This is a speculative risk assessment for the soccer world cup in Qatar, to identify a different set of hazards, risks and control measures at a project and strategic level, with many of the health and safety issues considered in terms of how they can affect the viability of actually staging the event. It also illustrates some classic elements about project event risk management, in that as the event nears completion, the level of uncertainty should be reduced, but the potential losses if the event was to be cancelled are huge. This assessment can also be considered strategic in relation to the timescales and the breadth of resources that need to be considered when planning for the event. Table 5.4 presents examples of the range of control measures that could be considered.

5.9 CONCLUSION

Control measures will always need to be considered as part of a dynamic process whereby there is a mix of control decisions, resources and methods employed to implement control measures. Sometimes controls need to be carefully mapped out and explored. At other times they rely simply on the person's experience and judgement to make the best decisions to ensure environments are safe, project schedules maintained, or the long-term viability of the organization and business is maintained.

In formulating the environment for safety, a balance has to be struck between safety, enjoyment and quality. Systems and procedures will bring control and identify standards of operation, but they do not necessarily in themselves lead to service improvement once those systems are implemented. They provide stability rather than innovation. A dynamic organization responding to customer expectations and providing an improving service needs to balance the controls from safety with the need to innovate and improve the customer experience on an ongoing basis.

Table 5.3. Example of controls for a tour operation to Burma (Myanmar).

Examples of hazards	Examples of risks	Examples of the control measures mix (the jigsaw)
Political: • terrorism • civil unrest/demonstrations (e.g. Rangoon) • ethnic tensions between Buddhist majority and Muslim minority (Mandalay Division, etc.) • attacks on religious buildings • political change • human rights abuses/ restrictions on freedoms • corruption	Injury/death from bombs or shootings (see incident/ frequency table for dates, outcomes and locations)	*Avoid* travel to destinations highlighted by government travel advice/ rated as high risk (e.g. tensions in Rakhine State, Kachin)
Social: • refugees or displacement of people • crime • community	Kidnapping	*Avoid* all demonstrations and large gatherings and do not take photographs or videos of the military, police or demonstrations
Transport: • roads in poor condition • sea and water transport does not follow international standards • aircraft crashes	Staff/clients arrested (drugs, illegal sex, drink driving)/deported	*Reduction*: take precautions on certain dates (e.g. risk of political unrest/terrorism on dates such as Armed Forces Day on 27 March and Martyrs Day on 19 July)
Diseases/health	Imprisonment/fines for drink driving, photographing military police	*Transfer*: • comprehensive medical insurance by participants • medical insurance, such as flying medic cover • cover cancellations of tours

(Continued)

Table 5.3. Continued.

Examples of hazards	Examples of risks	Examples of the control measures mix (the jigsaw)
Animals	Loss/theft of possessions/ physical assaults	*Monitor:* • government advice • political events (for improving or worsening situations) • disease outbreaks • tensions between groups
Environmental conditions: • humidity/heat • rain/flooding	Travel restrictions (frustrations and annoyance that attractions cannot be visited?)	*Equipment:* • sterile medical kits for first aid • satellite phones
Natural hazards: • earthquakes (e.g. in 2012, 45 miles north of Shwebo Township) • cyclones (April to October)	Ethical dilemmas/ reputational damage if a crackdown on human rights groups occurs/ ethical principles are compromised	*Communication:* • inform staff of risks • inform/check clients know risk beforehand and have time to put in place any relevant precautions (e.g. vaccinations) • check embassy/ consulate contact information is had
	Poor electricity supply/ problems charging electrical items (frustrations or inability to contact emergency numbers)	*Practices:* • avoid approaching animals • check food and water hygiene • vaccinations (e.g. tetanus) • carry copy of passport • avoid driving at night

(Continued)

Table 5.3. Continued.

Examples of hazards	Examples of risks	Examples of the control measures mix (the jigsaw)
	Cancellations because of political turmoil or natural disaster, such as an earthquake	
	Risk likelihoods increase at times of festivals or near government buildings, etc.	
	Contract diseases such as hepatitis A (water/food), hepatitis B (blood); Japanese encephalitis (animal-to-human transmission and mosquito bites mainly in Shan State in May to October); rabies (animal saliva/bites/scratches/licks from dogs, bats); tetanus (soil, manure, via open cuts, puncture wounds); typhoid fever (food and water, but low risk); malaria (mosquito bites in high-risk areas, but no risk in cities of Mandalay and Rangoon)	
	Flooding caused by cyclones leading to travel disruptions/cancellations	
	Tourists can visit Rangoon, Mandalay, Bago and Irrawaddy regions without restrictions; other destinations are subject to limitations (e.g. access by air or train but not by road)	

Table 5.4. Example of controls from a strategic assessment of the Qatar World Cup.

Examples of hazards	Examples of risks	Examples of the control measures mix (the jigsaw)
Political: • terrorism • civil unrest/ demonstrations • ethnic tensions in region over spilling borders • political change • human rights abuses/ restrictions on freedoms • corruption	Terrorist acts before event affect building schedules or result in losing sponsors	*Take* risk and maintain event
Social: • crime • community/culture clash	People projecting risks of Middle East on to Qatar, so not wanting to travel there	*Avoid*: • if instability in region grows? • playing at hottest times of year and day (winter world cup?)
Transport	Accusations of corruption make world cup less attractive to sponsors/ reduce revenues	*Reduce*: • political lobbying to change government policy on workers' rights • negotiate with government to have areas/fan zones where alcohol can be served • negotiate with human rights groups such as Amnesty International to show that the issues are engaged with • rules on injuries such as concussion • stadiums moved into other countries to help develop sport • engagement with women's rights

(Continued)

Table 5.4. Continued.

Examples of hazards	Examples of risks	Examples of the control measures mix (the jigsaw)
Diseases/health	Heat exhaustion and collapse of players or fans/ potential deaths (leading to reputational damage and accusations of putting money before safety)	*Equipment:* • cooling technology for stadiums • design of stadiums
Animals	Issues of women's rights undermining credibility for supporting the women's game	*Practices:* • ethical codes of conduct and practice adopted • rule changes allowing extra breaks during games to take on water
Environmental conditions: • heat	Culture clash/alcohol	*Training:* • volunteers recruited • security and police as to how to deal with fan behaviour
Natural hazards: • sandstorms	Offending local customs or country rules	
Club opposition to winter world cup	Brand damage/reduced commercial/sponsorship appeal	
	Reputational damage by failure to engage with ethical challenges and stories of abuse	
	Stories of human rights abuses of immigrant workforce	
	Disproportionate social impacts in relation to the small community and large influx of outside visitors	

(Continued)

Table 5.4. Continued.

Examples of hazards	Examples of risks	Examples of the control measures mix (the jigsaw)
	Protestors disrupt event	
	Financial losses	
	Compensation for disruption of league fixtures	
	Event cancellation	

DISCUSSION QUESTIONS AND TASKS

1. For an activity of your choice, identify the jigsaw mix of control categories, resources employed and methods of implementation. Represent this as a simple diagram.

2. For a chosen sector and activity, conduct research into the key documentation that needs to be identified in order to comply with safe risk practices. Try and distil the key points into a series of bullet points that can fit on one sheet of A4 paper.

3. How much detail should be written down in relation to control measures? Give examples for an activity of your choice.

4. Conduct a role-playing exercise for a worst-case scenario (e.g. death of a customer, facility closure, damage to a building, trip cancellation, etc.), running in real time to identify how effectively decisions are made in dynamic risk situations. Produce a short list of what was done well and what needs to be improved.

REFERENCES

APM (2004) *Project Risk Analysis and Management Guide.* APM Publishing, Biggleswade, UK.

Cloutier, R. (2002) The business of adventure tourism. In: Hudson, S. (ed.) *Sport and Adventure Tourism.* Haworth Hospitality Press, New York, pp. 241–271.

Fitzgerald, P. (2003) *Risk Management Guide for Tourism Operators.* Canadian Tourism Commission, Ottawa.

Gardiner, P.D. (2005) *Project Management: A Strategic Planning Approach.* Palgrave Macmillan, Basingstoke, UK.

Gifford, N. (1983) *Expeditions and Exploration.* Macmillan, London.

Heldman, K. (2005) *Project Manager's Spotlight on Risk Management.* Harbor Light Press, Alameda, California.

Heng, Y. (2006) *War as Risk Management: Strategy and Conflict in an Age of Globalised Risk.* Routledge, London.

HSE (1999) Management of Health and Safety at Work Regulations 1999. Available at: http://www.legislation.gov.uk/uksi/1999/3242/contents/made (accessed 19 February 2015).

HSE (2001) Reducing Risks, Protecting People, HSE's Decision-Making Process. Available at: http://www.hse.gov.uk/risk/theory/r2p2.pdf (accessed 20 August 2014).

HSE (2003) *HSG179 Managing Health and Safety in Swimming Pools*. HSE Books, Sudbury, UK.

IIRSM (2014) Core Competencies for Public Service Risk Management. Available at: http://www.iirsm.org/Resources/IIRSM/Documents/PDF/Alarm%20Full%20Version%20Final.pdf (accessed 19 February 2015).

ISO (2009) *Risk Management – Principles and Guidelines*. International Organization for Standardization, Geneva, Switzerland.

Masteralixis, P., Barr, C.A. and Hums, M.A. (2005) *Principles and Practice of Sport Management*, 2nd edn. Jones & Bartlett Publishers, London.

Sadgrove, K. (1997) *The Complete Guide to Business Risk Management*. Gower, Aldershot, UK.

SPARC (2004) Risk management of events. Available at: http://www.sportnz.org.nz/managing-sport/guides/risk-management-for-events (accessed 20 August 2014).

Spengler, J.O, Connaughton, D.P. and Pittman, A.T. (2006) *Risk Management in Sport and Recreation*. Human Kinetics Publishing Co., Champaign, Illinois.

UK Sport (2005) Major Sports Events – The Guide. Available at: http://www.uksport.gov.uk/publications/major-sports-events-the-guide-april-2005 (accessed 24 June 2013).

Wilks, J. and Davis, J. (2000) Risk management for scuba diving operators on Australia's Great Barrier Reef. *Tourism Management* 21, 591–599.

FURTHER READING

ABTA (Association of British Travel Agents) offers a great deal of practical advice for tourism, available at: http://abta.com/resource-zone/publication/health-and-safety-technical-guide

Air Safety Network gives useful information on aviation incidents to check out airlines for safety, available at: http://aviation-safety.net/index.php

American Camping Association has a variety of useful information on expeditions, safety and first aid, available at: http://www.acacamps.org

FIFA's guide to safety offers a great deal of practical advice on staging large-scale events, available at: http://www.fifa.com/mm/document/tournament/competition/51/53/98/safetyregulationse.pdf

International Institute of Recreation and Safety Management (IIRSM) provides information on a variety of incidents, standards and examples of good practice, available at: http://www.iirsm.org/

Kids Sport Network has a variety of useful information, such as guidance notes on doing criminal background checks, available at: http://www.ksnusa.org

National Travel Health Network and Centre (NaTHNac) has useful information on health and diseases, available at: http://www.nathnac.org/

Ready Campaign has information about natural disasters and tracks incidents, available at: http://www.ready.gov/earthquakes

Severe Weather Information Centre monitors severe weather around the world, available at: http://severe.worldweather.org/

SPARC (2004: 26) gives some useful notes on waivers, available at: http://www.sportnz.org.nz/managing-sport/guides/risk-management-for-events

Swimming Pool and Spa Alliance (SPASA) has a variety of useful information and guidance notes on safety, available at: http://www.spasa.org.au/

chapter 6

Designing Risk Forms, Documentation and Using Assessment Scales

CHAPTER OBJECTIVES

- To explain the importance of recording information in electronic or paper documents.
- To identify the key theories and concepts that should be considered when designing and utilizing forms.
- To identify and explain points of good practice in form design.
- To illustrate how forms can be designed and utilized at the operational, project and strategic levels of management.
- To explain the importance of developing checklist documentation.

Key concepts

Documentation; risk registers; compliance; risk process, risk analysis and assessment; checklists; crisis management and checklist manuals.

6.1   INTRODUCTION

This chapter focuses on what sorts of information should be recorded on paper or in electronic documents, and how it should be recorded. This aspect of risk management is not represented as a separate process stage, as it is an integral part of *all* of the risk process stages identified in Chapter 2. The discussion focuses primarily on how the information gathered from research, mind mapping and tool application can be distilled and presented in easy-to-read documentation, from where the key controls can be identified and formulated into checklists.

In this chapter, a key focus is the examination of some of the problems in documentation and how they should be managed. It is argued that when approached properly, documentation can form a key foundation for safety, operational, strategic and project risk analysis and assessment, helping to identify and monitor the key actions and decisions that must be taken to deal with the downside and upside risks.

6.2 THE IMPORTANCE OF FORMS AND DOCUMENTATION

Risk forms can often be poorly designed, inadequately completed and have numerous misapplications of concepts and theories. They can be disliked by staff, who see them as unnecessarily bureaucratic, adding to workloads, encouraging officiousness and removing the 'fun' from many adventure, sport and touristic activities.

These are important criticisms, but there are a number of reasons why completing forms and documentation is important, which can be summarized as:

- *Compliance.* In many countries, there is now a statutory requirement to conduct and record occupational workplace risk or hazard assessments.
- *Protection.* If a risk assessment has been done, with the information properly recorded and implemented, then if an incident does occur the documentation can form an essential part of an investigative audit trail to ensure proper practices were complied with, so helping protect from frivolous claims designed to gain financial compensation.
- *Checklists.* Completing forms helps distil the key controls that need to be taken; Gardiner (2005: 169) argues that if risks are written down they are more likely (not guaranteed) to be acted upon.
- *Communication.* Information which is recorded and used to develop checklists is a key element in the effective communication of risks to staff and other key stakeholders.
- *Monitoring.* If information is recorded it can make it easier to identify pieces of data that can be used to monitor the risks.
- *Evaluation.* Identifying risks and hazards can give a basis for evaluating how effectively businesses are being run.
- *Structure.* Recording information can give structure to a manager's thinking processes.
- *Quality.* Risk forms can form a crucial part of any quality system that ensures services are consistently delivered to an appropriate standard, which must include safety, but should also go far beyond it.

6.3 WHAT IS RECORDED AND WHEN?

What information needs to be recorded? Quite simply this will depend on:

- the level of complexity of the activity (e.g. a game of badminton compared with a large event);

- what is exposed to risk (e.g. people, money, reputation); and
- the scale of the risk exposure (e.g. number of people and type of risks, amount of money invested).

Where the activity or project is simple, with limited exposure to money, reputation and people, then the whole risk process could be recorded on a single piece of paper, if that. As the level of complexity and scale of exposure increase, so too will the need to record information gathered from analysis, research and assessments, which should lead to identifying a list of control measures or actions. A range of examples of the information that could be recorded at each project stage is given in Table 6.1.

Figure 6.1 gives a further illustration of how information recorded from different process stages is distilled down and fed into a summarizing risk register, which in turn can feed into further separate documentation, such as the shaded action checklists box, discussed in more detail in Section 6.6.

Looking at the Table 6.1 and Fig. 6.6, it really is important to reiterate that all of these process stages could be completed in a very short period of time and produce little paperwork. It would, however, be foolhardy to always take the minimalist approach when the risk complexity and exposure increase. To do this can be a symptom of poor management, showing a lack of desire or ability to engage more deeply in the analysis of the potential hazards and risks. This in turn can leave an individual or organization vulnerable to litigation if an incident was to occur, or even lead to just simple project and strategy failures, which can compromise the organization's viability.

A word of caution is needed when considering forms and documentation in response to incidents. When an incident occurs, a knee-jerk reaction can sometimes be to produce further documented procedures, after insurance companies highlight what they see as deficiencies in operational controls because of lack of a written procedure. But in reality an organization needs to balance its written and unwritten procedures in order not to swamp the useful information with peripheral information, which can be delivered through training and competence in other ways (see Chapter 5 for the discussion on competence and training).

6.4   EXAMPLES OF RISK SUMMARIZING FORMS, REGISTERS AND REPORTS

So how much detail is recorded can reflect the level of complexity of the project, the degree of risk exposure and even the politics of the country. The next critical question is just *how* should information be presented or documented? In this section, the prime focus is given to the form or document at the centre of Fig. 6.1. This document, sometimes called the *risk register*, *risk log*, *risk report* or even the *Job Hazard Analysis* (a form primarily used in America), has numerous variations in design, which can be found from different organizations, sectors and countries.

Table 6.1. Examples of possible documentation for each risk process stage.

Process stage	What may be recorded?
Stage 1: Context	• Notes of meetings • Mind maps identifying hazards and risks • Preliminary SWOT and PESTLE analysis • Stakeholders identified • Clarification of activity/project purpose • Preliminary recording of hazards, risks and control measures on a risk register/report
Stage 2: Analysis	• Research, case study analysis, consultation of guidance notes from government and professional bodies, etc. (see Chapters 5 and 7) • Analysis of job and key functions to identify exposure to hazards used for JHA (Swartz, 2001) • Application of tools to identify/understand causation factors, triggers, etc. (Chapter 4) • Recording of hazards, risks and control measures on a risk register/report (Chapter 6)
Stage 3: Assessment	• Incident frequency tables used to help calculate and allocate risk assessment values • Control measures prioritized based on assessments and recorded down on risk register/report (Chapter 5)
Stage 4: Control	• Action checklists clarifying who, what and when completed, etc., preferably on the risk register/report • Procedure guidelines/checklist produced if necessary • Participation registration forms, contact details, liability waiver forms, medical history/declaration forms, insurance details • Crisis manual/checklists
Stage 5: Monitoring and reviewing	• Risk registers updated if necessary • Record down any information identified as a key control measure, such as when and who last checked safety equipment or when training completed • Record down any accidents or near misses (regulatory obligation) • Track return to play if appropriate (e.g. when people return to activity after an injury such as concussion)

(Continued)

Table 6.1. Continued.

Process stage	What may be recorded?
	• Event safety guidelines, such as those produced by FIFA, identify such things as recording pre-event inspections, all key incidents relating to accidents and crowd control, and attendance figures

SWOT, Strengths, Weaknesses, Opportunities and Threats; PESTLE, Political, Economic, Social, Technological, Legal and Environmental; JHA, job hazard analysis; FIFA, Fédération Internationale de Football Association.

In essence, this form should be designed to encapsulate and represent the key hazards, risks, assessment values and control measures.

The problem can be that it is sometimes difficult to gauge if the forms used by an organization or sector simply reflect common practice – which does not necessarily equate with best practice or, for that matter, good practice. What therefore needs to be done next is to compare a variety of forms to try and identify examples of good and effective design and practice. For those who already use a set form, the encouragement is given to reflect on the different examples offered here in order to better understand why certain concepts and layouts may be used, or potentially how they could be further refined and improved.

6.4.1   Examples of a simple risk register log or report

In many operational health and safety assessments, it is perfectly feasible to record all the analysis, assessments and control measures on a single form, or even with some simple notes. Two examples are given from the UK and USA, to illustrate how relatively simple some forms can be and which can comply with regulations, such as those relating to occupational or work health and safety. The first example is produced by the RFU for England, which adapts the UK HSE risk process guidance notes, and is presented in Table 6.2.

The second example is produced by the US Occupational Safety and Health Administration (OSHA, 2002), which gives a sample form that can be used for job hazard analysis (JHA), shown in Table 6.3.

While the US example just uses the term hazard in a very broad way, failing to distinguish between a risk and a hazard, it still in essence does a similar job to the RFU example: they are attempting to identify hazards and risks, then identify some control measures to deal with them, all of which are clarified by various subsidiary questions. Although these forms are simple, if the background work is done for the different process stages, as illustrated in Fig. 6.1, the forms can help ensure compliance with both legal regulations and best practice.

Fig. 6.1. Examples of recorded information.

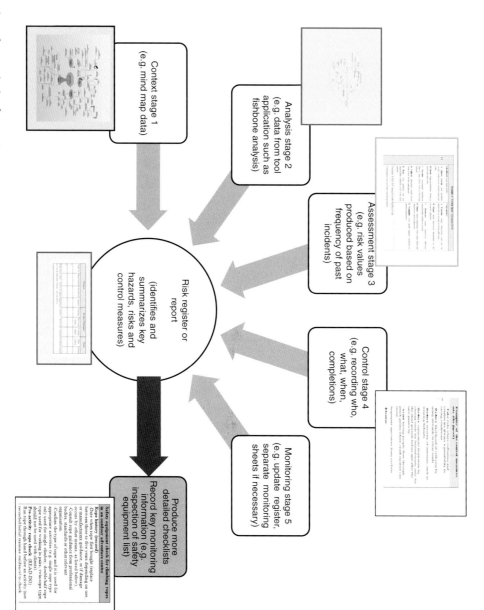

Context stage 1
(e.g. mind map data)

Analysis stage 2
(e.g. data from tool
application such as
fishbone analysis)

Assessment stage 3
(e.g. risk values
produced based on
frequency of past
incidents)

Risk register or
report
(identifies and
summarizes key
hazards, risks and
control measures)

Control stage 4
(e.g. recording who,
what, when,
completions)

Monitoring stage 5
(e.g. update register,
separate monitoring
sheets if necessary)

Produce more
detailed checklists
Record key monitoring
information (e.g.
inspection of safety
equipment list)

Table 6.2. RFU risk assessment pro-forma headings summarized. (From RFU, 2014.)

Step 1: What are the hazards?	Step 2: Who might be harmed and how?	Step 3: What are you already doing?	Step 4: How will you put the assessment into action?	Step 5: Review date
Spot hazards by: • walking around your workplace; • asking your employees what they think; • checking manufacturers' instructions; • contacting your trade association. Don't forget long-term health hazards.	Identify groups of people. Remember: • some workers have particular needs; • people who may not be in the workplace all the time; • members of the public. Say how the hazard could cause harm.	• List what is already in place to reduce the likelihood of harm or make any harm less serious. • What further action is necessary? • You need to make sure that you have reduced risks 'so far as is reasonably practicable'.	• Remember to prioritize. Deal with those hazards that are high-risk and have serious consequences first. • Action done by whom by when.	

RFU, Rugby Football Union.

Table 6.3. Job hazard analysis form (JHA). (From OSHA, 2002.)

Job location:	Analyst: (Name of person doing the assessment)		Date:
Task description: (What is involved with the activity? What are the key job tasks involved?)			
Hazard description: (This relates to asking a variety of scenario-based questions, such as what can go wrong, what are the consequences, how could it arise? Contributing factors? How likely is it that the hazard will occur? This information should come from staff meetings, discussions and analysing past incident data)			
Hazard controls: (These relate to putting in the control measures to remove or reduce the hazards)			

OHSA, Occupational Safety and Health Administration.

There are, however, some limitations that should be considered if such simple approaches are adopted, which are:

- people may use this as the only documentation or process engaged with, failing to conduct deeper analysis of situations;
- the simplistic use of the concept of hazard (see Chapter 2) may deter people analysing more deeply how risk events may come about, such as the key factors or triggers;
- there is a simple, narrow focus just on 'who' is at risk which, while vital for safety-related assessments, can mean opportunities are missed to analyse other operational areas of risks;
- while it can be useful for basic, simple activities, it is less suitable for more complex activities and projects, where there can be a greater range of hazards and more complex interaction of causation factors; and
- the forms may encourage a risk-averse approach to be adopted, as the emphasis is on focusing on the 'harm' that can be done, rather than the benefits that can be gained.

6.4.2 Developing more sophisticated safety and project risk forms

Where the risk assessments have to be done for more complex activities or projects that carry higher levels of exposure, it can be worthwhile considering using more sophisticated forms. The following examples of risk forms, presented in Tables 6.4, 6.5 and 6.6, are drawn from different countries and sectors and are designed for both project and safety risk assessments.

These forms are presented here not as definitive examples to be simply replicated by practitioners. They are used to illustrate both similarities and the differences. Comparing the different forms, the following points should be noted:

- although some of the terminology varies, all the forms attempt to refine the assessment of risk, by using the two key pillars of risk likelihood and risk consequences, and then crucially attempt to record the control measures;

Table 6.4. Project risk register (non-country specific). (From Gardiner, 2005.)

Project:				Project Manager:			Date:	
Risk no.	Description	Likelihood	Impact	Strategy	Previous status	Current status	Date closed	Owner
1.								
2.								
Risk status: red = active and impacting project; amber = active but contained without impact to cost and schedule; green = not yet active.								

Table 6.5. Risk identification form (for sport and adventure activities in New Zealand and Australia). (From Department of Sport and Recreation Government of Western Australia, 2007.)

Business/association/club/group			
Activity/event			
Risk ref. no.			
Risk (what can go wrong?)			
Existing preventive measures			
Consequence if risk occurs (select worst/or largest impact)			
Consequence rating	Likelihood rating		Level of risk
What can you do about it? (actions)	Due date	Status	
Level of risk after actions			
Consequence rating	Likelihood rating		Level of risk
Name		Date	

- the examples combine (usually by multiplying or adding values) a probability/likelihood rating and a consequences/severity rating to produce an overall risk rating;
- in risk registers used for project management, such as in Table 6.4, it can be less common to refer to the concept of a hazard, but this tends to reflect past practice, rather than a theoretical necessity;

Table 6.6. CIMSPA risk spreadsheet (for sport and leisure in the UK). (From CIMSPA, 2014.)

People at risk								
Name of centre/facility								
Hazards identified	How might people be harmed	Recommendations (based on industry practice)	Control	PLR	PSR	RRN	Further controls	Revised PLR, PSR and RRN

Probability Likelihood Rating (PLR) × Potential Severity Rating (PSR) = Risk Rating Number (RRN).

CIMSPA, Chartered Institute for the Management of Sport and Physical Activity.

- when looking at the forms relating to safety, all they may require is to broaden the *who* to also include *what*, which can mean they can easily be adapted for other areas of operational and project risk management;
- although the forms may have been written in a particular country or focus on a specific sector, they are easily transferable between both countries and sectors; and
- Table 6.6 shows a method to put in a revised risk assessment score after control measures have been put in place.

6.5 USING AN ASSESSMENT SCORING OR DESCRIPTION SYSTEM

In the previous section, the sample forms all separate risk into the two risk components of likelihood and its consequence, then combine these two elements to produce an overall risk rating. This initially seems very straightforward and an attractive way to make a more sophisticated assessment; the difficulty is that there can in fact be so many variations with how risk can be expressed, rated or scored. But what sort of scoring system is best, or most appropriate for the activity being assessed?

The first part of the answer is to remind readers that it is perfectly acceptable to produce a risk assessment without using any scoring/value system, as Section 6.3.1 illustrates. Having said this, using an assessment scoring or category description system is such common practice, with many professional bodies using a rating system, that it is necessary to explore them in more detail. This will be done by looking at variety of assessment scales in relation to likelihood (Section 6.4.1) and consequences (Section 6.4.2), with examples of both presented in Table 6.7, drawn from the different sectors and levels of management. How these two elements can be brought back together to produce an overall risk rating and used as guidance for selecting control measures is then examined (Section 6.4.3).

6.5.1 Comparing probability/likelihood scales

In Chapter 2, Section 2.3.3, it was explained that a key part of many definitions of risk relates to the notion of the chance of something occurring, with the term *probability* often used for numeric assessments and *likelihood* used for descriptive assessments. Examples of the various scales that can be used are presented in Table 6.7, which offers three-, five-, six- or ten-point scales to represent chance, probability or likelihood.

When comparing the likelihood/probability scales in Table 6.7 a number of observations can be made:

- Many combine both a numeric value with a qualitative description to better represent the likelihood.
- Using frequency over a set time period can make the numbers easier to understand, as examples 3 and 4 illustrate.

Table 6.7. Examples of likelihood and outcome scales.

Scale	Chance, probability or likelihood	Outcome, impact, consequence or severity
1–3	Example 1 – used in events (UK Sport, 2005: 45)	
	Probability: High Medium Low	*Impacts*: High Medium Low
	Impacts × Probability = Risks	
1–4	Example 2 – used in adventure (Haddock, 1999)	
	Probability ranking: 0 = very unlikely 1 = slight possibility 2 = medium possibility 3 = highly possible	*Seriousness*: 0 = of no consequence 1 = marginal 2 = quite serious 3 = catastrophic
1–5	Example 3 – used in tourism (Fitzgerald, 2003: 7)	
	1–3 = *low probability* (risk is considered remote, perhaps 1 in 1000) 4–5 = *medium probability* (risk is considered unlikely, perhaps 1 in 100 years) 6–8 = *high probability* (1 in 10 years) 9–10 = *extreme probability* (likely to occur in 1 year)	1–3 = *low consequence* (minor injury, low costs, no media involvement) 4–5 = *medium consequence* (moderate costs, minor injuries requiring hospital treatment, local or regional media coverage) 6–8 = *high consequence* (severe injuries, high costs can be expected, extensive media coverage is likely to harm reputation, potential for political involvement) 9–10 = *extreme consequence* (multiple fatalities, extreme costs could affect future viability of the business, negative repercussions for the business, international press coverage damages reputation)
1–5	Example 4 – used in sport (VicSports, 2014)	
	Likelihood (year timescale): A = *almost certain* (will probably occur, could occur several times per year)	*Consequence*: A = *extreme* (many objectives will not be achieved or several severely affected)

(*Continued*)

Table 6.7. Continued.

Scale	Chance, probability or likelihood	Outcome, impact, consequence or severity
	B = *likely* (high probability, likely to arise once per year) C = *possible* (reasonable likelihood that it may arise over a 5-year period) D = *unlikely* (plausible, could occur over a 5- to 10- year period) E = *rare* (very unlikely but not impossible, unlikely over a 10-year period)	B = *major* (most objectives threatened or one severely affected) C = *moderate* (some objectives affected, considerable efforts to rectify) D = *minor* (easily remedied, with some effort the objectives can be achieved) E = *negligible* (very small impact, rectified by normal processes)
	Correlate A–B–C–D–E rating for both likelihood and consequence on a priority risk-rating matrix	
1–5 (%)	Example 6 – used in event project management (SPARC, 2004: 13)	
	Likelihood: *Almost certain* (risk has a ≥90% likelihood of occurrence) *Likely* (risk has a 70–89% likelihood of occurrence) *Moderate* (risk has a 30–69% likelihood of occurrence) *Unlikely* (risk has a 5–29% likelihood of occurrence) *Rare* (risk has a <5% likelihood of occurrence)	*Impact*: *Extreme* (death, brain/spinal injuries, serious organ damage, permanent disability, emergency medical assistance, hospital for ≥6 weeks) *Major* (fractures, crush injuries, serious facial injuries, recovery of ≥6 weeks, emergency medical assistance, hospital care) *Moderate* (dislocation/simple fractures, medical assistance, participant does not continue event, recovery of 1–6 weeks) *Minor* (contusions, sprains, lacerations, minor first aid, participant continues event, less than 1 week recovery) *Insignificant* (bruises, grazes, participant continues, no recovery time or medical assistance)
1–6	Example 7 – used in sport and leisure (CIMSPA, 2014)	
	Probability Likelihood Rating (PLR): 1 = highly improbable 2 = remotely possible	*Potential Severity Rating (PSR)*: 1 = negligible injury 2 = minor injuries (single or repetitive)

(Continued)

Table 6.7. Continued.

Scale	Chance, probability or likelihood	Outcome, impact, consequence or severity
	3 = occasional 4 = fairly frequently 5 = frequent to regular 6 = almost certainty	3 = major injuries 4 = fatal injuries 5 = multiple fatalities 6 = catastrophic fatalities (e.g. stadium collapse)
	PSR × PLR = Risk Rating Number (RRN) RRN of ≤7 = green; RRN of 8–15 = amber; RRN of 16 –36 = red (note colour coding system also used)	
1–10	Example 8 – used in project management (Gardiner, 2005: 169)	
	Probability: 10 = virtually certain 1 = extremely unlikely	*Consequence*: 10 = severe impact 1 = negligible impact
	Probability × Consequence = Risk Exposure, with 100 = very high and 1 = very low exposure	

- There is no set time period that has to be used, as it can depend on the type of assessment done. Hence for more strategic assessments, the timescales may stretch over many years, while operational ones can be based on days, even hours.
- Examples 3 and 4 show how different exposure areas, beyond injuries, can be considered, such as time delays, media attention.
- At times it can be difficult to consider which elements should be given the probability; for example, is it the probability of the hazard of a hurricane occurring, or is it the probability the risk of an event may need to be cancelled?
- Although different examples are shown from tourism, sport, events and adventure these should by no means be considered as definitive standards for the sector.
- Use of numeric scales can give a superficial artifice of being more objective or scientifically sound. However, they can be constructed around analysing past incidents, cases, research, application of tools or just simply a person's heuristics and judgement, which means they can often be highly subjective (as discussed further below).

So which scale should be used? There is not necessarily a simply answer because each scale can have its own strengths and weaknesses. What will perhaps decide which scale is used (if at all) may depend much more on what is common practice for the industry sector, or even which of the different scales and qualitative statements actually make sense to the person making the assessment. Whatever scale is used, perhaps what is most important is to recognize is that variations exist which tend to represent received practice, rather than some serious theoretical impediment that can stop different scales being used in different sectors or levels of management.

6.5.2   Comparing consequence/impact scales

The second element of risk relates to the notion of the consequences, variously expressed as *impacts*, *outcomes* or *severity*, discussed in Chapter 2. This is a far more complex area to try and represent than likelihood. This is because it can be difficult representing all the different exposure areas that can be impacted, ranging from injuries to people, reputational impacts to the financial consequences of risks. It is, however, of critical importance as it sets the relative tolerance levels for taking risks based on the different exposure areas of what/who is at risk, how are they at risk and the degree of risk exposure (discussed in Chapter 2, Section 2.3.4).

In Table 6.7, various impact scales were illustrated. Looking at and comparing these examples, the following observations can be made:

- They all have a focus on the downside risks or negative consequences, leading to the question if it is possible to develop an upside scale in order to better fit in with the fourth-age risk paradigm. Although not represented here, for an example of how an upside assessment scale can be adapted one can examine the scales offered by PMBOK (2004), but even these can lack specific descriptive details.
- For safety assessments it is essential that the focus is given to the risks of injuries and death, but it should be noted that there can be variations in the values given and how severe the consequences are. For instance, example 6 in Table 6.7 uses the most extreme consequence value for a single death, while example 7 uses the most extreme consequence value for multiple fatalities.
- These variations illustrate how one can adjust scales to fit in with different levels of risk assessment, such as those that focus on short timeframes relate more to operations, while longer timeframes have more strategic implications.
- Consequences can be considered not only in relation to injuries, but also time, money, competiveness, etc.
- There is the potential that when a risk assessment process is engaged with, it can make sense to consider how a broader range of risk impacts can be covered as part of the review processes of operational and project management.

This last point needs further elaboration, as it is one of the key aims of this book to show how one can develop a risk approach and culture to deal with all aspects of risk management, not just those relating to safety. To reiterate the point, it seems sensible to review risk in a broader sense when resources are committed to doing risk assessments; such as when a work-based risk assessment is done to comply with legal regulations, the opportunity is taken to consider other risks to operations and projects.

To help with this end, it can be useful to try and represent the different exposure areas that can be impacted, represented on a chosen scale, whether this has three or ten points. For example, publications produced by Sport New Zealand (2004) and the Department of Sport and Recreation of the State Government of Western Australia (2007), both of which adapt the ISO (2009) scales, illustrate the variety of ways outcomes can be represented. These outcome exposure areas, with some additions, are represented in Table 6.8.

Looking at Table 6.8, the outcomes relating to time and money are the most easily quantifiable, while those relating to quality can be harder to specify. Furthermore, when considering which of these scales may be used or adapted (and there are many more variations), the critical point to appreciate is that they must be contextualized to the needs of the organization and the activities being assessed, as this clarifies what is tolerable and acceptable. For example, the financial scales given in Table 6.8 are purely illustrative and should be considered in relative terms, where a loss of $1,000 to $10,000 may be considered a minor loss to a large organization, but could in fact be catastrophic for a small entrepreneur and so not acceptable. The same point applies to timescales, whereby the perishable nature of a service (i.e. once the time slot has gone, it can never be resold) could mean that an hour's delay for a service can in fact be catastrophic as customers will leave and go elsewhere.

The other important comment to make is that many of the consequence scales that can be found tend towards the negative, downside risks, yet what is argued in this book is that consideration should always be given to the potential benefits of upsides. But how are these upsides, opportunities or gains to be represented? While in financial terms it can be easier to develop some scale of the gains from undertaking certain risks, for many of the other areas of exposure, as Collins and Collins (2013: 74) note, it is far harder to try and quantify or represent the benefits. The crucial point is to accept that engaging with activities and projects involves risks, which can produce gains, some of which can be measured, others of which are too intangible or unrealistic to measure with any degree of accuracy. The easiest way to do this is to state the potential benefits of the activity at the beginning of any risk form designed, which can then help put any identified negative consequences into some perspective. Examples of this are done in the contextualization section at the end of this chapter.

6.5.3   Combining and using representative matrices

The examples presented in Table 6.7 all combine the likelihood rating with the consequence rating, to produce an overall risk rating. Using the numeric value attached to each element, these are sometimes added, but more commonly they are multiplied, as examples 1, 7 and 8 illustrate. The theory behind doing this is that it can then provide some sort of ranking that can be placed in a matrix, which in turn can help prioritize the control measures that need to be put in place. Examples of this were discussed in Chapter 5, where it was explained how something that may be given a high likelihood and a high severity impact rating should be given immediate attention so this risk can be avoided.

There are, however, some problems with this common practice of multiplying likelihood with consequences that practitioners should be aware of. Kaplan and Garrick (1981: 11) note how

Table 6.8. Examples of exposure outcome/impact scales.

Sub-categories		1. Insignificant	2. Minor	3. Moderate	4. Major	5. Catastrophic
Physical and psychological	Serious injuries	No injuries	First aid treatment	Medical treatment required	Death or extensive injuries	Multiple deaths or severe permanent disablements
	Emotional	Minor irritation	Dissatisfaction and annoyance	Dissatisfaction, seeking refunds and poor rating reviews online	Anger, frustration and resentment, seeking additional compensation	Post-traumatic stress and litigation action for damages
	Time off	Less than 1 h	1 h to 1 day	1 day to 1 week	1 week to 1 month	More than 1 month or permanently off work
	Medical treatment	Self-treatment, e.g. cuts or bruises light	First aid required	Injury that needs medical treatment	Severe harm that results in disability/ impairment	Death
Equipment and buildings	Damage and repair times, delays and costs of repair, parts or replacement (see operational time factors also)	Minor knocks or scratches to equipment	Damage occurs, but operations not affected, more aesthetic loss	Damage that can be repaired and continue to utilize, but creates delays/ loss in value	Damage to equipment or building that prevents usage in the short to medium term	Loss of all equipment or physical resources, such as a vehicle or a building, with no possibility of future usage

(Continued)

Table 6.8. Continued.

	Sub-categories	1. Insignificant	2. Minor	3. Moderate	4. Major	5. Catastrophic
Financial	Specific	Less than $1,000	$1,000 to $10,000	$10,000 to $50,000	$50,000 to $150,000	More than $150,000
	Generic (adapt to size of organization)	Very insignificant losses which will hardly noticed	Some loss, but easily absorbed	Impacts on short-term revenues or profits	Significant financial loss that affects short-term viability of the organization	Bankruptcy
Reputation/ image	Media coverage	Unsubstantiated, low impact	Substantiated, low impact, low news profile	Substantiated, public embarrassment, moderate impact, moderate news profile	Substantiated, public embarrassment, high impact, high news profile, third party actions	Substantiated, public embarrassment, very high multiple impacts, high widespread multiple news profile, third party actions
	Members (none to collapse)					
	Governance/ public confidence					
	Stakeholder confidence	Some comments, but no residual legacy	Questions raised, but little or no effect on reputation	Reputation affected so people may consider alternatives	Credibility severely damaged and rebuilding confidence necessary	All credibility lost
	Political intervention and regulatory change					
Ethical	See also reputation	Minor ethical issues compromised ('little white lie' principle)	Questions raised as to the rightness and wrongness of activity	Ambiguity whether ethical guidelines or regulations are compromised	Ethical regulations or guides broken	Many or all moral/ ethical statements clearly contradicted

		Less than 1 h	1 h to 1 day	1 day to 1 week	1 week to 1 month	More than 1 month
Operations	Specific					
	General	Minor delays and inconveniences	Delays of some hours	Delays of some days	Postponement of activities to later date	Complete cancellation of activities
Competitiveness	Rankings, such as league position	Points lost, with no change to position	Slip of one or two places	Slide down rankings by five to ten places	Drop to the bottom of the league or band	Crash out of division or fall out of key banding area

this multiplication of the two elements can lead to distorted perceptions about the risks because something can lead to a low-probability/high-severity, or damage scenario being the same as a high-probability/low-severity or damage scenario (their preference is to represent it as probability *and* severity). For example, referring back to Table 6.7 one can look at example 7, which uses a six-point scale where the probability rating is multiplied by the severity rating to produce an overall rating, which is also colour coded using the traffic light system. Using this system could for example produce the following scores:

- a terrorist attack could be given a rating of a 6 (highly improbable value of 1 × catastrophic fatalities value of 6) or 12 (remotely possible value of 2 × catastrophic fatalities value of 6); and
- a slip on a wet surface could also be given a rating of 6 (almost certainty value of 6 × negligible injury value of 1) or 12 (almost certainty value of 6 × minor injuries value of 2).

Both these risk actions would only be given a low amber rating, which does not convey any sense of urgency or the prioritizing of resources. Looking at the two, it would be difficult to say that they are of the same value. In Chapter 7 and the discussion about perceptions, one could say that the terrorist attack is an example of dread risk; so while on paper the assessment may have the same value as slipping, in terms of people's perceptions and expectations, the two have completely different levels of acceptability.

To overcome this problem, it is of interest how various Australian/New Zealand organizations related to adventure, sport and tourism deal with it. Looking back to Table 6.7, in example 4, it should be noted that rather than numbers they use a letter system, which is an adaptation of the ISO (2009) international standard. Rather than adding or multiplying, they use the letters to read off a matrix, which can be used to prioritize resources and control measures. It can also be represented as a coloured heat map; this is replicated in Table 6.9.

The numbers given simply reflect an overall summary rating, which are:

- 1 = extreme – extreme risks likely to arise with potentially serious consequences requiring urgent attention;
- 2 = major – major risks likely to arise with potentially serious consequences requiring urgent attention or investigation;
- 3 = medium – medium risks likely to arise or to have serious consequences requiring attention; and
- 4 = minor – minor risks with low consequences that may be managed by routine procedures.

Using this matrix applied to the terrorism versus slip example used earlier (both placed on the matrix in Table 6.9), the ratings would be:

- a terrorist attack could be given an E likelihood rating (rare) and an A consequence rating (extreme), which would mean it is placed in a medium risk category, requiring attention; and
- a slip could be given an A likelihood rating (almost certain) and an E rating (negligible), which would mean it is also placed in a medium risk category, requiring attention.

Table 6.9. Example of a risk matrix. (VicSports, 2014.)

Likelihood		Consequences				
		A	B	C	D	E
	A	Extreme (1)	Extreme (1)	Major (2)	Major (2)	Medium (3) (slip)
	B	Extreme (1)	Extreme (1)	Major (2)	Medium (3)	Minor (4)
	C	Extreme (1)	Major (2)	Major (2)	Medium (3)	Minor (4)
	D	Major (2)	Major (2)	Medium (3)	Minor (4)	Minor (4)
	E	Medium (3) (terrorist)	Medium (3)	Minor (4)	Minor (4)	Minor (4)

Initially, this seems little better than in the previous example, as it still ranks them the same. If however, the likelihood rating for terrorism is adjusted to a D rating, this moves it to a major risk; while for the slip, if the likelihood rating is moved down to a B, it gives it a minor rating. While far from perfect, these slight adjustments do at least better convey the risks and what may need to be done in comparison with the first example, when similar adjustments were made but did not change the overall rating.

6.6 DEVELOPING A SINGLE FORM AND KEY ELEMENTS FOR GOOD DESIGN

The problem with designing risk forms is that there can be so many variations it can be difficult to decide what should and should not be included in a form. One should be cautious about saying that one definitive approach should be adopted. It is, however, possible to identify points of good practice that can be used to understand better any existing forms used or to help improve and refine them. Some of the points to consider are:

- *Identify the benefits.* While this may not appear on the main risk register that identifies and summarizes all the key hazards, risks and control measures, it is always worthwhile reflecting on the benefits of interacting with hazards and taking risks, which is in keeping with a fourth-age risk paradigm. Examples from PMBOK (2004) can be examined for how to potentially develop an upside scale.
- *Anatomy of risk.* In Chapter 2, the anatomy of risk diagram was presented, which identifies some of the key concepts that can be utilized to analyse risks. The risk register can record the key hazards and risks, with the analysis of causation and triggers done on separate documentation if necessary, such as producing event and fault tree analysis diagrams, as illustrated in Fig. 6.1.

- *Use hazard headings.* Use of the concept of a hazard heading in safety assessments should be regarded as essential, as it is often an important part of best practice or legal compliance in certain countries. The recommendation though is to view them as the source of the risk, rather than the cause, as causation should be examined and analysed separately and more critically.
- *Hazard headings for project and strategic forms?* Although it is not common practice in project or strategic risk forms to refer to the concept of a hazard, there are no theoretical reasons why it cannot be used. The lack of use tends to reflect how practices have developed rather than theoretical barriers. Indeed, at times it can be a simple question of re-categorizing or labelling concepts and terms that may be commonly used, such as viewing external environmental PEST factors as hazards, as they are a source of risks.
- *Use a risk heading.* It is vital that the risk is identified, named, even described. In the USA, organizations conducting a JHA may not explicitly refer to risks, as they are implicitly implied, but it is encouraged to think and use risk headings as it can help refine the analysis and potential control measures.
- *Separate risk into likelihood and consequences.* Many risk forms may simply have a single risk category, heading or value. The danger of this is that it can be unclear what the key basis of the rating value is. Thinking about likelihood and consequences, whether they are given a rating or not, is still invaluable as this can help focus attention for the control measures, such as whether controls should focus on reducing the likelihood, the severity or both.
- *Identify how risk changes with control measures.* Sometimes this is done by repeating the process, but it can be simplified by just clarifying if the risk score given is with or without controls.
- *Using a control heading.* This is one of the most critical parts of the risk form. While the assessments can be highly subjective, the critical point relates to what are you going to do about the risks, which, as discussed in Chapter 5, can range from doing nothing and taking the risks, to transferring them, avoiding them or reducing them, with reduction relating to either reducing the chance of occurrence or reducing the severity of impact.
- *Named and dated.* Recording the date and who completed the assessment sheet is invaluable for reviewing and checking controls are implemented.
- *Layout.* Forms should be designed so that they are easy to read and summarize data. Remember, reference can be made to more detailed documents, scenario exercises, etc., which may appear in the appendices of a report.
- *Is it necessary to use an assessment scale?* Their common usage means that an assessment scale should always be considered. For activities that are relatively simple, with a low exposure of risks, then using scales may not be necessary. In other instances, what governs the use of a scale can be what the industry sector practice is or what is recommended by professional bodies. Table 6.10 gives a quick summary of some of the pros and cons of the different scales.
- *Mix assessment scales with numbers and descriptors?* The best assessment scales use numbers to help summarize the risk, but will try and elaborate on the score or value with descriptions of what the risks may relate to, making it more tangible to readers.

Table 6.10. Pros and cons of different assessment scales.

Positives	Negatives
Using no scales	
• Quick, easy and can focus on the key risks and the control measures • Reflects common practice for simple activities	• Can be difficult to prioritize resources for more complex risks • Failure to use a value assessment score may be viewed as poor analysis and assessment
Using qualitative scales only	
• Risks are more tangible and easy to understand	• Can miss many risks and the possible impacts and may be harder to summarize
Using numeric/quantitative scales only	
• Easy to interpret and understand • Appear objective and neutral	• Numeric scores given can still be highly subjective • May not fully convey the complexity of the risks • Risk values can fail to consider how perceptions of other key stakeholders may differ
Using a 1–3 point scale	
• Quick and easy to use • Common usage in industry sectors	• Too simplistic and lacks subtlety • OGC (2002: 87) warns that with a three-point scale it can be difficult to decide which are the most significant risks needing attention
Using a 1–5 point scale	
• Popular in practice • Has more range to express different aspects of risk	• Can be tempting to select the middle point on the scale
Using a 1–6 point scale	
• Good range of scale and used by some key professional bodies, meaning it has become a standard in some countries and sectors • No clear middle value, so a better sense is given about the direction of the risk score	• Can be harder to explain all the differences in the scale

(Continued)

Table 6.10. Continued.

Positives	Negatives
Using a 10-point or percentage scale	
• Good range of values and can offer the most precise expression of risk probability • Used in projects where more traditional scientific disciplines are encountered, such as in medicine or engineering	• Can be harder to get some of the qualitative expressions for the different scales • More difficult to relate it to consequences

6.7 DEVELOPING CHECKLISTS

In Fig. 6.1 it was illustrated how a lot of documentation and data feeds into an overall summarizing form. The last shaded box in Fig. 6.1 shows how the risk register can in theory generate additional, separate documentation. What this section does is explore additional documentation as it relates to the development of checklists.

6.7.1 What are checklists?

Checklists are likely to be familiar to many, from simple shopping lists, management to-do lists, to following the checks to be done before a piece of machinery is used. They can have a superficial simplicity to them, which can mean they are regarded as unimportant or as something that adds to workloads. This is wrong. The use of checklists can be considered a critical part of controlling risks, acting as both an aide-memoire and a mechanism to check that controls are implemented. They have also become a critical part of quality control systems, which opens out into a whole new subject area, well served by literature, but will not be discussed here in any detail.

Gawande (2010) is a leading advocate of the use of clear and simple checklists to deal with the problem of complexity. This advocacy was informed by his experience as a surgeon and the highly complex surgical procedures that have developed, where if one small detail is overlooked it really can mean the difference between life and death. Box 6.1 gives more details on how he developed a surgery checklist and what students, practitioners and managers can learn from this. Adapting Gawande's work, here are some key points that can be considered when thinking about checklists:

- The risk register can in some instances suffice as a checklist, whereby it acts as the document wherein the identified risk controls are checked for completion, dated and who completed the task.
- In other instances, separate checklists and procedures may need to be developed.
- Care must be taken in designing checklists as they should ensure any critical steps that can lead to an incident are not ignored.

Box 6.1. The surgical safety checklist

Some reading this may think why is a checklist about surgery safety appearing in a book about adventure, events, sport and tourism? It is used because it demonstrates a number of important points which any student, practitioner or manager should reflect on. When Dr Gawande was approached by the World Health Organization (WHO) to help reduce certain surgery risks, he showed a willingness to learn from others, unconnected with medicine. The discussions with people in aviation, construction and the event sectors were particularly important as they shared an important attribute with surgery: complexity. Gawande looked at how the aviation industry deals with complexity in relation to training, flying and crisis situations. The result of this consultation and, just as importantly, testing of various checklists was the production of what initially seems a remarkably simple and short checklist, which can be found on the WHO website. Although short and simple, it nevertheless has had profound impacts in terms of the number of health services that have adopted this checklist around the world. In all, he developed nineteen key checklists that appear on one A4 sheet of paper, a sample of some of the checklists appearing below:

Before induction of anaesthesia (with at least nurse and anaesthetists)	Before skin incision (with nurse, anaesthetist and surgeon)	Before patient leaves operating room (with nurse, anaesthetist and surgeon)
Has the patient confirmed his/her identity, site, procedure and consent? Yes	Confirm all team members have introduced themselves by name and role	Nurse verbally confirms: Name of the procedure Completion of instrument, sponge and needle counts
Is the site marked? Yes Not applicable	Confirm the patient's name, procedure and where the incisions will be made	
Etc.	Etc.	Etc.

Interestingly, through the refinement and testing process, not all the checklist points included were based on simple probability, such as the incident of operating on the wrong person or the wrong part of the body. Although these are very rare events, because of the high attention such incidents receive and the severity of the impact on reputation, credibility and expensive litigation, such checks were kept in (the dread risks).

The results have been credited with saving thousands of lives, but by no means are they fool-proof. For example, in their comparative study of UK and African hospitals, Aveling *et al.* (2013)

(Continued)

> **Box 6.1.** Continued.
>
> showed the approach could vary in how effectively it was implemented, identifying such factors as: scarce resources; long hours; and the problems when senior people do not offer leadership to support the checklist, which in turn dilutes the safety culture. Any student, practitioner and manager of adventure, sport, tourism and events should look at this example and ask themselves what they can learn from both Gawande's approach and design to make activities safer and more enjoyable, just as Gawande looked outside his area of work.

- Checklists can range from DO–CONFIRM (i.e. confirm you have done an action) to READ–DO (i.e. read what has been written and do it).
- If it is an operational checklist, identify points where verification can be confirmed.
- Checklists should be clear and concise, where it is easy to read what has to be done and checked off (aim for a single page of no more than ten points).
- Checklists help structure the communication processes.
- People must be utterly disciplined in adhering to the checklists of actions where failure to complete an action can result in a catastrophic risk event.
- No one should see themselves as 'above' or too experienced to adhere to a checklist. Memory and knowledge can be imperfect, so learn to trust procedures.
- The key is not necessarily about remembering everything, but remembering where to access information.
- Checklists must be tested with staff to ensure they avoid being vague, imprecise and too long. Running live scenarios is useful for testing and refining procedures.
- Checklists should make reference to industry or regulatory standards.
- Waivers (discussed in Chapter 5), although they do not remove liability, can be turned into checklists to remind people of the risks and to check that they have adopted any recommended measures (e.g. safety equipment, medical declarations, securing belongings, etc.).

The examples of checklists presented in Table 6.11 illustrate how one can go from the step of recording a control measure on a risk register, to providing a more detailed checklist to help implement and monitor the control. The two examples show a range of READ–DO and DO–CONFIRM checklists, which in turn can sometimes link into another checklist.

Although some of these checks seem quite long, adding to workloads, they can in fact be done very quickly and easily. For example, in the rope safety equipment check in Table 6.11, the rope history is initially recorded, noting the date of purchase and its type. This is to help keep track of when it needs to be replaced and to try and avoid the wrong rope being used in activities. The initial guidance on how staff should do a pre-activity rope check may be done in staff training sessions, which may be signed off to confirm the training has been done, but then staff would do this as a matter of course, only recording or making a record of any serious incidents the rope is involved in. Safety inspections, which have set dates allocated for them, should be recorded. Obviously, not all equipment needs to go through this checklist type process, but any pieces

Table 6.11. Examples of simple checklist items to consider in a checklist form.

Children's sport activity	Safety equipment check for climbing ropes in an outdoor adventure centre
Pre-activity check (confirm that following recorded): • proof of police checks for staff • proof of first aid for staff • proof of coaching qualifications • in-house customer care training done (see separate checklist)	*Rope history* (record): • date when rope first bought (replace after 3–5 years depending on use, or manufacturer's guidance, or if damage occurs by other means, as listed below) • consult rope guidance from professional bodies, standards or other relevant organization • confirm the type of rope and its use for appropriate activities (e.g. single rope type only used for single climber; double/half rope type used for working in pairs; twin rope type should not be used with clients)
Activity checklist (recorded DO–CONFIRM): • all children are signed in • no child can begin activity until registration form completed (which confirms parent/guardian contact details given; declares any medical conditions; medication available if necessary, e.g. inhaler for asthma) • all children are signed out (see separate checklist for missing child)	*Pre-activity rope check* (READ–DO) Run rope through hand before an activity (not recorded/initial training guidance) to check for: • fraying of strands • fuzziness/abrasion marks • discoloration • irregularities • burn/melt marks • stiff sections • ensure rope is properly stored away from sunlight, heat sources, chemicals and properly coiled in a bag
During activities (not recorded, READ–DO, unless any incidents occur, such as an accident) Coaches should ensure that they: • introduce themselves • check that all safety equipment is worn if appropriate • explain what will be done • do warm-up activities (see separate guidance checklist on warm-up routines)	*Incident checklist* (record) Report and record rope history if it is involved in any of the following: • a high/hard fall • exposed to a rock fall • grit, sand or dirt has worked into fibres which cannot be cleaned • exposed to extreme heat • exposed to chemicals • exposed to sunlight for long periods

(Continued)

Table 6.11. Continued.

	Safety equipment check for climbing ropes in an outdoor adventure centre
	Six-monthly rope check (signed and dated) Check for: • discoloration/chemical marks • fraying of strands • fuzziness/abrasion marks • irregularities • burn/melt marks • stiff sections • check incidents if rope sustained a hard fall involving people falling from a great height or over a sharp edge • confirm rope condition/recommendation (remove or use for other low-risk activities)

of equipment where the failure can have catastrophic implications (e.g. failures in alarms, life vests, first aid equipment) should be considered for the application of systematic checklists in terms of training, inspection and history.

In relation to the child safety example presented in Table 6.11, again the list may seem long, but the initial short list is used as a mechanism for tracking because of the profound implications if an incident was to occur and if one of the control measures was not properly implemented. The checklist for children in terms of contacts and medical conditions can be dealt with by a simple tick or initial next to their names as they sign in and sign out. If a child fails to sign out, then this can initiate referral to another checklist of actions (discussed in the next section on crisis checklists). The activity checklist is designed for staff training and as an aide-memoire for staff and would not really need to be recorded down.

6.7.2   Developing crisis checklists and manuals

Simply put, crisis or catastrophic events can be understood as those risk events classified as having an extreme severity of outcome which, although rare, can have the potential to affect the future viability of the organization. Examples can relate to such things as: spinal injuries; deaths of participants; transport accidents; natural disasters, such as earthquakes, tsunamis; terrorist attacks; and political instability. How the organization responds to the crisis can have huge implications in terms of its reputation, credibility or finances, or the continuation with operations.

Crisis management is another discrete subject area, whereby only a few key points will be considered here in relation to checklists. Gawande gives some useful insights into how the aviation industry and pilots are trained to use and adhere to checklists during crisis situations. Many of the checklists are designed to prevent a crisis, such as some obvious or mundane DO–CONFIRM actions like checking brake lights are off, controls run free and seatbelts are secured. If a crisis such as sudden engine failure does take place, pilots are trained to consult a series of checklists, which they must run through systematically.

The crucial point to appreciate is that at times when a crisis situation occurs it can be difficult for staff to know the correct procedures and actions to take, particularly when a serious accident or incident has occurred. While people working in the emergency services are trained to deal with critical incidents, most people working in the industry sectors simply may not have encountered a critical incident before (it is hoped they never will). So the answer is to have a crisis manual, where a simple checklist of actions are identified that deal with key critical incidents such as the death of a participant, extreme weather, or equipment failure forcing an activity or event to be cancelled. When developing a crisis manual, along with the more specific crisis checklists for specific scenarios, the following points should be considered:

- key emergency contacts should be provided for emergency services and senior managers identified as part of the crisis team;
- a checklist can refer to another checklist of actions, which must again be clear and concise, such as the 'non-normal' crisis checklists that pilots use (Gawande, 2010: 86);
- staff should be trained in how to deal with checklists in a crisis situation, just as airline pilots are trained to stay cool under pressure and consult the checklists in a systematic manner;
- crisis checklists can be developed from developing various crisis scenarios (see Chapter 7 for examples), exploring what may happen if things go wrong;
- when developing crisis checklists, ensure there is a clear chain of command, staff training, insurance, etc.;
- develop checklists for key crisis events, such as how staff deal with the death of a participant (details of how this may occur do not necessarily need to be explained here) or if someone is lost or kidnapped; and
- provide clear lines of responsibilities of who has to deal with the media, if relevant (a separate training checklist will be given, to cover the key points of condolences, praise and a promise to find answers).

To illustrate these matters, a range of checklist crisis points are presented in Table 6.12. These could be used for the basis of some simplified, properly designed checklist sheets.

6.8 CONTEXTUALIZATION FOR THE SECTORS

The following examples consider how some of the points discussed in this chapter can be applied to the different sectors. It is not possible to show all the information that would have been recorded from the research conducted and tools applied. What is presented is just a simplified form, using the five-point risk rating scale of example 4 highlighted in Section 6.5 and

Table 6.12. Examples of points to consider for crisis-related checklists.

Simplified training checklist for staff dealing with the incident of a participant collapse/not breathing (not recorded)	Senior manager/crisis response leader checklist for death of a participant (signed and checked)	Missing person/child simplified points (record/tick/initial as actions are gone through)
• Was it as a result of collision or exertion?	• If rumour heard, verify the incident with police/coroner	• Check all people doing activity have returned/signed out
• Environmental conditions (e.g. extreme heat, storm)	• Once families have been officially informed, contact to express condolences/offer support (see separate letter)	• Confirm person is missing (e.g. not just forgotten to sign out)
• Any medical conditions known (e.g. diabetes, heart conditions) that medication can alleviate? (See separate guidance checklists for diabetes, asthma, heat exhaustion, etc.)	• Convene crisis response team (discuss scripts for staff announcements, media if necessary and parental letter)	• Ring relevant contact numbers available or guardian/parent number on consent form
• Check for any dangers nearby (e.g. electric cable)	• Notify key stakeholders listed in crisis manual	• Determine when and where the person was last seen and by whom
• Attempt to rouse/call person	• Prepare script for responding to enquiries	• Can the last location be searched safely?
• If collapse not related to collision, tilt head back and check breathing/clear airways	• Designated senior manager to deal with media (sympathy, praise, investigate, confidentiality) (separate checklist)	• Possible scenarios can be: accident, abduction (children), kidnapping considered in relation to evidence collected so far (see separate checklists)

• If not breathing, call for help: emergency services and equipment (e.g. defibrillator/spinal board)	• Collect all relevant case study materials, such as training policies, risk assessments	• If suspected child abduction call emergency services to initiate their crisis plan (see separate checklists)
• Check airways for blockages	• Call team meetings and review the case study details	• Dealing with parents, family and friends (see separate checklist)
o Begin CPR (see separate training checklist)	• Offer counselling services to key stakeholders if necessary (separate checklist and organizations)	• Can staff assist in search without compromising other people's or their own safety?
o If no heartbeat, use defibrillator if available	• Parent/relative contacted about funeral services/memorials	
o Keep going until emergency services arrive	• Implement follow-up responses	
• Inform emergency services of suspected conditions/cause	• If litigation/criminal prosecution initiated (see separate checklist)	
• Designated responsible person to ensure group is kept safe and checking in/ signing out procedures are maintained		

(Continued)

Table 6.12. Continued.

Simplified training checklist for staff dealing with the incident of a participant collapse/not breathing (not recorded)	Senior manager/crisis response leader checklist for death of a participant (signed and checked)	Missing person/child simplified points (record/tick/initial as actions are gone through)
Post-crisis situation		
• Notify designated senior manager who will initiate post-incident crisis measures (see separate checklist)		
• If death has occurred, do not ring guardian/ parents/relatives as this must done by proper authorities (see separate checklist for accidents requiring hospitalization)		

CPR, cardiopulmonary resuscitation.

presented in Table 6.7, which can be revisited in order to recall what the letters and numbers refer to. It would be recommended that when people complete risk registers, they are presented in a landscape format as it is easier to add columns and read the information.

6.8.1   Children's rugby

Table 6.13 gives a range of possible hazards and risks for children playing rugby. This assessment would be relatively easy to complete by any experienced player or coach using his/her own experiences, but would be greatly aided by additional research of governing body regulations and any incident data. For example:

- Pollock (2014) suggests that children have a one-in-six chance of being seriously injured during a season, with 'serious' being defined by such parameters as needing hospital treatment, or a prolonged absence from the game. Over two-thirds of the injuries will come from tackling.
- Fuller (2007) notes that forwards are more likely to suffer catastrophic injuries, because of the role they perform, with the scrum most likely to cause the injury.

6.8.2   Adventure trek in a rainforest

A range of possible hazards and risks that a group trekking in a rainforest may be exposed to is presented in Table 6.14. It should be considered how such things as the type of group would affect the exposure. For example, while one may expect that a more experienced group may be at less risk, their skill level may in fact mean they will try more challenging activities which could have a higher severity of impacts. Research would have involved accessing a variety of databases, as highlighted in Chapter 4.

6.8.3   New hotel development in a developing country

The risk exposure of a hotel development in comparison with a package tour is different because there is a greater degree of captive investment (see Chapter 2, Section 2.3.4) with the hotel and longer timescales are involved in building it. As with any project, the nearer the completion of the hotel construction, the more there is to lose. It should be noted that with some of the political risks, the company can take relatively few control measures beyond insurance or monitoring situations. In terms of the background research, this would involve a more complex gathering of key country data, such as economic performance and political trends, in order to better assess the future conditions and stability of the country. An example of some risks and hazards are given for the strategic risk assessment in Table 6.15.

6.8.4   Cultural festival for a city

Events are projects, whereby in the early stages of the risk management process they will focus on hazards stemming from the external business environment, examples of which are

Table 6.13. Example of a risk register and assessment for children's rugby.

Risk register (summary)

Risk benefits: Fitness, satisfaction, fun, teambuilding, grow the sport, social well-being, financial gain, community club and social activities for parents and children

Hazard	Who/what	Risks description	Risk rating (consequences and likelihood)	Controls
Goals	Players	Collision resulting in bruising, breaks and concussion	Bruising: C band for likelihood/E band for consequences	Purchase padding for lower part of goalposts
	Club		Concussion: C band for likelihood/B band for consequences (major risk)	
	Reputation		With control measures: for bruising, C band likelihood/E band consequences with padding (medium risk)	Ensure they are fitted at each game (see separate training checklist)
	Membership		With control measures: for concussion, B band likelihood/C band consequences (major risk)	
Game play relating to: • running • tackling • scrum • Team imbalances (strength, skill and experience)	Injuries because of uneven contest/fun removed/no skill development	Strains/muscle tears	With control measures (e.g. warm-ups): D band likelihood/C band consequences (medium risk)	Ensure proper warm-ups are done (see separate checklist)

Collision injuries of bruising, breaks (e.g. nose, cheek, arm, leg), concussion and spinal injuries	For concussion and spinal injuries: C band likelihood/B to A band consequences	Qualified referees to be used in competitive game	
		Referee to enforce RFU/IRB rules governing dangerous tackling (see separate checklist of guidance points)	
Dangerous tackling/high arm	Etc.	Spinal injury suspected: initial spinal injury first aid (see separate checklists)	
Fighting		Suspected concussion: person must leave field and not play for at least a week (see concussion checklist guidance notes)	
		Under-14s to avoid scrums (see separate guidelines on law variations by age grade)	
Etc.		Etc.	

RFU, Rugby Football Union; IRB, International Rugby Board.

Table 6.14. Example of a risk register and assessment for an adventure jungle trekking expedition.

Risk register (summary)

Risk benefits: Excitement, new venture, education, challenge, commercial gain, personal satisfaction, skill development, physical, social and mental well-being, educational such as leadership skill development

Hazard	Who/what	Risks description	Risk rating (consequences and likelihood)	Controls
Animals (bats, dogs, etc.)	Staff	Bitten by animals/insects and risk of disease/illness or death	Bitten: D band likelihood (with control measures)/A band consequences for suspected rabies	Vaccinations (see separate medical checklist)
Diseases: • malaria • dengue fever	Customers	Waterborne disease risks from food and water	D band likelihood (with control measures)/A band consequences (D with medication)	Avoid contact/approaching animals
Etc.	Reputation	Medication side-effects		Mosquito nets/covered at night
Political instability demonstrations:	Ethical	Etc.		Initiate CASEVAC (casualty evacuation) for suspected bites (see separate checklist)
• curfews • terrorism				
Etc.	Financial losses	Delays or cancellations because of changed Foreign & Common- wealth Office advice	D band likelihood/A band consequences for cancellation (control measures cannot change ratings)	Flying doctor medical insurance (part of CASEVAC)

Equipment	Restrictions on movement/travel, etc.		Anti-malaria tablets taken (monitor behaviour) Alternative destinations considered (3-month notice) Monitor political situation Etc.

Table 6.15. Example of a strategic risk register for a hotel investment.

Risk register (summary)				
Risk benefits: Financial gain, new market, growth, brand reputation, creating stimulating new experiences, cultural differences, market leader in the country				
Hazard	**Who/what**	**Risks description**	**Risk rating (consequences and likelihood)**	**Controls**
Political instability	Hotel	Delays in building	D band likelihood (with control measures)/A band consequences	Monitor political conditions (track and record key events)
Government policy	Reputation	Hotel is expropriated		Track various government advice sites (see separate checklist)
Demonstrations	Shareholders	Hotel is damaged in conflict		Insurance
Terrorism	Financial	No customers		
Criminal gangs				
Poor infrastructure/ sanitation				

presented in Table 6.16. As the project nears completion, the risk management process will begin to change, concentrating more on operational and safety issues, such as how the flows of people for an event can be managed safely, reducing delays and allowing attendees to enjoy the event. The exposure level, as noted before, will also change; the closer the event date, the more that can be lost in terms of money and, indeed, credibility. Just a few of the many possible hazards and risks are considered here, noting how they change and the project life cycle develops.

Table 6.16. Example of a risk register for a cultural event

Risk register (summary)				
Risk benefits: Commercial gain, brand enhancement, raising city profile, community well-being, enjoyment, job creation				
Hazard	**Who/what**	**Risks description**	**Risk rating (consequences and likelihood)**	**Controls**
Contractors	Reputation	Contractors stop operating	D band likelihood (with control measures)/A band consequences	Use of flexible, temporary pavilions
Natural environment	Brand	Accidents to workers and adverse publicity and delays	D band likelihood (with control measures)/A band consequences	Ensure contractors used have a sound track record (investigated)
Artists	Finances	Facilities not ready	D band likelihood (with control measures)/A band consequences	Ensure contractors comply with regulatory and industry standards
		Structures damaged by weather		Alternative suppliers researched for crisis contingency
		Failing to secured named artists reducing attractiveness of event/low attendance	C band likelihood (with control measures)/B band consequences	Develop contingency for emergency venues (see separate crisis plan checklist)
				Monitor key indicators to decide if crisis measures need to be implemented in good time

(*Continued*)

Table 6.16. Continued.

				Venues designed with sheltered areas
				Ensure high-profile artists are secured early on to act as leverage to attract other artists
				Etc.

6.9   CONCLUSION

So how important is it to record and document the information gathered from applying the different process stages? The answer is that it depends on the level of complexity of the activity, the scale of exposure and what is exposed to risk. In theory, for simple activities, operating with experienced people, very little may need to be recorded, with the all elements of the process stage completed relatively quickly. Using a simple risk register form can be both the beginning and the end of the risk assessment, with no additional documentation required, unless any accidents or incidents occur.

As the level of complexity of the activity increases and one moves into the realms of project and strategic management, the need for recording and documentation becomes essential. This is to not only help in the analysis, but to also to monitor risks and track the implementation of control measures. To aid in this process, one should think about how forms are designed, completed and if an assessment scale needs to be used, appreciating that they can always be prone to various subjective influences and biases. From this form, to check that control measures are being implemented and training is done, the use of checklists can be of critical importance; this can help in assuring both consistent and safe practice, which can be extended into the area of crisis management.

While there are variations between sectors and countries, there are, however, no theoretical impediments for preventing the use of many of the key concepts highlighted and some of the points of good practice. The key is consistency in concept application and usage, using forms and documentation to deliver better quality and safe services.

DISCUSSION QUESTIONS AND TASKS

1. Study the WHO surgical checklist and identify what is good and bad about it. Research the news stories and the impact it has had. For your chosen sector, how can this be adapted for an activity?

2. Find out more about quality control and how it this can relate to risk and checklists.

3. Examine a number of case studies relating to aviation incidents and consider the role of training, checklists and the control of emotions.

4. Examine a number of news clips of politicians or senior managers dealing with a crisis situation and consider if they follow key principles of a crisis response (condolences, praise and a promise to investigate).

5. Go online and try and find at least three different-looking examples of risk forms. Compare and contrast them, paying particular attention to how they have used certain concepts, whether an assessment scale is used and the visual design of the form.

REFERENCES

Aveling, E., McCulloch, P. and Dixon-Woods, M. (2013) A qualitative study comparing experiences of the surgical safety checklist in hospitals in high-income and low-income countries. *BMJ Open* 3, e003039.

Cagno, E., Caron, F. and Mancini, M. (2007) A multi-dimensional analysis of major risks in complex projects. *Risk Management* 9, 1–18.

CIMSPA (2014) *Risk Assessment Manual 5th Edition (IMSPARAM)*. Chartered Institute for the Management of Sport and Physical Activity, Loughborough, UK.

Collins, L. and Collins, D. (2013) Decision making and risk management in adventure sports. *Quest* 65, 72–82.

Department of Sport and Recreation, Government of Western Australia (2007) Can You Risk It? An Introduction to Risk Management for Community Organisations. Includes Community RiskBase User's Guide. Available at: http://www.dsr.wa.gov.au/support-and-advice/organisational-development/management-and-planning/risk-management (accessed 12 December 2014).

Fitzgerald, P. (2003) *Risk Management Guide for Tourism Operators*. Canadian Tourism Commission, Ottawa.

Fuller, C.W. (2007) Catastrophic injuries in rugby union: an assessment of the risk (final draft). Available at: http://irbplayerwelfare.com/pdfs/CI_Risk_Assessment_EN.pdf (accessed 20 September 2014).

Gardiner, P.D. (2005) *Project Management: A Strategic Planning Approach*. Palgrave Macmillan, Basingstoke, UK.

Gawande, A. (2010) *The Checklist Manifesto: How To Get Things Right*. Profile Books Ltd, London.

Haddock, C. (1999) High potential incidents – determining their significance. Tools for our trade and a tale or two. Wilderness Risk Management Conference Proceedings. Available at: http://www.nols.edu/nolspro/pdf/wrmc_proceedings_99_high_potential_haddock.pdf (accessed 18 January 2015).

ISO (2009) *Risk Management – Principles and Guidelines*. International Organization for Standardization, Geneva, Switzerland.

Kaplan, S. and Garrick, J.B. (1981) On the quantitative definition of risk. *Risk Analysis* 1, 11–27.

OGC (2002) *Management of Risk: Guidance for Practitioners*. UK Office of Government Commerce, London.

OSHA (2002) *Job Hazard Analysis, OSHA 3071, 2002 (Revised)*. US Department of Labor, Occupational Safety & Health Administration, Washington, DC.

PMBOK (2004) *A Guide to the Project Management Body of Knowledge*, 3rd edn. Project Management Institute, Newtown Square, Pennsylvania.

Pollock, A. (2014) *Tackling Rugby: What Every Parent Should Know*. Verso Books, London.

RFU (2014) Risk Assessments. Available at: http://www.englandrugby.com/governance/legal-and-admin/risk-assessments/ (accessed 20 February 2015).

SPARC (2004) Risk management of events. Available at: http://www.sportnz.org.nz/managing-sport/ guides/risk-management-for-events (accessed 20 August 2014).

Standards New Zealand (2004) New Zealand Handbook: Guidelines for Risk Management in Sport and Recreation. SNZ HB8669:2004. Available at: http://www.sportnz.org.nz/assets/Uploads/ attachments/managing-sport/strong-organisations/Risk-Management-Toolkit.pdf (accessed 20 August 2014).

Swartz, G. (2001) *Job Hazard Analysis: A Guide to Identifying Risks in the Workplace*. Government Institutes, Rockville, Maryland.

UK Sport (2005) Major Sports Events – The Guide. Available at: http://www.uksport.gov.uk/publications /major-sports-events-the-guide-april-2005 (accessed 24 June 2013).

VicSports (2014) Guide to developing risk management plans for sport and active recreation clubs. Available at: http://www.myfootballclub.com.au/fileadmin/user_upload/Sport_and_Recreation_ Organisations_Guide_to_Developing_Risk_Management_Plans.pdf (accessed on 20 February 2015).

FURTHER READING

Albrighton, L. (1993) Emergency response – planning for crisis management. *Safeguard: Journal of Occupational Safety and Health* July issue, 17–19.

Australian Sports Commission (2013) *Sporting clubs guide to a safe workplace*. Available at: http:// www.ausport.gov.au/__data/assets/pdf_file/0005/526064/33004_Workplace_Safety_Guide_ web.pdf

CIMSPA, in the Shop folder, extracts and details can be found for the risk assessment manual, available at: http://www.cimspa.co.uk/

Comcare, an Australian Government agency, has a useful travel risk assessment checklist, available at: http://www.comcare.gov.au/Forms_and_Publications/forms2/safety_and_prevention_forms/ safety_and_prevention/travel_risk_assess_checklist

European Agency for Health and Safety at Work (EU-OHSA) provides details about documenting the risk process, available at: https://osha.europa.eu/en/topics/riskassessment/documenting_risk

FIFA produces various guidance notes that can be developed into various control or crisis check-lists. *Dealing with sudden death,*available at: http://www.fifa.com/mm/document/afdeveloping/ medical/01/07/26/86/fifapcmaform.pdf. Warm-up guidelines, available at: http://www.fifa.com/ aboutfifa/footballdevelopment/medical/playershealth/the11/index.html

JISC provides some invaluable useful guidance notes on project risk management. Examples of assess-ment scales, available at: http://www.jiscinfonet.ac.uk/infokits/risk-management/qual-analysis/. Example of a stakeholder form, available at: https://docs.google.com/document/d/1QE8jG_ t6GWt8zFkY5Xtvey7kjcxiafOGbtzsJUkMrFE/edit. Examples of a risk log or register, available at: http://www.jiscinfonet.ac.uk/infokits/risk-management/identifying-risk/risk-log/

St John Ambulance (UK) gives first aid advice for the unconscious and not breathing adult, available at: http://www.sja.org.uk/sja/first-aid-advice/unconscious-and-not-breathing.aspx

UK HSE provides many examples of risk assessments, available at: http://www.hse.gov.uk/index.htm

US Sailing provides example of waivers as a form of checklists, available at: http://www.ussailing.org/ racing/youth-sailing/junior-olympics/jo-manual/additional-resources-and-forms/

WHO Surgical Safety Checklist, available at: http://www.who.int/patientsafety/safesurgery/checklist/en/

chapter 7

Risk Perceptions and Decision Making

CHAPTER OBJECTIVES

- To explain the limitations of classical rational models of decision making.
- To explain how perceptions of risk influence risk decision making.
- To identify the factors that can influence risk perceptions for practitioners and key stakeholders.
- To develop an explanatory model giving an overview of filters that can shape perceptions.

Key concepts

Derived utility; prospect theory; risk homeostasis; heuristics; heuristic traps; T-CUP; role of emotions; culture of fear; media amplification; flow theory.

7.1 INTRODUCTION

Why is it possible for two people to look at the same sport, adventure or travel activity, yet make completely different assessments of the risks? The answer is not a simple one, but the question is vital for practitioners to ask because: (i) it enables them to understand why customers, clients and other key stakeholders can view risks so differently from themselves; and (ii) it can help them be aware of their own limitations in risk analysis and assessments, guarding against hubris or excessive overconfidence.

What is therefore explored in this chapter is how various factors interact and entwine to shape both practitioners' and stakeholders' perceptions of risk. To explore these factors, a variety of theories and concepts are used, drawn from different scientific disciplines, particularly those of psychology, sociology and economics. This is done to show the breadth of factors that can potentially influence perceptions about risk, with these perceptions influencing how risk is dealt with. It is a discussion that is relevant for all levels of management, from the operational to the project and the strategic, for all the different industry sectors.

7.2 THE LIMITATIONS OF OBJECTIVE RISK ASSESSMENTS REVISITED

From the discipline of economics, the *theory of derived utility*, while not purely about risk taking, helps illustrate a classic underpinning theory used to try and understand human behaviour. At its core is the belief that people, when buying goods and services, will act rationally, in the sense that they will choose the good or service where the most utility (or benefit) is delivered (or derived). The implications in terms of risk should be obvious, in that people are undertaking a form of risk assessment in relation to seeking opportunities for gains or avoiding losses. This belief in rational behaviour is one which can be extended to management, whereby a manager can make rational decisions by collecting statistical data, observing patterns, performing statistical assessment calculations and then making objective decisions free from emotional bias. This type of decision-making theory can be described as *normative*, in that it describes a directed form of behaviour as to how customers and managers should act in certain situations (Timmermans, 2010: 368).

As explained in Chapter 3, there are numerous problems with this notion of objective risk and rational decision making (Adams, 1995: 23; Eduljee, 2000: 16). There it was explained how the differences between the *objective* risk assessment (the assessment which in theory is based on scientific evidence and research) and *subjective* risk assessment (the assessment based on experiences and managed through judgement) are often blurred and even contested, with Adams (1995) calling these areas of dispute *virtual risks*.

These limitations mean it is vital to develop a more realistic descriptive model of how risk is analysed, assessed and dealt with by both practitioners and other key stakeholders, such as staff or customers. Three reasons can be given for why this is important:

- *Risk should not just concentrate on formal management processes*. This distinction between the objective and the subjective risk can place too much emphasis on the formal risk management process, which can fail to recognize that decisions about risk are in fact constantly being made that do not rely on complex probabilistic assessments and form filling.
- *Subjective customer perceptions can be more important than expert practitioners' objective assessments*. It is easy to find examples of how people do not always make decisions which maximize utility or benefits. The implication for managers is that if they are in the business of providing services for profit, or to achieve social objectives, it is vital they understand their customers', clients' and stakeholders' perceptions of risk, even

though these may be based on misunderstandings, distortions or simple ignorance, as it is these perceptions that influence their behaviour and actions to purchase goods and services.

- *Practitioners should be aware of how their assessment of risk can become distorted or wrong.* Many decisions about risk are not necessarily objective, but can be shaped by cultural systems, instinct, intuition and experiences. Appreciating these subjective influences can help managers recognize that they are fallible, so helping them to have a degree of humility and guard against hubris.

Consideration of these many factors can be an important part of the early context stage of the risk process, as not only does it help identify key stakeholders, it also encourages analysis of how different stakeholders may perceive risk, which in turn may influence their decision to buy or use services offered.

7.3 EXPLAINING THE VARIATIONS IN RISK PERCEPTIONS: A MODEL

There are many interacting factors that influence both practitioner and customer perceptions of risk. To help convey this complex array of factors, a simple model is developed, represented in Fig. 7.1. The model draws on a range of literature from different scientific disciplines, but Adam's (1995, 2011) work on the theory of 'filters' and Slovic's (1991, 1999) theories on risk perceptions are particularly influential.

The model begins with the risk situation or scenario. This refers to the decisions and actions that need to be made, which can range from the immediate decisions required to deal with adventure, sport or travel-related activities, to those for a longer-term business plan. Next, a number of broad categories are developed to help bunch or theme the many possible influencing filters that may shape perceptions, which are represented as the surrounding circles. These categories are:

- knowledge, information and heuristics (Section 7.3.1);
- emotions and skill levels (Section 7.3.2);
- personality and behaviour (Section 7.3.3);
- the stake (Section 7.3.4); and
- culture (Section 7.3.5).

These create a complex interactive cocktail of influences shaping judgement and perceptions, which in turn affect the decisions and actions taken by practitioners, customers and other key stakeholders. The filters can act to both inhibit behaviour and direct it. Very importantly, the model considers how the decisions are made to avoid losses or make gains and benefits. Each of these sets of factors is explored in more detail in the following sub-sections.

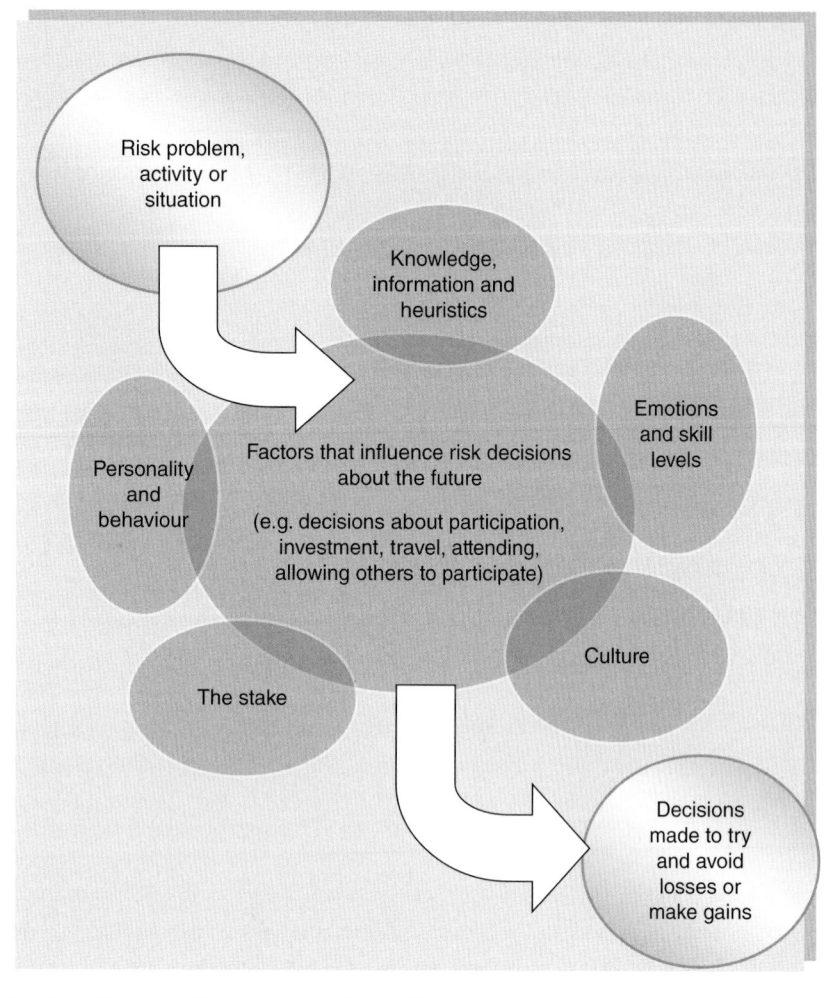

Fig. 7.1. How do we make decisions about risk?

7.3.1 Risk perceptions filters: knowledge, experience and heuristics

In Chapter 3, it was explained that while researching past incidents is a key theoretical principle underpinning risk management practices, the reality is that many practitioners may not have enough time for research, or there may be very few precedents or previous cases that can be found. The result is that people will fill in the gaps based on their own knowledge and experience. This process is known as *heuristics*: making decisions based on personal experiences, rather than just pure calculations (Kahneman and Tversky, 1979; Lanchester, 2010). It is decision making also based on numerous unconscious rules (Merna and Faisal, 2005: 24) which are shaped by experiences gained through trial and error.

It should be appreciated that analyses, assessments and decisions based on heuristics are not necessarily less accurate in comparison with a more objective assessment based on a systematic data collection process. Indeed, in relation to many operational, dynamic risk situations (see also Chapter 8) that managers, coaches, instructors, teachers or tour leaders may find themselves in, heuristics are vital bedrock from which to make decisions as operating conditions change.

While valuable and giving a good description of how risk assessments are actually made, there are many limitations that practitioners should be aware of, which Collins and Collins (2013: 77), citing McCammon (2004), describe as *heuristic traps*. These can be described as:

- *Inexperience*. The capacity for reflection on past experiences can be limited if people are inexperienced.
- *Habituation*. Practitioners and clients can become overfamiliar with certain risks, which creates a false sense of security, leading them to 'switch off', 'drop their guard' or become overconfident in activities.
- *Poor learners*. Some people may be poor at reflecting and learning from previous incidents or mistakes made.
- *Scarcity of opportunity*. If something is seen as unique, it may encourage more risk taking. Maybe because of time (people have the free time only on that day), conditions (e.g. new snow, sunny weather), or the opportunity to be first for a new market investment, all could influence the decision to take risks.
- *Consistency of alignment*. People can sometimes become hardwired into a project and find it difficult to change their minds, or may not want to lose face, or appear inconsistent, so bad decisions may be followed up with more bad decisions.
- *Halo effect*. At times people may have a heightened trust and belief in the manager, instructor, coach, guide or other expert in the field.
- *Acceptance*. People may not contest issues because of a desire to be accepted in a group.
- *Social facilitation/impacts*. People feel emboldened to test or show new skills or abilities to other members in a group.

7.3.2   Risk perceptions filters: role of emotions and skill levels

The need for emotional arousal is a critical element in creating memorable and satisfying adventure, sport, tourism and event experiences. While vital and positive ingredients for good experiences, perhaps paradoxically, emotions in decision making are sometimes seen as things that interfere with good risk analysis, assessments and cloud judgements, leading to poor decision making.

In his book *The Decisive Moment*, Lehrer (2009) gives a very readable account of the role emotions play in critical decision making. He begins by using Plato's metaphor of the mind being pulled by a chariot with two horses, with the rational mind represented by the well-bred and behaved horse, while the other horse is unpredictable and difficult to control, representing an old argument that emotions interfere with clear thinking

(Lehrer, 2009: 16). The importance of this 'control' of the dark horse can be found in many fields of work. For example, among those who may find themselves in crisis situations, such as pilots, soldiers, doctors, emergency service workers or top-class sport athletes (see Section 7.4.2 and Clive Woodward's T-CUP principle), a key part of their training is to learn how to control certain emotions, such as feelings of panic, in order to act calmly and make good decisions.

What is of interest in Lehrer's work is how he uses some remarkable case studies to illustrate that, at times, reacting to emotions can be a critical part of good decision making, as Box 7.1 illustrates. While his work does not offer any clear guidelines as to when to control emotions or when they should be acted upon, it still gives a deeper understanding into why people making decisions based on their 'gut instinct' (people reacting to the feelings they have, rather than what they necessarily actually know), like many successful entrepreneurs do (Boyne, 2003: 14), can actually lead to decisions that produce gains. Lehrer also observes how different working environments influence the emotions and mood of people, which in turn can further shape their perceptions of risk.

Box 7.1. When acting on your 'gut instinct' can make for the best decisions

Lehrer (2009) discusses a variety of case studies to illustrate this tension between emotions and rational decision making. One case study stands out.

Lieutenant Riley was monitoring radar signals during the Iraq war of 1991. He had been looking at the blips of the allied planes coming and going for hour after hour, for many days. On one of these monitoring sessions, one radar blip caused a pulse of fear. He could not explain it, because for all intents and purposes one blip looked the same as another. He had very little time to act owing to the speed of the target, so he decided to act on his fear and gave the order to fire some intercepting missiles that destroyed the target. After a long wait, the target turned out not to be an allied aircraft but a hostile Silkworm missile, with Riley's decision saving the lives of many people on *HMS Gloucester*. When it was analysed how Riley was able to make such an important decision, initially nothing was found in the radar blips that could explain how he interpreted such a difference between the missile and the plane blips, as they seemed to be exactly the same. Was it simple luck? Not quite, as Klien (1999), who investigated this case, found out. It was because there was an almost imperceptible difference in the timing of the hostile missile's appearance on the screen (it flew lower, so was picked up later), compared with the planes. Riley had unconsciously evaluated the situation, which is why he felt fear, and his decision to act on those fears helped save lives.

This case study offers an interesting paradox: sometimes we need to control emotions in decision making, while at other times these emotions help us to act on those moments of intuition which can bring rewards or benefits.

There are various books and journal articles which explore the role of sensation seeking and emotional arousal further, giving many useful insights about risk perceptions and behaviour. For example, Scitovsky (1986) argues how excitement is a primitive emotion, intimately tied in with our survival; and how people in the developed world, having satisfied many of their basic needs, have lost a key challenge in their lives (i.e. survival), but the need for stimulation is not necessarily diminished. He goes on to use his theory to try and gain insight into such activities as adventure sports and certain forms of criminal behaviour, such stealing cars to race (sometimes known as joyriding) rather than for financial gain.

Csikszentmihalyi (1992) attempted to try and understand the general condition of human happiness, developing his theory of *optimal flow experience*. He defined flow as a feeling and state of mind where the level of skill is balanced in relation to the level of challenge. If the challenge (mental or physical) is too difficult, then anxiety can set in; if too easy then boredom occurs. When there is the match or balance between skill and challenge, then this is described as *flow*, with the best moments often happening when people are stretched physically and mentally. Echoing Scitovsky, the idea of skill is an interesting point for practitioners in the industry to consider, together with his point that satisfaction is not always gained immediately with the act itself, but is gained with later reflection. This theory helps explain why people may need to do activities that have greater risks, as there is a need to maintain the challenge in order to experience arousal and flow. It should also be noted how there is an element of homeostasis here (see Section 7.3.3), whereby an increase in people's skill levels does not necessarily mean the risk of an accident will decrease.

While overcoming challenging activities, both physically and mentally, can produce immense satisfaction derived from the arousal that has taken place, one should be cautious about making the assumption that it is the risk that motivates people. As Cater (2004) argues, it is a 'false idea' that risk motivates people. People may know there can be risk of death or injury from an activity, but that is not part of the attraction; rather it is overcoming the challenges, and the feelings of excitement and satisfaction this can bring, placing trust in their own skills or the organizers, which makes the risk tolerable and so accepted.

7.3.3 Risk perception filters: personality and behavioural influences

While considering personality differences and the influence on risk-taking behaviours seems obvious, it is not necessarily supported by a great deal of conclusive research. For example, it is sometimes suggested that younger people and males may have a higher propensity to take risks, but as Slovic (1999) highlights, research into the extent that this is shaped by biology or social factors has produced mixed results. There are, however, a number of related behavioural theories which offer a firmer foundation for gaining insights into both practitioners' and customers' risk decision-making processes. These are:

- homeostasis;
- hindsight bias;
- severity of outcome versus degree of situational control; and
- prospect theory.

As part of his *risk thermostat* model (discussed in Chapter 3), Adams (1995, 2011) adapts Wilde's (1994, 2001) theory of *homeostasis*: the idea of a system always trying to balance or stabilize itself. The example often used to illustrate this idea of homeostasis looks at the impact of legislation requiring people to wear safety belts in cars; this, so the argument goes, does not necessarily see a reduction in the number of deaths because it gives people a false sense of security and may encourage them to drive faster, thereby increasing the likelihood of an accident. Although the evidence for this situation is limited and often disputed, it does raise an interesting point that has many relevant applications to adventure, sport and tourism, as the examples given in Box 7.2 illustrate. It offers a useful point for reflecting on whether new safety equipment or procedures will encourage greater risk taking, thus negating any accident reductions which may gained.

Slovic's (1991, 1999) work is commonly cited in many reports and journal articles on risk and safety. In his work he identified many useful theories that can be invaluable to help students and practitioners understand how risk perceptions are framed. A number of important points are worthwhile summarizing in relation to both Slovic's work and the many writers who have adapted it to different industry sectors, such as Heng (2006: 46), Fuller (2007) and Gigerenczer (2006). The key points are:

- Risks are more likely to be tolerated if they yield some form of benefits, such as pleasurable experiences or financial gains.
- The tolerance for risk becomes less acceptable, the more that the risk is dreaded and unknown.
- *Dread risks* relate to those events where the outcomes are catastrophic to the individual, such as severe injury or death, or for society, when large numbers of people die. This dread of the outcomes evokes emotions of fear, even terror, which in turn creates an expectation that governments or organizations do more to control these risks as they are not deemed acceptable or tolerable.
- *Catastrophic risks* relate to the dread risks that are the sudden, highly visible events where large numbers of people are injured or killed, which have a low likelihood but a highly severe impact.
- *Catastrophic events* are rare and can have dramatic impacts on behaviour, such as the impacts on global tourism patterns after the 9/11 terrorist attacks on America (Gigerenczer, 2006). The demands for actions to deal with these risks can be strong, but not always proportional to the probability of risk.
- *Stealth risks* relate to those risks where the deaths take place over a longer time (the delay effect), so the impact on behaviour is less dramatic, such as cases relating to skin cancer from too much exposure to the sun.
- In relation to sport, tourism and to a lesser degree, adventure, while they have many risks, they also yield many benefits, are more familiar and less likely to be dreaded; therefore there may be less demand for government intervention.

> **Box 7.2.** Equipment, technology and homeostasis in relation to sport, tourism and adventure
>
> The theory of homeostasis raises some intriguing questions into how new technologies and equipment influence the decisions about risk taken by people involved in sport, adventure and tourism. What can be of interest is how new technologies add to the dynamics of the risk situation, whereby the intention of reducing the likelihood or severity of injuries is balanced out, or nullified by increased risk taking, or a new set of risks coming into play (the boomerang effect discussed in Chapter 3).
>
> Haddock (1999) discusses the theory in relation to adventure activities, illustrating how new procedures or devices designed to make activities safer can in fact encourage more risk-taking behaviour, as people become too confident in the ability of the new equipment or procedures to protect them. This debate about the impact of technologies and risk reduction has also been very evident in skiing. Dying in a ski accident still has a very low likelihood, despite some of the high-profile cases of people dying or being severely injured. Yet one interesting trend observed is that even with more people wearing ski helmets, the number of head injuries has been going up as a percentage of total ski injuries reported. Furthermore, the likelihood of death or serious injury increases significantly when people ski off-piste, particularly in relation to being caught in an avalanche. Part of the reason why the numbers of head injuries and avalanche incidents have gone up, it is speculated, is because of new equipment such as helmets, GPS (Global Positioning Satellite) systems (which allow people to track and time the speed they are going down a mountain) and air bags (which inflate if someone is caught in an avalanche). In the latter case, sometimes an avalanche is started on purpose so that a person can be filmed being caught in the avalanche and then later dug out (with these people known as 'avalanche cowboys'). All of this has encouraged greater risk-taking behaviour, because it increases the confidence to go off-piste for the thrill of skiing on untouched snow on remote parts of the mountain.
>
> Some interesting research has also been conducted on the impact of safety equipment in the game of American football. While the introduction of helmets reduced the number of deaths, it has been speculated that because wearing helmets encouraged players to tackle harder, head injuries still occurred, which has been linked to brain disease in later life. Aspects of these debates can also be seen in other sports such as rugby, where it has been conjectured that the introduction of some lightweight padding may encourage more risk taking, resulting in more injuries and thereby negating any gains in reducing injuries.

- Natural catastrophic risks such as tsunamis and volcanic eruptions can have a higher tolerance than man-made events, such as terrorist attacks.
- The tolerance of risk is affected by the severity of outcome, the degree of freedom and the situational control that people have to deal with the risks.

The last three factors are worthwhile exploring in more depth as they have some important implications for the sectors. In terms of *severity of outcome*, Sonmez *et al.* (1999) and Moore (1983: 147) argue that people's decision to take a risk can be influenced more by the severity of the outcome, rather than the probability. This is commonly illustrated by the following examples: (i) people are more scared of flying than driving, even though the latter, statistically speaking, is more likely to cause death or injury; and (ii) the often cited, but never properly verified case of people being more scared of a shark attack than coconuts – even though coconuts are reputed to cause more injuries, it is the former that has a greater impact on behaviour because of the stronger emotions aroused. What is of interest here again is how emotions, such as fear, can distort perceptions and influence behaviour, which no amount of statistical evidence can assuage.

The *degree of freedom* people have to take the risk, along with the amount of *situational control*, are also important considerations, whereby the more control people have, the less they fear the risk (which gives an insight into the driving/flying fear paradox discussed previously). Sjöberg *et al.* (2004: 13) note for example how drivers can overestimate their driving skills and underestimate hazards, using the term *unrealistic optimism* to describe this behaviour. Lupton (1999) also observed how pilots who fought in World War II, and flew both fighters and bombers, were less scared of flying a fighter because they felt more in control of their destiny, even though statistically they were more likely to be killed in a fighter plane in the early stages of the war.

Prospect theory was developed by Kahneman and Tversky (1979). They argued that people's decision to select different actions can depend not necessarily on the derived utility or benefits, but on how the risk is framed or presented. Simply put, they argued that people are more likely to be risk averse if the outcomes are framed around the notion of loss; if, on the other hand, the risks are framed around the idea of gains, people can be less risk averse, even though in reality the outcome would be exactly the same as before. This theory has some interesting implications for managers in relation to how they communicate risks, whether it is to try and encourage people to adopt certain policies or control measures, or influencing people's decision to participate in an activity. As Watts (2003) states: 'people love to win, but they hate losing more'.

7.3.4 Risk perception filters: the stake

The stake is intimately related to what in the organization or service is exposed to risk, and the three key elements of who or what is at risk, how it is risk and the degree of risk exposure are discussed in Chapter 2. This can be summarized as the *stake*, which has the potential to shape perceptions and influence decisions. Thus an outdoor leader should understand how the risk will vary for the participants depending on whether they are children or adults, which also can carry different reputational stakes if something was to go wrong. Alternatively, the stake will vary depending on the degree of captive investment held in particular countries, such as if the service needs investment in buildings or physical equipment. Clearly, understanding the nature of the organization, its key stakeholders and the purpose of the activity or project is a critical part for understanding what is at stake and how it can affect the tolerance and acceptability of risk.

7.3.5   Risk perception filters: social cultural theories and media amplification

The disciplines of sociology and anthropology have produced a number of very influential writers on the subject area of risk who give additional insights into how society can influence risk perceptions. For example, Ulrich Beck's (1992, 1998) theory of the *risk society* and *reflective rationality*, Douglas and Wildavsky's (1983) *cultural theory of risk* (explained in Box 7.3) and Furedi's (2002) *culture of fear* all give some critical insights into how risk perceptions are framed. There is not the scope to fully discuss their work here, but a number of key points can be highlighted, which are:

- *Social construction of risk*. Risk is a social construction whereby 'perceived risk' is intimately tied in with cultural forces, such as the media, which help to identify what people fear and by how much (Frosdick, 1997: 34; Sjöberg *et al*., 2004: 5).
- *Risk averse*. In the modern world, many of these writers argue people are becoming more risk averse, whereby every death, every accident and every misfortune can be blamed on someone who in turn can be 'chargeable' (Douglas, 1985: 60; cited in Lupton, 1999: 45).
- *Reduced risk tolerance?* The tolerance for certain risks has diminished, with Furedi (2002: 8) arguing that society has become governed by the *precautionary principle*, whereby the management of the world is more conservative and cautious. Sometimes this principle is taken to what can seem ridiculous lengths, where everything we are exposed to in our everyday lives can be presented as 'hazardous', creating a culture of fear, which in turn can encourage people, the media and governments to adopt risk avoidance strategies.
- *Media amplification*. Furedi is also critical of the media and how it amplifies and transforms people's fear of risks by the language used; such as how rare events can be turned into normal risks and their dangers exaggerated by the use of such terms as 'plague', epidemic' and 'syndrome' for health-related stories, and the idea that people are 'at risk' (Furedi, 2002: xii).
- *Media outrage*. Brown (1999: 274) observed how the media conveying a sense of outrage in relation to adventure accidents would be amplified if: the people involved are young; there is an unfamiliarity with the actions; there is a level of ignorance of the dangers by the participants; standards are compromised; and the culture is risk averse and is motivated to apportion blame. These points are relevant not only for adventure, but all sectors.
- *Governments overwhelmed*. Amplification can mean governments become overwhelmed by the need to respond sympathetically and try and make things better. The result is that this can cloud the process of choosing the best response and can make the option of 'no action' appear both uncaring and irresponsible (BRC, 2006: 11), which can result in over-regulating activities.

Many of these arguments have filtered into mainstream discussions in relation to how modern societies should manage risk and if there is too much regulation. While there are plenty of exponents of the risk-averse society, it is at times perhaps too deterministic, simplistic even, where examples are selectively chosen to support the theory. What it does highlight is the tension between being risk averse, leading to risk avoidance, and the argument about the importance and necessity of risk in people's lives. Furthermore, while the media plays a critical role in shaping risk perceptions, which can distort or inflate risks, its importance in exposing examples of poor working practice, or alerting people to risks they may not have been aware of, should not be forgotten; as the example of the controversy of the NFL and concussion, discussed in Chapter 3, illustrates.

Box 7.3. Explaining Douglas and Wildavsky's (1983) group/grid model

In essence, Douglas and Wildavsky's (1983) theory relates to examining two key dimensions, developing a model that has become known as the *group/grid model*. The easiest way to understand the model is to consider how different cultural groupings may view risk, whereby the groups are divided up using two key dimensions: (i) the sense of 'group'; and (ii) the sense people feel free or constrained by society, labelled as 'grid'. By relating these two dimensions, it is possible to identify four key groups (Fatalist, Hierarchy, Individualism, Egalitarianism) which are usually represented in a four-way matrix, as seen below (adapting Frosdick and Mars, 1997: 113; Oltedal *et al.*, 2004). The higher their sense of group, the more are people's behaviours modified by consideration of the need to conform to the norms (the informal rules or expected codes of behaviour) of the group. In terms of the grid relating to freedom, the higher their grid placement, the more constrained people feel by the rules and regulations imposed by society and governments.

FATALIST (low group/high grid)	HIERARCHY (high group/high grid)
Characteristics: little activity to social life; little attachment to groups; life is a lottery	*Characteristics*: emphasize the natural order, where authority is to be respected; people should conform closely to group rules and norms; everyone is viewed as having a place; scientists and their opinions are to be respected; nature is self-preserving
Risk is viewed indifferently where they have little control over dangers, or as a random chance event	
Example: football fans who feel they have little control over the risks, but the pleasure outweighs the negative risks	*Risk* is accepted as long as decisions are justified by governments and experts
	Example: government, police, licensing authorities who issue rules and regulations

(Continued)

Continued.

INDIVIDUALIST (low group/low grid)	EGALITARIAN (low grid/high group)
Characteristics: fear things that put constraints on their freedom to act; dislike government regulation; support free markets, competition and self-regulation; nature/the environment can look after itself; strive to exert control over the environment *Risk* is viewed as opportunistic in the long term *Example*: clubs, businesses, governing bodies that give priority to commercial activities over safety	*Characteristics*: fear developments that accentuate inequalities; sceptical about expert knowledge and institutions misusing power; support greater taxation to reduce inequalities; strong group loyalties and bounds; human nature is or should be about cooperation, sharing and trust; nature is to be respected; if it cannot be proved to be safe, assume it is dangerous *Risk* is seen as something negative generated by economic developments, such as risk derived from new technologies *Example*: football supporter groups and resident pressure groups more concerned about environmental risks and quality of life

7.4   CONTEXTUALIZATION TO THE INDUSTRY SECTORS

This section uses the key filters identified in Fig. 7.1 to reflect on how they can relate to the different sectors, with additional references made to research and a variety of examples.

7.4.1   Adventure contextualization

Managing the perceptions of risk is a critical area in adventure, which, of all the sectors, is perhaps the most challenging. The following points can be considered when reflecting on the different filters:

- *Knowledge, experience and heuristics*. For adventure leaders and instructors the use of heuristics is a vital part of their decision-making process, where they may have to make decisions in rapidly changing conditions. It is vital that they are aware of some of the heuristic traps, which Collins and Collins (2013: 77), citing McCammon (2004), illustrate in relation to skiing and avalanches. These writers note how the scarcity of opportunity, such as a fresh fall of snow and people having a limited amount of time, can tempt people to take risks. Trust in the instructors and the instructors having done similar activities previously without incident can also create overconfidence and lead to the risks being ignored.
- *Personality and behaviour*. The theory of the risk thermostat/homeostasis is very important in adventure activities, whereby new technologies, such as satellite communications and the possibility to be rescued from remote environments by helicopter, may encourage more risk taking.

- *Emotions and skill level.* Creating stimulating emotional experiences is critical in adventure and outdoor activities, particularly where there is a learning element involved with the activity. Consideration can also be given to how the need to maintain challenge as skills develop also changes the risk dynamic, such as increasing the level of severity if an accident occurs, because people may be going faster, climbing higher, exploring deeper, etc.

- *Culture.* Adventure has illustrated a number of the debates about risk in society, whereby after certain incidents some feel that the increase in regulation in some countries impinges on people's ability to gain the benefits of adventure. This is particularly relevant in relation to the discussions about childhood development, individual freedoms and the case study about Lyme Bay discussed in Chapter 11, where the media amplification transformed the issue and influenced subsequent regulation. There are also some interesting applications of the group/grid theory, where there may be Individualists (see Box 7.3).

7.4.2   Sport contextualization

For some sport activities there can be a challenging dynamic between the key stakeholders, where their interests are not always the same. This can relate to governing bodies that may compromise on issues of safety for financial reasons, or how a sponsor's interest may shape the decisions about risk.

- *Knowledge, experience and heuristics.* A coach's experience can be very important in shaping training practices. The available heuristics can be a vital point to learn from, but there have also been instances where training practices and approaches are shaped by a coach's own experience as a player, which may mean they replicate dated, unsafe practices, such routines for heading a soccer ball or poor warm-up exercises (e.g. there are stories of how, in the past, footballers would head old gym medicine balls to build up their neck muscles, but this creates a severe risk of concussion and later brain disease).

- *Personality and behaviour.* Safety equipment in sport has been shown to have mixed impacts, whereby it may reduce some injuries but increase others, as the example of American football illustrates. It is a debate also evident in rugby, whereby there is some speculation that wearing some protective gear can lead to harder tackling because players believe they are better protected. There are also some interesting explorations of prospect theory in relation to how sports people can be motivated more by the fear of losing, such as the embarrassment of losing to a weaker team or opponent, rather than the desire to win.

- *Emotions.* In sport there are some interesting paradoxes in relation to the role of emotion. For example, Clive Woodward, the coach of the England rugby team that won the 2003 Rugby World Cup, would explain to his players the importance of T-CUP (thinking clearly under pressure). A key part of their training was about how to control and channel their emotions to allow them to make the correct decisions. This pressure for top athletes not to be overwhelmed by their emotions can be contrasted with the theory of the sport event acting as a catharsis for fans and spectators: the old Greek classical theory that sport or cultural events could provide an opportunity to experience intense emotions that can act as a form of purging and releasing of pent-up frustrations and anger.

- *Culture.* The grid/group theory has had a number of interesting applications such as how the Individualist group may dominate and influence practices. For example, how attempts to control negative stories to avoid damaging the brand have backfired (see Chapter 3 and the NFL case study); and how, after accusations of corrupt practices in the awarding of the 1996 Atlanta Olympic Games, the Olympic brand was damaged, which in turn risked the attractiveness of the Olympic brand to sponsors, encouraging the International Olympic Committee (IOC) to change its practices. Other areas to explore relate to the decision to take the risks of cheating, which can range from diving for a penalty in a football match, to taking drugs to improve performance, because of the potential rewards that can be gained.

7.4.3 Tourism contextualization

Beirman (2003) and Anson (1999) argue it is absolutely critical for tourism organizations to understand tourists' perceptions of risk, particularly in relation to how tourists and travellers can have perceptions about different destinations that are highly distorted, based on little evidence.

- *Knowledge, experience and heuristics.* For many potential tourists, the lack of direct experience of travelling to certain destinations means that the available heuristics for them are limited and dependent on secondary sources, such as media stories. Experienced travellers, on the other hand, can frame travel and any news stories within their own experiences: although knowing that the hazards and risks exist, because they have travelled there safely before, they feel confident that the risks can be managed and are worthwhile taking because of the gains from visiting the destination. Indeed, Williams and Baláž (2013) note how the uncertainty about tourism in terms of the destination and the future conditions is compounded by the characteristics of being a service (i.e. perishable, heterogeneous, intangible and inseparable). One interesting observation to be made is that some travellers can actually be ignorant of many of the risks, as they have not sought to investigate them, and so can be willing to travel to certain destinations in a cocoon of ignorance.

- *Personality and behaviour.* Dimanche and Lepetic (1999) noted how risk perceptions of crime in Florida were inflated by the media after some dramatic attacks on tourists, leading to a drop in tourism, while at the same time the general crime figures were actually falling for the State. What is of interest here is how the severity of outcome, shaped by the media, was more influential on demand than the probability of occurrence. There are many other examples of this pattern, such as Carter's (1998) research into how people's perceptions of African countries are often reduced down to a 'single, undifferentiated territory' of a dangerous African continent, which relates to Lepp and Gibson's (2003) use of Enders *et al.*'s (1992) concept of the *generalization effect*, or the transferring of the problems of one country to another. Dread risk and catastrophic events are also interesting areas for exploration, such as the impact on tourism after natural disasters or terrorist attacks. A homeostasis effect is often evident, in that many can be deterred from travelling to the destination facing the crisis but demand for travel is redirected elsewhere, such as the growth in domestic tourism in America after the 9/11 terrorist attacks (Gigerenczer, 2006).

- *Emotions.* While noting that tourists can be risk averse, Bowen and Clarke (2009: 200) also talk of 'feistiness' to try and capture something of the resilience of tourists and their behavioural adaptations to crisis events. Emotional experiences should also be considered a critical ingredient in creating many satisfying and rewarding tourism experiences. The tourism industry can, however, be prone to emotive and shocking news stories which can deter many people from visiting destinations where incidents such as disasters or acts of terrorism have occurred.

- *Culture.* When looking at the research literature, one can find a variety of interesting examples of how people can build up distorted perceptions of the risk of travel to a destination, often amplified by the media, which many writers such as Stone (2001: 181), Fallon (2003) and Sonmez *et al.* (1999) argue is of critical importance.

- *Stake.* Williams and Baláž (2013) note how the importance of the risk decision is further amplified by the relative importance attached to holidays, in terms of their cost in proportion to household income and need for recreation to restore and have a break from work, meaning people may be more risk averse in their choice of destination (another good example of prospect theory).

7.4.4 Events contextualization

Large events, because of the scale of the risks to which a government, people or even the country brand may be exposed, pose some difficult challenges in risk management and perceptions.

- *Knowledge, experience and heuristics.* An event is a project, so it can be prone to some of the heuristic traps noted in Section 7.3.1. Here the heuristic trap of consistency of decision making can be of interest, whereby people involved with a project can sometimes become hardwired into a decision, finding it difficult to change their minds. The result is that bad decisions may result in more bad decisions, as they do not want to show that they may have made a mistake. The decision of FIFA to stage the 2022 World Cup in Qatar is an interesting example in this respect; much concern has been expressed about the risks of staging the event there, particularly in relation to the heat, along with accusations of corruption.

- *Personality and behaviour.* One interesting observation about sport events relates to the use of prospect theory and how questionnaires and referendums that seek a community's approval for events can be used to shape the response. Andersson *et al.* (2004) examined how questionnaires designed to test people's support for staging sport events in Norway could get different results, depending how the risks of the events were framed. They noted people's willingness to accept an event was 40 times higher than their willingness to pay, which they argue is explained by prospect theory (Andersson *et al.*, 2004: 157), saying the willingness to accept giving up something you already have is given higher value than the willingness to pay for something you don't already have.

- *Emotions*. Events need to tap into emotions for the fans, but the excitement of a bringing an event can sometimes cloud thinking. Also, on the day of an event, one needs to consider how the event is managed because that can impact on the intensity of the emotional experience.

- *Culture*. Frosdick and Mars (1997: 109) observed how stadium safety in the UK was sometimes dominated by Individualism (low group/low grid) before the 1989 Hillsborough disaster, where there was far more concern about the financial imperatives, keeping costs down and disliking outside interference. The result was a culture of simple compliance based on adhering to the basic legislation, but doing nothing more; a culture which did nothing to reduce accidents – indeed, with the response of erecting physical barriers in the stadium to deal with the problems of hooliganism and pitch invasions, it only increases the risk of a tragedy. Aspects of dread risk are also worth exploring here in relation to the huge amounts spent on security for large-scale events which is driven by the severity of outcome, not necessarily the probability of occurrence, such as the devastating impact on people, the government's reputation and the damage to the country's brand if a devastating terrorist attack was to take place at a large sporting event.

7.5 CONCLUSION

Risk is a social construct, which can be shaped by the prism of emotions, culture and previous experiences. These various factors act to both direct and inhibit behaviour, whereby people are willing to take risks if they perceive there are gains or benefits to be had or if it means losses are avoided. The idea of the rational decision maker, be they the practitioner or customer, represents an ideal, not the reality. This is clearly illustrated by the model developed which attempts to encapsulate the variety of social and psychological factors that can shape people's perceptions of risk, which is relevant for managers, customers and other key stakeholders.

While the many filters have been discussed separately, they are intimately connected. For example, cultural factors, such as media amplification, can create a sense of fear, which in turn can make customers more risk averse in their behaviour (prospect theory). Alternatively, the seeking of emotional arousal and flow experiences are key factors motivating or directing behaviour, whereby the development of skills leads to taking on greater challenges, which in turn means more risks are taken (the theory of homeostasis). These emotional states are also shaped by other factors, such as previous experiences (heuristics), the degree of control, the severity of outcomes and the freedom to choose.

Understanding how different groups or stakeholders may perceive risks should be regarded as a critical part of the contextual stage of the practical risk management process. This has benefits in relation to ensuring the organization and service is market oriented (i.e. understanding the needs and wants of customers), together with developing appropriate communication strategies to either help put the risks in context or help deal with perceptions that may be based on poor information and highly distorted. To do this is not only good risk management, but also just plain good management.

DISCUSSION QUESTIONS AND TASKS

1. Discuss how much new technologies and safety equipment actually reduce risk or simply increase the level of risk taking. Find examples, such as stories of the avalanche cowboys or the issue of concussion in sport, to illustrate your answer (relate this to the theory of risk homeostasis).

2. Are people in the developed world becoming more or less risk averse? What is the evidence to support both sides of the argument?

3. Conduct a search on risk-related stories in the media pertaining to the different industry sectors and reflect on how they amplify the risks and contribute to a culture of fear.

4. For a chosen activity of your choice, as part of the context process stage, identify some of the key stakeholders (e.g. customers, coaches, guides, customers, sponsors) and consider how their perceptions may be shaped by the following filters (summarizes Fig. 7.1):

Filter	Concepts and theories to consider
Knowledge, experience and heuristics	Previous knowledge Possible heuristic traps: inexperienced, habituation, poor learners, scarcity of opportunity, consistency of decision alignment, halo effect, acceptance, social facilitation
Personality and behavioural	Homeostasis; severity of outcome Degree of control; freedom; unrealistic optimism; prospect theory
Emotions	T-CUP; type of emotions clients seek; high or low client skills
Culture	Risk averse; culture of fear; media amplification (relate to activity and clients); precautionary principle; group/grid theory
Stake	Financial, time or emotional investment; who (people); what (buildings, reputation, equipment, etc.); project life-cycle stage

REFERENCES

Adams, J. (1995) *Risk*. UCL Press, London.

Adams, J. (2011) Not a 100% sure? The 'public' understanding of risk. In: Bennett, D.J. and Jennings, R.C. (eds) *Successful Science Communication: Telling It Like It Is*. Cambridge University Press, Cambridge, pp. 90–100.

Andersson, T.D., Rustad, A. and Solberg, H.A. (2004) Local residents' monetary evaluation of sports events. *Managing Leisure* 9, 145–158.

Anson, C. (1999) Planning for peace: the role of tourism in the aftermath of violence. *Journal of Travel Research* 38, 57–61.

Beck, U. (1992) *Risk Society: Towards a New Modernity*. SAGE Publications, London.

Beck, U. (1998) *World Risk Society*. Polity Press, Cambridge.

Beirman, D. (2003) *Restoring Tourism Destinations in Crisis*. CAB International, Wallingford, UK.

Bowen, D. and Clarke, J. (2009) *Contemporary Tourist Behaviour*. CAB International, Wallingford, UK.

Boyne, R. (2003) *Risk*. Open University Press, Buckingham, UK.

BRC (2006) *Risk, Responsibility, Regulation: Whose Risk Is It Anyway?* Better Regulation Commission, London.

Brown, T.J. (1999) Adventure risk management. In: Miles, J.C. and Priest, S. (eds) Adventure Programming. Venture Publishing, State College, Pennsylvania, USA, pp. 273–284.

Carter, S. (1998) Tourists and traveller's social construction of Africa and Asia as risky locations. *Tourism Management* 19, 349–358.

Cater, I. (2004) Playing with risk? Participant perceptions of risk and management implications in adventure tourism. *Tourism Management* 27, 316–325.

Collins, L. and Collins, D. (2013) Decision making and risk management in adventure sports. *Quest* 65, 72–82.

Csikszentmihalyi, M. (1990) *Flow: The Psychology of Optimal Experience*. Harper & Row, New York.

Dimanche, F. and Lepetic, A. (1999) New Orleans tourism and crime: a case study. *Journal of Travel Research* 38, 19–23.

Douglas, M. (1985) *Risk Acceptability according to the Social Sciences*. Routledge, London.

Douglas, M. and Wildavsky, A. (1983) *Risk and Culture: An Essay on the Selection of Technological and Environmental Dangers*. University of California Press, Berkeley, California.

Eduljee, G.H. (2000) Trends in risk assessment and risk management. *The Science of the Total Environment* 249, 13–23.

Enders, W., Sandler, T. and Parise, G.F (1992) An econometric analysis of the impact of terrorism on tourism. *Kyklos* 45, 531–554.

Fallon, F. (2003) After the Lombok riots, is sustainable tourism achievable? In: Hall, C.M., Dallen, J.T. and Duval, D.T. (eds) *Safety and Security in Tourism: Relationships, Management and Marketing*. Haworth Press, Inc., Binghamton, New York, pp. 129–158.

Frosdick, S. (1997) Risk as blame. In: Frosdick, S. and Walley, L. (eds) *Sport and Safety Management*. Butterworth-Heinemann, London, pp. 33–66.

Frosdick, S. and Mars, G. (1997) Understanding cultural complexity. In: Frosdick, S. and Walley, L. (eds) *Sport and Safety Management*. Butterworth-Heinemann, London, pp. 108–114.

Fuller, C.W. (2007) Catastrophic injuries in rugby union: an assessment of the risk (final draft report). Available at: http://irbplayerwelfare.com/pdfs/CI_Risk_Assessment_EN.pdf (accessed 18 September 2014).

Furedi, F. (2002) *Culture of Fear: Risk Taking and the Morality of Low Expectations*. Continuum, London.

Gigerenczer, G. (2006) Out of the frying pan into the fire: behavioral reactions to terrorist attacks. *Risk Analysis* 26, 347–351.

Haddock, C. (1999) High potential incidents – determining their significance. Tools for our trade and a tale or two. Wilderness Risk Management Conference Proceedings. Available at: http://www.nols.edu/nolspro/pdf/wrmc_proceedings_99_high_potential_haddock.pdf (accessed 18 January 2015).

Heng, Y. (2006) *War as Risk Management: Strategy and Conflict in an Age of Globalised Risk*. Routledge, London.

Kahneman, D. and Tversky, A. (1979) Prospect theory: an analysis of decision under risk. *Econometrica* 47, 313–327.

Klien, G. (1999) *Sources of Power: How People Make Decisions*. MIT Press, Cambridge, Massachusetts.

Lanchester, J. (2010) *Whoops! Why Everyone Owes Everyone and No One Can Pay*. Allen Lane, London.

Lehrer, J. (2009) *The Decisive Moment: How The Brain Makes Up Its Mind*. Cannongate Books Ltd, Edinburgh.

Lepp, A. and Gibson, H. (2003) Tourist roles, perceived risk and international tourism. *Annals of Tourism Research* 30, 606–624.

Lupton, D. (1999) *Risk*. Routledge, London.

McCammon, I. (2004) Heuristic traps in recreational avalanche accidents: evidence and implications, *Avalanche News*, no. 68. Available at: http://citeseerx.ist.psu.edu/viewdoc/download?doi=10.1.1.386.301&rep=rep1&type=pdf (accessed 11 December 2014).

Merna, T. and Faisal, F.A. (2005) *Corporate Risk Management: An Organisational Perspective*. Wiley, Chichester, UK.

Moore, P.G. (1983) *The Business of* Risk. Cambridge University Press, Cambridge.

Oltedal, S., Moen, B., Hroar Klempe, K. and Rundmo. T. (2004) Explaining risk perceptions. An evaluation of cultural theory. Available at: http://www.svt.ntnu.no/psy/Torbjorn.Rundmo/Cultural_theory.pdf (accessed 20 November 2014).

Scitovsky, T. (1986) *Human Desires and Economic Satisfaction: Essays on the Frontiers of Economics*. New York University Press, New York.

Sjöberg, L., Moen., B. and Rundmo, T. (2004) Explaining risk perception. An evaluation of the psychometric paradigm in risk perception research. Available at: http://www.svt.ntnu.no/psy/torbjorn.rundmo/psychometric_paradigm.pdf (accessed 10 August 2014).

Slovic, P. (1991) Beyond numbers: a broader perspective on risk perception and risk communication. In: Mayo, D. and Hollander, R. (eds) *Acceptable Evidence: Science and Values in Risk Management*. Oxford University Press, Oxford, pp. 48–65.

Slovic, P. (1999) Trust, emotion, sex, politics, and science; surveying the risk-assessment battlefield. *Risk Analysis* 19, 689–701.

Sonmez, S.F., Apostolopoulos, Y. and Tarlow, P. (1999) Tourism in crisis: managing the effects of terrorism. *Journal of Travel Research* 38, 13–18.

Stone, M. (2001) Scourges that strike at the heart of global business. In: Pickford, J. (ed.) *Mastering Risk, Volume 1: Concepts*. Pearson Education Ltd, Harlow, UK, pp. 181–186.

Timmermans, H. (2010) On the (ir)relevance of prospect theory in modelling uncertainty in travel decisions. *EJTRIR* 10, 368–384.

Watts, G. (2003) The trouble with risk. EurekAlert. Available at: http://www.eurekalert.org/pub_releases/2003-07/bpl-tco070203.php (accessed 20 October 2014).

Wilde, G.J.S. (1994) *Target Risk*. PDE Publications, Toronto, Canada.

Wilde, G.J.S. (2001) *Target Risk 2: A New Psychology of Safety and Health: What Works? What Doesn't? And Why?* PDE Publications, Toronto, Canada.

Williams, A.M. and Baláž, V. (2013) Tourism, risk tolerance and competences: travel organisation and tourism hazards. *Tourism Management* 35, 209–221.

FURTHER READING

John Adams has a series of essays where a variety of interesting topics are explored in relation to risk management, available at: http://www.john-adams.co.uk/papers-reports/

Berry, L. (2011) *The Art of Living Dangerously: Risk And Regulation*. Joseph Rowntree Foundation, York, UK. Available at: http://www.jrf.org.uk/sites/files/jrf/risk-regulation-approaches-full.pdf

HSE myth of the month, available at: http://www.hse.gov.uk/myth/mythofthemonth.htm; the common sense approach to risk report, available at: http://www.hse.gov.uk/aboutus/commonsense/index.htm

Kasperson, R.E., Renn, O., Slovic, P., Brown, H.S., Emel, J., Goble, R., *et al*. (1988) The social amplification of risk: a conceptual framework. *Risk Analysis* 8, 177–187.

Moss, S. (2013) Natural childhood. Available at: http://www.nationaltrust.org.uk/document-1355766991839/ (accessed 5 July 2014)

Pedersen, D.M. (1997) Perceptions of high risk sports. *Perceptual Motor Skills* 85, 756–758.

Sandseter, E.B. (2009) Risk play and risk management in Norwegian preschools–a qualitative observational study. *Safety Science Monitor* 1(2), article 2, available at: http://www.academia.edu/3410019/Risky_Play_and_Risk_Management_in_Norwegian_Preschools_-_a_Qualitative_Observational_Study

chapter 8

The Law of Tort and its Relevance for Risk Management

CHAPTER OBJECTIVES

- To identify the key concepts of tort.
- To understand how tort is a very important legal area for managers.
- To use exemplars to explain the principles of tort.
- To demonstrate how the law of tort is a key element in the toolbox of risk management of an organization.

Key concepts

Definition of tort; how tort operates; the importance of negligence to risk management; defences against tort; tort in other countries

8.1   INTRODUCTION

There is a difference between criminal and civil prosecutions and although criminal prosecutions seem to have far more gravitas when it comes to health and safety, civil prosecutions can also be just as damaging to an organization. In most cases, UK civil cases usually follow criminal ones as the compensation awarded by UK criminal courts is somewhat poor (Bereavement Award Act, amended 2013, compensation for loss of life is now set at £12,890) (FAA, 2014); however, the punishments in criminal cases, if found guilty, can be very punitive in terms of imprisonment. Some argue that currently UK criminal law compensation payments are very derisory and hence if a criminal prosecution is successful then a civil prosecution is almost certain to win, usually providing a larger fiscal compensation. Also if a criminal prosecution fails then a civil action may well be successful as the body of proof required is far less. Thus civil actions are more likely to be faced by managers than criminal actions and tort negligence is a civil action that will affect many managers. It is also within the civil courts that large sums of money are paid out in damages, which has been a cause for concern in terms of insurance premiums protecting against negligence claims, resulting in what some commentators have argued is a 'compensation culture' (Hawkes, 2013). It must be noted that this chapter is designed to provide a summary and overview of how tort works. It is not a legal text and for more detailed aspects of tort the reader needs to seek and research legal texts in the relevant country where he/she resides.

8.2   TORT

Tort is an important litigious area for any manager of tourism, leisure and sport, and will probably affect his/her responsibility more than any other subject in relation to the operation of products and facilities. Most accidents subsequently resulting in legal action are usually motivated by this aspect of the law, with the majority of tortuous actions being those of negligence.

8.2.1   What is tort?

Put simply, tort is a 'wrong' or 'civil wrong' (Pannett, 1997; Okrent, 2009; Giliker and Beckwith, 2011) and is part of Common Law which in the UK dates back to the 19th century. Tortuous litigation has grown in importance, especially as a means of awarding damages to a person or property. The use of tort is established upon the concept of the 'neighbour principle' and the perspective that it is easier to prove than a criminal action. This is because the balance of evidence is based upon the *balance of probabilities* for civil actions (51% likely) and not *unreasonable doubt* (90% near certainty) as required in criminal actions. Most tort cases usually follow a criminal prosecution, especially when these have been successful. If a 'case' has been proved in a criminal court then it is easier to win an action in a civil court, where the evidence requires only a balance of probabilities in favour of a plaintiff. It should be noted that the discussion on tort in this chapter is based upon a UK perspective; however, the countries of Australia, Canada and New Zealand also have tort legislation that is mainly based upon the UK understanding of tort. The main differences regarding tort legislation in these countries is discussed later in Section 8.9.

Negligence claims in the UK have increased since the late 1980s, possibly connected to a change in law in the European Union, whereby cases of tort can be brought to court in terms of *strict liability in tort*. Essentially this means that any 'wrong' can be attributed to the 'point of sale', not necessarily the agent who created the wrong. So for example, if a person was to sell a packet of crisps that was found to be faulty and harmed a customer, the customer could take the vendor to court (see Box 8.1). They in turn could take the manufacturer to court and so on,

---

Box 8.1. Ginger ale and the snail

The principal legal case often cited as the precedent for tort in the UK is the 'Snail and the Ale', *Donoghue versus Stevenson*, 1932 (Frosdick and Walley, 1997; Pannett, 1997). This case demonstrates that a company/person could be held liable even though the wrong to a customer is not caused by their immediate or unintentional action. In summary, the case derives from the following narrative: a snail was found in a bottle of ginger beer by a customer who subsequently claimed that its discovery had affected her psychological state. The discovery was alleged to be a great shock, especially as the customer had consumed part of the beer before realizing the presence of the snail. The customer subsequently took the vendor to court claiming damages based on psychological harm and won the case. This set the precedent for future claims based upon negligent actions in the UK and was used by other countries that followed English Common Law. Although this is not a sports or tourism precedent, it is still cited for the purpose of prosecutions within this sector.

---

the rationale being that prosecution is easier for the consumer. The rise in negligence claims (duty of care) also seems to reflect changes in society whereby paying customers expect a 'duty of care' and responsible actions from a company and its employees.

8.2.2 Definition of tort

It is important to understand the concept of tort and the ideas giving rise to its outcomes. It can be defined as follows:

> Tort obligations are owed by one person to another and embody norms of conduct that arise outside contract and unjust enrichment. Tort enables the person to whom the obligation is owed to pursue a remedy on his own behalf where breach of a relevant norm infringes his interests to a degree recognised by the law as such an infringement. (Murphy and Street, 2012: 3)

In terms of the tourism, leisure and sports industries, it is usually about an expected level of care provided by a person or company. It does *not* relate to any *breach of contract* which is covered by other types of litigation. Put simply, it is an action or non-action that falls below what an average person would expect, resulting in significant detrimental loss. It also includes vicarious links, meaning that a person or company may still be liable even though not actually present at the time of the damage or loss. However, the customer must show the person or company is closely linked (proximity) to the loss.

There are many different types of tort that can be brought against a defendant including defamation of character, trespass, economic loss, wrongful imprisonment, nuisance and *negligence*.

8.2.3 The tort of negligence

This is perhaps the most important element of tort. Negligence is usually the action most frequently used to take a person or company to court and is related to a 'duty of care' owed by the defendant to the plaintiff (Pannett, 1997). How then is negligence measured in tort cases? Normally, it is based upon the premise of a 'reasonable man'. The court uses this concept to try and establish what types of actions/non-actions by the defendant are related to failure of the service or good. A number of criteria are used to appraise the actual event and establish whether reasonable care was used by the person or company. A key element of this is the idea of 'foreseeability' (see Boxes 8.2, 8.3 and 8.4). Could the company or person have foreseen the actual event and if so, what did they do to ensure that such an event did not occur? The law, in many respects, is basically asking: 'What would a normal/average person do in these circumstances?' (Moran, 2010).

8.3 THE RELEVANCE TO A MANAGER

It is important to try and envisage the position of a *reasonable and prudent person*, using this assumption as a proxy for assessing the appropriate health and safety actions of the company and the standards that have been put in place to ensure that the offered product is as safe as possible (see Boxes 8.2, 8.3 and 8.4). However, under a civil action it would still be expected that the manager has ensured appropriate regulations have been incorporated and actioned,

---

Box 8.2. Mountain bikes and negligence[1]

An interesting case with which the author was involved concerned a company who offered its clients the use of mountain bikes as a part of an adventure tourism weekend. In this particular instance, a client sustained injury while riding a mountain bike and a claim of negligence was made against the company. The accusation was based upon the company's 'assumption' that all clients knew how to ride a mountain bike and could do so confidently. The plaintiff claimed that as the bike was different from other types of bikes he had ridden, this led to him losing control and falling, sustaining significant injuries. This incident changed the approach of the company, resulting in it not *assuming* that everyone was proficient in riding a bike and ensuring that customers were given instructions and assessed for competency before allowing them to use its bikes. In the author's opinion this is rather absurd given that 'common sense' seems to have been somewhat ignored in this case, allowing for the fact that much of the population can ride a bike; also it was the customer's individual choice to undertake such an activity. This is one case of many that the author feels illustrates the ridiculous, litigious culture proliferating the UK during the 1980s and 1990s. Thankfully this now seems to be changing.

Such cases illustrate how difficult it can be for companies to delineate what constitutes 'common sense'. Under English law this is further complicated by the system whereby decisions are often made based upon precedents, rather than in European law, which is defined by codes and rules, often appearing to have greater clarity in terms of rulings.

[1] From Jenkins, I.S. (2014) Consultancy Notes.

Box 8.3. Lyme Bay

The Lyme Bay tragedy of March 1993 involved the St Albans Centre, Dorset, a UK-based adventure tourism company, and is very different from the bike example cited in Box 8.2. Like many other disasters it could have been prevented if sufficient attention had been paid to what constitutes a 'reasonable and prudent' person. Four teenagers died during a canoeing trip in Dorset while they were crossing Lyme Bay in open canoes, and a further eleven casualties were involved in the tragedy (Dunn and Bennett, 1993; Smithers, 2000). From the writer's perspective this was an incident waiting to happen as the UK adventure industry had not been properly regulated since its inception, meaning that anyone could set up an adventure tourism business without prior knowledge, appropriate qualifications or competency in adventure tourism activities (higher-risk leisure product). In essence there were a number of factors that conspired to create this tragedy:

- unqualified staff;
- inadequate/poor risk assessments;
- inadequate equipment;
- lack of appropriate experience;
- lack of preparation for the expedition;
- lack of understanding of foreseeable events;
- lack of appropriate funding;
- poor understanding of risks; and
- failure to heed and act upon past accidents.

In summary, this incident was reflective of the state of the UK adventure tourism industry, highlighting the lack of validation and vetting of competent operators. It was also the first time in the UK that a company director was found guilty of negligence, receiving a custodial sentence. The magnitude of the incident produced a public outcry, resulting in the adventure tourism industry becoming one of the most heavily legislated industries in the UK, on a par with the nuclear industry (somewhat heavy handed in the author's opinion). This legislation, The Activity Centres (Young Persons' Safety) Act 1995, established the AALA (Adventure Activities Licensing Authority) in 1995 (HSE, 2013a), meaning that all providers offering similar activities to young persons under the age of 18 had to be vetted and approved. Recently, that legislation is being considered for repeal (HSE, 2013b), but it seems evident that without a new vetting system the industry remains unsure as to how to inform and reassure the public about which companies are safe providers. It is also interesting to note that although the industry complained about the introduction of this legislation there has not been a repeat of an incident similar to the Lyme Bay tragedy; perhaps vindicating the success of the legislation. It should also be mentioned that the HSE was uncomfortable with such stringent legislation and it appears that the majority of support for it came from the DfE (Department for Education).

Box 8.4. Everest's death zone: Out There Trekking (OTT)

Another tragic case is that of OTT, where the cause of blame was not easily identified, resulting in an unproven civil case. Mike Matthews, aged 22, was a customer who attempted to climb Everest with an adventure tourism company, Out There Trekking (OTT). Sadly, Mr Mathews died during the descent (BBC, 2006a,b) with his family taking out a law suit against the company, alleging negligence. The allegations were that the company had not provided an adequate level of supervision or equipment in order for the customers to safely reach the summit of Everest (Douglas, 2001). To an extent the evidence demonstrated some support for this view. However, it became evident that Mr Matthews had contributed to the problem by refusing to follow instructions, increasing his risk of exhaustion, which may have contributed to his death. There was evidence to suggest that the equipment (oxygen cylinders) was faulty which may have meant that oxygen was not being fully supplied to the customer when needed. There also appeared to be some confusion and conflicting instructions given for the final ascent to the summit. However, the company had never lost a client and considering the high risk ratio (one out of seven people will die trying to ascend) on Everest, this seemed to indicate a good and competent safety record with sound management practices. Added to this scenario is the perspective that climbing Everest involves entering what is known as the 'death zone', in which many experienced climbers have been killed while attempting to reach the summit. This suggested the customer must recognize the inherent risk to life that this type of activity entails.

The main issue for consideration was whether the company failed in its 'duty of care'. The evidence suggested that OTT had carried out proper procedures although there were allegations of faulty equipment and improper supervision. The business of taking customers into a 'death zone' is itself something of a customer care paradox, yet companies continue to operate in such risky environments. The question needs to be asked whether customers fully understand the risks they are facing. Undertaking a high-risk activity means there are few guarantees that customers will not be seriously injured or die; customers therefore have to accept that high risks may include death, which possibly explains the judgement made in this case.

Finally, it is interesting to observe that even though OTT received adverse publicity following the death of Mr Matthews it did not change its name, which is what usually transpires if a company's name is tarnished. (For more information on this case, see the television documentary *Lost in Everest's Death Zone* which was originally made for Channel 4 in the UK.)

In summary, this case is an example of a high-risk activity in which a company is not necessarily guilty of negligence, even though a death occurred. As one mountain guide said in the documentary: 'Anyone who enters the death zone on Everest is on their own.' Do customers really understand and appreciate the risks they are undertaking?

including further amendments to legislation or codes of practice. The idea of a 'reasonable and prudent person' seems to be a workable solution and one commonly understood by the average consumer. Even so, there is still much debate on the effectiveness of this concept in deciding negligent actions (Moran, 2010).

8.3.1 Tort and acts of commission

Tort is not a single entity. There are different degrees and types of actions or non-actions that can result in a wrong to an individual, these are:

- *Malfeasance*. This is a deliberate act or lack of the act of commission, resulting in a wrong, leading to a detrimental outcome for the person.
- *Misfeasance*. Another aspect of tort can be regarded as an unintentional, but badly performed act of commission, resulting in loss or injury to a person.
- *Nonfeasance*. This can be defined as a lack of action, unintentionally resulting in damage or loss to an individual.

These legal terms are used to decide what gave rise to the wrong and in the case of negligence, usually relate to non-actions or actions performed poorly; rarely are actions deliberately undertaken to cause injury. It is asserted that non-actions can be as damaging as actions and indeed, in many negligence cases these non-actions can be more important than actions that are poorly effected. The *Herald of Free Enterprise* ferry disaster of 1987 is an example of a lack of action resulting in tragedy, vis-à-vis the failure to close the bow doors leading to the sinking of the ship.

8.3.2 Tort can be an aide-memoire

The idea of the reasonable and prudent man (see also Chapter 5) is a concept that can be adapted for risk assessment to help identify possible future incidents. The law requires that a company or person takes actions akin to those of a normal person in order to minimize risk to the customer and employee. The key element for tort cases is that of *foreseeability*, that is: 'would a normal person have seen the possibility of an accident or incident'? However, there are also caveats to this, as not everyone has 'common sense', expected of a reasonable and prudent person; therefore it should not be assumed that all employees know exactly how to act as a reasonable and prudent person. It is implicit that a manager should ensure appropriate training and actions for all employees relating to what characterizes a reasonable and prudent action. A court of law will want to comprehend what knowledge, skills and perceptions an employee had when responsible for the services or goods which led to a customer injury.

8.4 TORTS BASED ON NEGLIGENCE

Negligence claims, especially within developed economies, have grown exponentially over the last 40 years, not only in the tourism, leisure and sport industries but across the whole spectrum of goods and services. Protection against negligence is therefore a wise, if not an essential precaution to take. As indicated, in many cases protection simply means acting reasonably; it does not mean unreasonable protection needs to be in place. So how exactly is negligence in tort defined?

8.4.1   Definition of negligence in tort

> Negligence is therefore measured by the conduct of the defendant relative to that of a notional moral exemplar, 'reasonable man'. Negligence does not require 'fault' on the part of the defendant, in the sense of moral blameworthiness, however it does require fault insofar as a defendant's conduct is not of the standard of reasonable man. (Pannett, 1997: 8)

8.4.2   A reasonable and prudent person

The concept of a 'reasonable and prudent person', although apparently straightforward and simple to recognize, has a number of characteristics and particular actions which need to be undertaken to ensure that negligence does not occur. These are divided into the following:

- *Appropriate knowledge.* It is important that the person providing the service or good has had appropriate training and knowledge of the product they are providing and is up-to-date with changes and developments affecting the service or product.
- *Competency and experience.* The employee or company must also be able to provide a level of competency and experience appropriate to the service being offered. They should have been trained in the activity and be aware of risks and safety issues relating to the product/ service provided.
- *Physical ability.* It is also expected that the person delivering the service should have the physical capacity to carry out the actions related to the good or service. If the activity is high risk then there is a duty to ensure that the person supervising such an activity has a commensurate physical capacity to carry out the pursuit.
- *Skill level.* The person should have the appropriate skills and experience to deliver the service or good purchased by the customer. If he/she does not, this could be deemed to be a breach in the duty of care to the customer.
- *Perception.* It is expected that the person or company providing the goods would do so with an ability to foresee reasonable risks and to assess whether these would be detrimental to the product or the service being provided. The law expects that a company will act as an 'average person' (including, where appropriate, equivalent professional levels) would behave in this position. It is expected that precautions and actions should be taken currently, not retrospectively, to prevent any foreseeable damage or loss to customers.

8.5   PROVING TORT

Not all aspects of injury or loss can be attributed to tort. The tortuous process will require affirmation of a 'test' including some essential elements that need to be present. The test is composed of the following three elements that must also be time contingent.

1. *Duty of care.* It must be established that there was a 'duty of care' between the plaintiff and the defendant which does not refer to any contract. There has to be 'proximity', meaning a sphere of influence that is not tenuous, to the injury or loss. This is directly related to the neighbour principle, whereby the company or person must be either directly or indirectly linked to a duty of care. It does not mean that a company/employee has to be directly in contact with the person, but that the 'sphere of influence' of a good or service is linked significantly to the employee or the company.

2. *Breach of duty.* Furthermore, it must be established that the 'duty of care' was not performed and therefore constitutes a breach, causing the person's loss or injury. There are generally three parts to a breach of duty:

- foreseeability;
- appropriate standard of care; and
- comparison of defendant to standard of care.

3. *Significant damage/loss.* As discussed earlier in this chapter, the loss to the plaintiff must be of a serious nature, which is again critical to whether a tortuous prosecution would be successful.

- *Serious injury.* The injury sustained by a person must be seen as being of a serious nature and of a level that would significantly affect the plaintiff's life. It can be either a serious physical or psychological injury. Psychological injuries are frequently harder to substantiate than a physical injury as most physical injuries have an immediate effect upon an individual. However, the key constituent is the idea that the injury has a permanent and detrimental result.
- *Permanent effect.* The injury must be considered to be long term and permanent in nature, significantly affecting the lifestyle of the plaintiff. An interesting point to note is that this effect does not have to be immediate but may have the potential to be detrimental to a plaintiff's future health. A good example of this is injury linked to illnesses such as arthritis; a broken bone might heal but may cause further disease in the future, e.g. arthritis. In order to establish this, it is usually necessary to have expert witness reports, substantiating the possibility of a disease permanently affecting the plaintiff in the future.

8.6   POSSIBLE DEFENCES AGAINST TORT

Not all cases brought to court will be successful and there are certain defences that can be used against a case of tort. The following are a selection of the most frequently used:

- *Contributory negligence.* This attempts to establish whether the plaintiff contributed partially or wholly to his/her loss/injury (see Box 8.2). The justification is that the plaintiff acted carelessly and in an unsafe way, contributing to the accident resulting in his/her loss or injury.
- *Comparative negligence.* This is an approach used by the defence, endeavouring to offset the damage (compensation) made to the plaintiff. It is based upon third parties being in 'proximity' (directly connected) to the damage or loss to the plaintiff. It usually involves at

least one other company or person who may have supplied the goods or service resulting in the loss or damage also being considered negligent.

- *Vicarious liability.* This is where a person may claim that the responsibility for the accident lies with another individual, such as an employee not being liable but the manager, if a breach of his/her duty of care is proven. It is not always the employee or person providing the service that will be responsible for the loss; it may well be a systemic failure in the health and safety policy of the company that caused the accident or incorrect advice given by a manager. An example of this is the case of Lyme Bay where the Director of the company was found responsible and negligent, rather than the manager or instructors who had immediate contact with customers.

- *Waivers.* Some companies hope that ensuring customers sign a waiver concerning injury or loss absolves them from liability. However, this is not the case if the company is found to have been behaving negligently. The law expects that a company should act responsibly and if the client is injured due to company irresponsibility, a waiver is no defence even if the client has signed a form stating that all risks and injuries are his/her personal responsibility (Callandera and Page, 2003). Essentially, a waiver indicates to the customer the potential dangers that may be encountered while participating in an activity or purchasing a service or good.

- *Act of god.* This is where an event resulting in injury has occurred through circumstances that could not have been controlled or regulated; for example, a lightning strike. However, even if a customer has been seriously injured or perhaps killed by such an occurrence, some responsibility still lies with the company to ensure appropriate protection. If the service or activity is provided in a weather zone that experiences frequent lightning strikes, then the provider must take precautions, as far as possible, to protect customers. The term 'rain check' comes to mind and is related to this type of situation; allowing swimmers to continue in an outdoor leisure pool when there is a thunderstorm overhead would be considered negligent behaviour. It is necessary for the company to ensure that risk assessments have identified severe weather conditions as risk and have implemented procedures in place which will reduce the likelihood of injury or loss to customers.

- *Volition of risk, high-risk activity.* Certain activities require higher competences than others, necessitating participants to be more aware of possible perils and hazards (Horton, 2010). The law does not expect companies to have 'zero risks', but it does expect them to have an MRE (minimum risk environment). It is clearly the case that certain activities involve much greater risks than others. For example, parachuting and other types of air activities would be considered to be in a high-risk category. It is therefore necessary for a company to match this level of risk with a higher duty of care, ensuring that possible risks have been identified and minimized (see Box 8.4). In high-risk activities there is usually little 'room for error', so equipment, training and staff need to be of a higher standard than required for ordinary levels of risk. However, it is also expected that the customer will also assume more risk and have higher competences compared with other activities. In this situation some element of risk is assumed by the customer, which can be used as a defence against particular injuries/incidents related to such activities; for example, when climbing Mount Everest, there is no guarantee of survival.

- *Government protection.* Before 1947, in the UK certain organizations were protected under state legislation from prosecution. However, since 1987, even the Armed Forces in the UK can now be prosecuted under tort relating to a duty of care. However, it still remains a contentious area and in certain countries such as Canada is still being challenged.

8.7 SPECIAL CONDITIONS

The evidence needed to prove that a tort has occurred will change when considering vulnerable individuals and their exposure to risk and injury. In essence, a higher 'level of protection' and 'duty of care' are required if an activity or service is being provided to children or persons whom the law considers to be vulnerable (see Box 8.3). This means that certain aspects of the product need to be reviewed and delivered at a higher level of performance. For example, if a company is taking a group of children for adventure activities, there is a need to ensure that ratio levels of supervision are much higher and appropriate for the level of the activity. Review of the governing body's codes of practice is necessary to ensure that higher levels of supervision are made. For example, an increase from 1:20 to 1:10 or even lower in the ratio of staff to participants may well be necessary, especially if the activity is seen to be of a higher risk. It may also be necessary for the company to adjust equipment so that the customer is able to fully use it, especially where physically challenged individuals are taking part in activities such as sailing and climbing.

In reality, the company and its members of staff are acting in *loco parentis* for children, meaning they are 'de facto' parents with the responsibility to act as a reasonable and prudent parent would. However, some volition can be attributed to the child under tort but the level of the test (reasonable man) is adjusted pro rata if a child is believed to have acted negligently. It must also be remembered that under the law no child is considered cognate under the age of 7, therefore closer protection and care are required at all times.

8.7.1 Time limitations

A tort action does have a time limit related to the loss or injury incurred, which is usually 3 years from the discovery by the plaintiff of the injury or loss or a maximum of 6 years from the incident date.

8.8 WHERE TO ACCESS APPROPRIATE KNOWLEDGE AND TRAINING

It is important that an organization acquires the appropriate level of training and knowledge before offering activities to the public. Often the simple use of government legislation and codes of practice will suffice with the adjunct of accessing information relating to the particular activity either through a governing body or being a member of a professional association. This is also the case if an organization is offering a new activity; it is necessary to use the experience and knowledge that an organization has in order to assess the risk and also provide appropriately qualified staff and supervision (see Box 8.4). This can be acquired by combining information from other similar activities to the one being offered. There are a number of sources that can be used to ensure negligence does not occur by accessing appropriate information (see Fig. 8.1).

8.9 TORT IN AUSTRALIA, CANADA AND NEW ZEALAND

8.9.1 New Zealand

New Zealand has taken a different approach to injury compensation through tort. Although initially this existed in New Zealand, it has been replaced by an insurance compensation scheme (Palmer, 1994) introduced in 1972. This was a novel approach to the issue of risk and risk management and who is deemed responsible for injury, but it does have certain advantages. It appears that out of all the Common Law legal systems, New Zealand is the only one which has adopted such an approach to tort and following reviews; the system is still in existence today. A number of reasons were put forward for adoption of this system; however, there are protagonists who continue to suggest that tort offers a better method of redressing wrongs to individuals. That said, other countries have also looked at it: Australia considered it; America too especially in terms of medical negligence; and as recently as 2009 Scotland (which has a different legal system from England and Wales) was also looking at the possibility

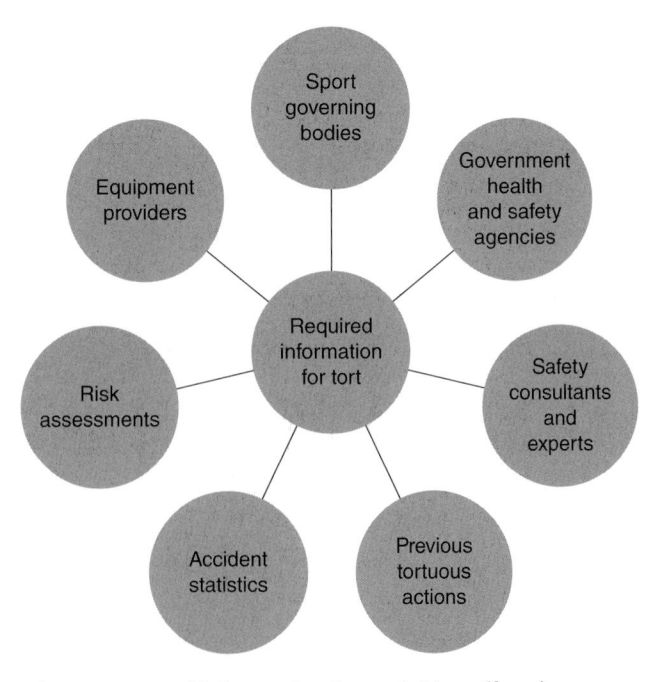

Fig. 8.1. Appropriate sources of information for activities offered.

of introducing a similar system, initiating a consultation paper. In essence individuals who are injured and lose earnings are compensated fully and cared for by this system. It is considered a lot fairer with more people being eligible than under tort. It also eliminates the heavy legal expenses which a tort action incurs. In essence, the state pays for the insurance system through employer and employee contributions and it is estimated to cost all individuals NZ$1 a day (Palmer, 1994). However, critics argue that it also removes responsibility away from the activity provider and that there has been an increase in the number of accidents, although hard evidence supporting this claim is difficult to find.

8.9.2 Australia

Australia has a system similar to the UK in terms of tort, which is unsurprising as Australia's legal system was introduced from English Common Law and reflects this. Therefore most of the discussion above follows in essence the aspect of Law of Torts in Australia. However, there have been some alterations to this law (Law Vision Pty, 2008) depending upon the state legislation that has been passed. Perhaps the most notable difference is the Civil Liability Act 2002 (NSW, 2002a) which has changed the law of tort to include a three-stage test, replacing the notion of a reasonable person, but following much of the ruling established by Lord Atkins on tort. However, the words 'reasonable' and 'foreseeability' are still used in judgements of negligence. See below for an example of the changes within the Act:

> Division 2 Duty of care
> 5B General principles
> (1) A person is not negligent in failing to take precautions against a risk of harm unless:
> (a) the risk was foreseeable (that is, it is a risk of which the person knew or ought to have known), and
> (b) the risk was not insignificant, and
> (c) in the circumstances, a reasonable person in the person's position would have taken those precautions.
> (2) In determining whether a reasonable person would have taken precautions against a risk of harm, the court is to consider the following (amongst other relevant things):
> (a) the probability that the harm would occur if care were not taken,
> (b) the likely seriousness of the harm,
> (c) the burden of taking precautions to avoid the risk of harm,
> (d) the social utility of the activity that creates the risk of harm.
> 5C Other principles
> In proceedings relating to liability for negligence:
> (a) the burden of taking precautions to avoid a risk of harm includes the burden of taking precautions to avoid similar risks of harm for which the person may be responsible, and
> (b) the fact that a risk of harm could have been avoided by doing something in a different way does not of itself give rise to or affect liability for the way in which the thing was done, and
> (c) the subsequent taking of action that would (had the action been taken earlier) have avoided a risk of harm does not of itself give rise to or affect liability in respect of the risk and does not of itself constitute an admission of liability in connection with the risk.' Civil Liability Act 2002 No 22 Section 5C (NSW, 2002a,b)

There are also changes in time lapses relating to claims for injury; for most Australian States it is 3 years but in others it can be up to 6 years (Law Vision Pty, 2008) and some recent rulings have been reflective of the US system rather than English Common Law.

8.9.3   Canada

Canada's federal system of government reflects its historical past, basing the legal system upon English Common Law. It has a similar system to England in terms of tort (Linden, 2007) and the information contained within this chapter would generally be found relevant to risk management and protection against tort cases, with the exception of Quebec which has a Civil Code including aspects of negligence. Canada does practise some of the tests established by English Common Law systems such as the Ann's Test but the UK has further modified this test, which Canada has considered and debated (Linden, 2007). In essence the theme and overriding principles of negligence in tort are very similar to the English system although finer points relating to judgement decisions can be different in terms of compensation to the plaintiff. It should also be noted that tort cases are extremely portable and English cases are used in Canada and other countries which use English Common Law.

8.10   CONCLUSION

This chapter has outlined the main guiding principles of negligence through tort, which is possibly one of the most important pieces of civil law that a manager will have to deal with. As can be seen from the text, in essence, the law is only asking that a manager behave in a reasonable and prudent manner and act with thought and foresight, no more! Perhaps it can be likened to the example of a glass of water placed near the edge of the table: we all know it is likely to be knocked off; by leaving it there the chances of an accident are increased, so if you suspect something might cause an accident, take some action to prevent it from happening. The following quote is an excellent summary of the purpose of tort and an appropriate ending for the chapter:

> Tort law compensates, deters, educates and provides psychological comfort to many. It reflects and reinforces our values of respect for the individual. It can act as an ombudsman focusing public attention on social problems, and as an empower of individuals wronged by the powerful forces in our society. (Linden, 2007: 25)

DISCUSSION QUESTIONS AND TASKS

1. What are the key elements that a manager should ensure are in place to prevent any tortuous action being brought against an organization?
2. What are the key publications that a manager should be aware of to ensure adequate knowledge of activities he is managing?

3. What has given rise to the growth in tortuous cases in the UK?
4. Why is non-action just as important as commission in the law of tort?

REFERENCES

BBC (2006a) Everest death charges dismissed. Available at: http://news.bbc.co.uk/2/hi/uk_news/england/london/5197628.stm (accessed 16 January 2014).

BBC (2006b) Everest trip 'beset by problems'. Available at: http://news.bbc.co.uk/2/hi/uk_news/5197542.stm (accessed 16 January 2014).

Callandera, M. and Page, S.J. (2003) Managing risk in adventure tourism operations in New Zealand: a review of the legal case history and potential for litigation. *Tourism Management* 24, 13–23.

Douglas, E. (2001) Death on Everest. The youngest Briton to climb Earth's tallest mountain never made it back. Now his family and the guides who led him there are locked in a bitter dispute. Available at: http://www.theguardian.com/theobserver/2001/nov/11/focus.news (accessed 17 January 2014).

Dunn, P. and Bennett, W. (1993) The School Canoe Tragedy: Schoolchildren's adventure at sea that turned: Father tells of survivor's anger at delay in being rescued after wind drove canoes away from shore. Available at: http://www.independent.co.uk/news/uk/the-school-canoe-tragedy-schoolchildrens-adventure-at-sea-that-turned-father-tells-of-survivors-anger-at-delay-in-being-rescued-after-wind-drove-canoes-away-from-shore-1499565.html (accessed 17 January 2014).

FAA (Fatal Accidents Act 1976) (2014) 1A Bereavement. Available at: http://www.legislation.gov.uk/ukpga/1976/30/section/1A (accessed 22 August 2014).

Frosdick, S. and Walley, L. (1997) *Sport and Safety Management*. Butterworth-Heinemann, London.

Giliker, P. and Beckwith, S. (2011) *Tort*, 4th edn. Sweet & Maxwell, London.

Hawkes, S. (2013) Britain's compensation culture is out of control, insurance chief warns. Available at: http://www.telegraph.co.uk/finance/newsbysector/banksandfinance/insurance/10221301/Britains-compensation-culture-is-out-of-control-insurance-chief-warns.html (accessed 22 August 2014).

Horton, D. (2010) Extreme sports and assumption of risk: a blueprint. *University of San Francisco Law Review* 38, 559–664.

HSE (2013a) Adventure Activities Licensing Regulations 2004 – Guidance for Enforcing Authorities. Available at: http://www.hse.gov.uk/foi/internalops/ocs/300-399/331_5.htm (accessed 17 January 2014).

HSE (2013b) Update on proposal to abolish the AALA – September 2013. Available at: http://www.hse.gov.uk/aala/update-on-proposal-to-abolish-aala.htm (accessed 17 January 2014).

Law Vision Pty (2008) The Law of Torts. Available at: http://www.lawvision.com.au/uploads/PDFs/Tort%20Law%20.pdf (accessed 21 August 2014).

Linden, A.M. (2007) The Triumphs and Trials of Canadian Tort Law, Lecture to Canadian Bar Association, Calgary, Alberta, August 14, 2007. Available at: http://www.mjswm.com/JPM/Torts2/files/The_Triumphs_and_Trials_of_Canadian_Tort_Law.pdf (accessed 22 August 2014).

Moran, M. (2010) The reasonable person: a conceptual biography in comparative perspective. Keynote Essay presented at *Symposium on Who is the Reasonable Person?*, December 2010, Lewis & Clark College, *Portland, Oregon*.

Murphy, J. and Street, H. (2012) *Street on Torts*, 13th edn. Oxford University Press, Oxford.

NSW (New South Wales) (2002a) Civil Liability Act 2002 No 22. Available at: http://www.legislation.nsw.gov.au/inforcepdf/2002-22.pdf?id=5e88bb05-5ac9-6ed8-ccbf-eaca0a94aa7f (accessed 21 August 2014).

NSW (New South Wales) (2002b) New South Wales Court of Appeal – Civil Liability Act 2002 (NSW) annotation. Available at: http://nswca.jc.nsw.gov.au/courtofappeal/Other/Civil_Liability_Act_Annotations/Civil_Liability_Act_Annotation.html (accessed 21 August 2014).

Okrent, C. (2009) *Torts and Personal Injury Law*, 4th edn. Delmar Cengage Learning, New York.

Palmer, G. (1994) New Zealand's accident compensation scheme: twenty years on. *University of Toronto Law Journal* 44, 223–273.

Pannett, A. (1997) *Law of Tort*, 8th edn. Pitman, London.

Smithers, R. (2000) Incidents which led to guidelines. Available at: http://www.theguardian.com/uk/2000/aug/08/education.educationnews (accessed 17 January 2014).

FURTHER READING

Fitzgerald, B. and Harrison, J. (2003) Law of the surf. *Australian Law Journal* 77, 109–116 – applies the aspect of negligence to the case of surfing.

Giliker, P. and Beckwith, S. (2011) *Tort*, 4th edn. Sweet & Maxwell, London – provides a good general over view of tort in the UK.

Horton, D. (2010) Extreme sports and assumption of risk: a blueprint. *University of San Francisco Law Review* 38, 559–664 –gives details on the aspect of volition of risk and tort.

Palmer, G. (1994) New Zealand's accident compensation scheme: twenty years on. *University of Toronto Law Journal* 44, 223–273 – gives more detail of the New Zealand injury compensation scheme.

chapter 9

Risk and Safety Management

CHAPTER OBJECTIVES

- To present and explain safety and management systems used in different countries.
- To evaluate the legislation and processes that specific countries use to ensure safety standards.
- To understand the mechanisms used to establish health and safety management.
- To appraise societal perception relating to death and injury.
- To understand the main issues affecting the organization of health and safety management.

Key concepts

Safety management systems for UK, New Zealand, Canada and Australia legislation; management culture and corporate social responsibility; good practice in safety management; accidents and management of safety.

9.1 INTRODUCTION

Safety and safety management have become very important issues in many developed countries. Within these societies any deviation from what is considered to be the 'norm', namely protection from and prevention of accidents, injuries and death, is met with a number of negative responses. One of the most influential of these originates from the media (see media amplification in Chapter 7), which appears to provide a vocal stimulus for alerting the public to such incidents. It is evident that the effects of the media are felt by many organizations, particularly private companies and government agencies. Companies that are perceived to have an image of *unsafe practices* usually receive a lower return of income, which can ultimately result in bankruptcy. Injuries to workers or customers are now seen as unacceptable by most Western societies and governments. Serious injuries and accidents, whether at the workplace or a place of business, are nearly always followed by an investigation exploring the causes and, in many cases, directing blame at the company or employees who may have caused these events to occur. Most people regard an accident as an unforeseen event/circumstance, whereas in reality most accidents are preventable and therefore do not concur with this generic understanding. The following discussion attempts to illustrate some of the strategies used to develop and ensure a safe environment for customers or employees within developed countries.

9.2 CUSTOMER AND SOCIETAL EXPECTATIONS OF SAFE ENVIRONMENTS

Death often appears remote from everyday life in Western societies. But this is not necessarily reflective of other cultures, where death is perhaps more accepted and an important fact of life to be celebrated. The Buddhist tradition sees death as an essential part of being alive and one which gives a clear perspective to life. It is also interesting to note that by the age of 18 years (in Western societies) the majority of people will not have been privy to death (with notable exceptions) even though many aspects of death are present throughout the media.

It is also argued that a consumer society does not accept sudden death as a natural outcome of living. In many cases this is unsurprising as people are living longer and life expectancy is increasing throughout the developed world. With advancements in science and better living conditions, most of us expect to at least have our three score years and ten. This has certainly become the norm for Western society, where current life expectancy has risen to an average age of 81 years. Only 50 years ago the average life expectancy was some 15–20 years less (Winterman, 2008).

The growth of a litigious culture also appears linked to the increased importance of the consumer, with society becoming more protected and monitored, particularly in terms of health and education (see Chapter 7). It is argued that this further exacerbates the notion that death and injury are not normal occurrences and must have some root cause or responsibility outside that of an individual's actions. Perhaps this is the central focus of issues relating to safety management; society is now meant to protect its citizens from harm and any accidents are therefore someone else's fault. Someone or something must be responsible for a negative outcome such as injury or death. With the growth in safety workplace legislation, there is an increased move towards corporate responsibility, protecting individuals from unscrupulous exploitation and ensuring that some responsibility for *wrongs* has to be taken by an individual or organization.

It is asserted that industrialization and the development of a consumer society have increased the dislocation of people from their natural environments. Furthermore, the past 150 years show that the diversity of work roles (industrialization) exposed more employees to dangerous environments resulting in death and serious injuries; for example, mining disasters and other industrial tragedies. The response to these has been increased legislation to ensure protection of the workforce, heightening expectations of protection. A hundred years ago, many employees worked in agriculture and manufacturing where injury and death were far more frequent than today. The shift in employment towards service sector jobs has further removed people from exposure to immediate harm, again increasing the perception that death and injury are infrequent occurrences, unlike a century ago.

Another factor increasing the perception of protection is, as already mentioned, increased life expectancy. The introduction of state-funded healthcare systems in many countries around the world, as well as improved living conditions, has had a significant impact on longevity and survival rates, again reducing awareness of death and injury within society. Consequently, we can argue that the 21st century could be termed the safest in history, especially for developed countries. Recent news coverage of National Health Service failures also seems to heighten the notion that longevity is a *given* or a *right* for everyone.

Another aspect of the consumer society relates to the view that if one pays for a good or service then there is some responsibility on the person providing it to ensure a minimum of risk for the purchaser. In essence this is the very basis of the litigation culture we are experiencing today. The 'Snail and the Ale' scenario (see Box 8.1) is possibly one that every manager and student of safety management will know very well (Coleman, 2009), setting a precedent for many UK negligence claims under the precept that an individual or a company has done wrong to another individual. It is somewhat remarkable that this case set the tone for the litigation culture that is so rife today in developed countries. This legal case demonstrated that the psychological pain suffered from an unintentional action was the basis for what is now a global industry (litigation) affecting us all. Even though many of us have never made a negligence claim, we are all affected by increased insurance premiums for standard items such as motor insurance, personal injury insurance and liability insurance for companies.

So the development of the consumer society and the move to a service sector economy, helped by the protection of the state and its many institutions, has heightened our lack of acceptance of death and injury. Consequently, it is argued that the basis of sound health and safety management is now perhaps more difficult for companies, as consumer expectations are so much higher. However, one aspect which is lost in the current debate seems to be where does individual responsibility of the consumer/customer lie?

9.3   SAFETY MANAGEMENT AND ELEMENTS OF GOOD PRACTICE

As noted above, safety management has been an evolving paradigm emerging from industrialization and post-modern society, resulting in today's situation where over 70% of the workforce is employed in the service sector. In the UK there have been several important milestones in the management of safety, perhaps the most notable being the establishment of the HSE (Health and Safety Executive) in 1974. It was a moment to celebrate the importance of safety management in terms of protecting both employees and the consumer. 1974 can also be attributed with the accelerating move towards a post-modernist society with the establishment of a service economy. It was a time of exponential tourist and leisure growth that is key to the central focus of health and safety in this book.

9.3.1   Risk and safety in the EU

Although the UK has its own health and safety legislation, since joining the EU many of the current safety regulations and legitimate actions relate to edicts emanating from the European Parliament. The control of health and safety has three types of EU parameters that a nation state has to incorporate into its health and safety structures. These are known as Directives, Guidelines and Standards:

- A *Directive* is a document that is legally binding but can be adapted and incorporated by a nation state into its own structures, whereas *Regulations* are much more specific and have to be enabled by an individual nation state. In many cases health and safety legislation has been communicated via directives.
- A *Guideline* is not legally binding, but designed to help implement aspects of Directives that have been enacted by the EU.
- A *Standard* is a specific document detailing expected characteristics of products or services within the EU, including specifications from the European Committee for Standardization (CEN), European Committee for Electrotechnical Standardization (CENELEC) and European Telecommunications Standards Institute (ETSI), which are organizations that design the standards that should be used throughout the EU and relate to the Directives. The idea is to ensure harmonization of products and services across the EU; therefore national standards agencies must verify that their approved standard for the product is equivalent to or greater than the EU standard.

The organization which is responsible for safety in the EU is the European Agency for Safety and Health at Work (EU-OSHA), which comes under the DG (Directorate General) Employment Social Affairs and Inclusion (EU-OSHA, 2014a). As the organization's name indicates, safety is primarily a 'work-based' theme and other safety aspects are dealt with through this 'work maxim', for example leisure and home accidents. This corresponds with the UK model of health and safety.

The idea is that the EU standardizes the European market so that all states are competing at the same level, with similar structures for health and safety. The safety document dealing with these topics is the *EU Strategic Framework on Safety and Health at Work 2014–2020*, although there have been others. These policy documents relate to EU legislation on safety and health with the most recent legislation emerging from the EU highlighted below.

Individual directives tailor the principles of the Framework Directive to:

- specific tasks (e.g. manual handling of loads);
- specific hazards at work (e.g. exposure to dangerous substances or physical agents);
- specific workplaces and sectors (e.g. temporary work sites, extractive industries, fishing vessels);
- specific groups of workers (e.g. pregnant women, young workers, workers with a fixed duration employment contract); and
- certain work-related aspects (e.g. organization of working time).

The individual directives define how to assess these risks and, in some instances, set limit values for certain substances or agents (EU-OSHA, 2014b).

The EU and EU-OSHA are now firmly integrated within UK legislation and management of health and safety. It is asserted that the UK had much of the EU legislation already in place based upon the work of the HSE, which has been managing safety since 1974. But what the EU safety legislation does is ensure that other member states have to provide the same level of protection as that of the UK. The EU is also a useful benchmark, both statistically and legislatively, to evaluate the protective measures taken on health and safety by sovereign states within Europe.

9.3.2 UK Health and Safety Executive

Established in 1974 and designed to look after aspects of work safety within the UK, the HSE covers the areas shown in Table 9.1.

As already briefly discussed, the HSE seemed to reflect changes in society and the move towards a more consumer-led economy. As can be seen from Table 9.2, within the context of the

Table 9.1. Work areas covered by the Health and Safety at Work Act 1974. (From HSE, 2013.)

Construction	Offshore
Nuclear	Health and social care
Agriculture	Catering
Biocides	Waste and recycling
Woodworking	Food
Education	Motor vehicle repair
Quarries	Chemicals
Explosives	Diving
Cleaning	Tree work
Entertainment	Hairdressing

Table 9.2. SIC (Specific Industrial Classification) covered by the Health and Safety at Work Act 1974. (From HSE, 2013.)

A	Gas – supply
Agriculture	Glass and glazing
Air transport	H
Armed forces	Hairdressing
B	Health and social care services
Biocides	
C	Heavy clay and bricks
Catering and hospitality	L
Cement	Laundries and dry-cleaners
Ceramics	Leather
Chemicals	Local government
Cleaning	Logistics
Concrete	M
Construction	Manufacturing
D	Mining
Diving	Molten metals
Docks (ports)	Motor vehicle repair
E	N
Education	Nuclear
Engineering	O
Entertainment and leisure	Offshore oil and gas
Explosives	P
F	Paper
Fire and rescue services	Pesticides
Food and drink manufacture	Plastics
Footwear	Police
G	Ports
Gas – domestic	Printing
Gas – LPG (liquefied petroleum gas)	Public services

(*Continued*)

Table 9.2. Continued.

Q	S
Quarries	Stonemasonry
R	Surface engineering
Railways	T
Recycling	Textiles
Refractories	Tree work
Retail	W
Rubber	Waste management
	Woodworking and furniture

HSE the leisure and tourism industry was not explicitly recognized but is covered by a number of SIC (Specific Industrial Classification) categories.

The development of a safety policy was also underpinned by the UK government's legislation. At about the same time as the formation of the HSE, the Health and Safety at Work Act 1974 was introduced, strengthening the view that it was necessary to protect employees (HSE, 2013) and, to some extent, customers. So 1974 saw the introduction of a raft of safety measures by the UK government, aiming to ensure that injury, accidents and death were minimized both in the workplace and to some extent protecting consumers.

The emphasis of the legislation was on employees and employers, which raises the question: to what extent does this affect consumers who are visiting a workplace for leisure and tourism activities or to purchase goods? It appears from the initial UK legislation that the premise seemed to be that if there are safe environments for workers then it necessarily follows that there will be safe environments for customers. It is asserted that this seemed to be clearly the tone of the Health and Safety at Work Act of 1974.

It is evident that almost all Western societies, including Australia, Canada and New Zealand, have similar safety institutions reflecting the importance of ensuring that workers and vicariously consumers/citizens are protected from unsafe working environments; indeed many of the safety management features of the HSE are common in these countries. The following section explores how different countries have provided safe environments for their workers and citizens.

9.3.3 Australia, Canada and New Zealand safety legislation

Although the UK is an exemplar of safety management provision, other countries have followed suit in the protection of their citizens. This has been done through the introduction of health and safety legislation. As with the UK, the main emphasis for protection seems to be with the employees and employer, again supporting the principle that consumers are to be protected vicariously by ensuring a safe working environment. Australia has an Occupational Health and Safety Act of 2011 (SWA, 2014a,b,c) which can be found for each of its Territories. Safe Work Australia is considered to be analogous to the HSE and is a strategic body providing polices and details of safety management within Australia. However, authority still resides with the State to ensure and enforce regulations. In Australia in January 2012, the Work Health and Safety Act 2011 and the Work Health and Safety Regulations 2011 were introduced effectively replacing the earlier legislation of:

- The Occupational Health and Safety Act 1991;
- The Occupational Health and Safety (Safety Standards) Regulations 1994; and
- The Occupational Health and Safety (Safety Arrangements) Regulations 1991.

At the same time, new codes of practice were introduced, preserving some of the older safety codes which will be reviewed or revised in the future (SWA, 2014b). To oversee the development of safety management in Australia, an independent government statutory body called Safe Work Australia (as noted above) was established to develop national policy on health and safety for employees and workers' compensation. However, it does not have the responsibility of enforcing these laws, which differs from the powers of the HSE in the UK.

New Zealand also seems to have emulated both the UK and Australian approaches, with the establishment of government systems to ensure that consumers and workers are protected from injury. It has implemented various pieces of legislation to help reduce risks to employees, such as the Health and Safety in Employment Act 1992 and The Purpose of the Hazardous Substances and New Organisms (HSNO) Act 1996 (WSNZ, 2014a). Its controlling organization is WorkSafe New Zealand (WSNZ, 2014a). 'We carry out the health and safety functions previously carried out by the Ministry of Business, Innovation and Employment (MBIE) and earlier the Department of Labour. We also carry out new functions as described in the WorkSafe New Zealand Act 2013' (WSNZ, 2014b), again mirroring the HSE model in the UK.

Similarly, Canada also ensures a safe environment for its workers and follows a comparable model to the UK. The Canadian Centre for Occupational Health and Safety (CCOHS) is a government organization designed to prevent accidents and ensure safety. It was formed in 1978 and reports directly to the Ministry of Labour. 'A "not-for-profit" Federal Department Corporation, CCOHS is governed by a tripartite Council – representing government, employers and labour – to ensure a balanced approach to workplace health and safety issues' (CCOHS, 2014). This organization seems to be the main government agency for ensuring safe working and consumer environments in Canada. Canada is somewhat different from the UK as it has health and safety legislation specific to its Provinces and Territories; however, there is an overarching Federal Act on health and safety management. The Federal Act is called Canada Labour Code Part II and Regulations, affecting some 10% of employees, whereas the Provincial and Territorial Acts affect the majority of employees (CCOHS, 2008).

9.4   PUBLIC AND PRIVATE SAFETY MANAGEMENT

There is both an assumption and an imperative that private and public organizations should provide safe environments for employees and consumers based upon the Health and Safety at Work Act 1974. However, there are no guarantees and the legislative culture of the last 40 years has given credence to this, indicating that all work environments must fulfil these requirements. In the UK a number of case studies can be identified that illustrate safety failures in tourism, adventure tourism and sport environments.

The most important unit at the time was SaiL (Safety In Leisure Research Unit), based at Swansea Metropolitan University, formerly West Glamorgan Institute of Higher Education. It was funded and supported by many members of the UK leisure industry including the HSE. Unfortunately at the end of the 1980s other safety problems were being reported, heightening awareness of difficulties relating to safety management (see Box 9.1). The UK press seemed littered with leisure- and tourism-related disasters such as the Bradford fire, the Heysel Stadium disaster, together with the infamous Hillsborough Stadium tragedy. Furthermore, during the 1980s there was a series of transport accidents, including the sinking of the *Herald of Free Enterprise* (BBC, 2012), the Lockerbie bombing, the King's Cross fire and the Channel Tunnel fire. These events increased the public's perception of poor safety provision and an apparent lack of risk management.

Box 9.1. Health and safety management: key elements

- It is evident that most countries have health and safety management controlled either by government or quasi-government departments, as in Australia, the UK, Canada and New Zealand.
- The main focus of legislation is primarily upon aspects of employment and the workplace.
- There is little, if any, legislation related directly to tourism, adventure tourism or sport.
- The 1980s and 1990s saw a burgeoning of leisure and tourism accident reports which seemed to indicate that there was a need for better safety management.
- In the UK the first ever leisure legislation was introduced after the tragedy of Lyme Bay. The adventure tourism industry became as heavily legislated as the nuclear industry.
- There was a clear paucity of accident data, further compounding problems of what types of risk the public were facing.
- In the wake of negative media coverage of the 1980s, there was a need for safety organizations to be established to identify the real nature of accidents relating to tourism, adventure tourism and sport.
- There is still a lack of coordinated data on accidents although several attempts have been made to collect this via HASS (Home Accident Surveillance System; UK) and EHASS (European Home Leisure Accident Surveillance System; EU).

The first investigation for SaiL was into waterslide safety in the UK. Its report identified that there were some potentially dangerous waterslides (Box 9.2); however, with appropriate safety management, these leisure facilities could be safely enjoyed by customers. In addition, the Unit also established that serious injuries were not as frequent as reported by the UK press.

Perhaps the most significant disaster for the leisure and tourism industry in the UK was the Lyme Bay tragedy of 1993. This event was the impetus for a significant change in attitudes towards leisure safety and resulted in a substantial amendment to the law. This was the first time ever in UK legislation that a law had been introduced specifically for a particular sector of the tourism industry. The result was that parts of the tourism/leisure industry became as heavily regulated as the nuclear industry; a moot point which the HSE has always been uncomfortable with.

Box 9.2. Case study of waterslides in the UK

The 1980s and 1990s provide some exemplars highlighting the problems of safety and risk management, combined with the public's increasing expectations of a risk-free environment at most leisure facilities. In addition, the Lyme Bay tragedy of March 1993 in the UK also emphasized the failure of current legislation to prevent death and injury to children while undertaking higher-risk activities. Even though the UK's HSE does cover most elements of the leisure and tourism industry, it is difficult to legislate for specific activities that might pose high risk and are difficult to define under the HSE remit. However, some activities have been identified as being of greater risk than others (namely fairgrounds) possibly due to the high number of accidents that occurred prior to the establishment of the HSE. Fairgrounds are a special case for which the HSE has developed specific legislation for inspecting such facilities and the companies providing them.

The introduction of waterslides to the UK in the 1980s was a result of their popularity in the USA. Ironically, this introduction was also accompanied by a growing concern for leisure safety (Stevens and Jenkins, 1992). Many UK leisure facilities began to introduce waterslides which were met with public excitement and enthusiasm (Stevens and Jenkins, 1992). However, during the mid- to late 1980s news stories began to emerge of serious injuries to customers eventually leading to a fatality. The media capitalized on such stories with newspaper headlines vilifying facilities, many of which were ill-equipped to deal with adverse press allegations mainly as a result of a paucity of accident data. It is perhaps interesting to note that this was more than 10 years after the formation of the HSE (1974), suggesting that the HSE was unable to manage the exponential consumer boom and the emergence of multiple leisure products. At this time in the UK there was a lack of accident data available on leisure facilities, further exacerbating the problems relating to the real nature of accidents on waterslides and other related leisure and tourism facilities. This prompted the emergence of new research investigating allegations of unsafe practices and increased exposure to risk.

9.5   CONCEPTS AND MANAGEMENT OF SAFETY

9.5.1   Importance of accidents to the manager

As can been seen from the previous sections, accident data/incident data are essential elements of the safety management toolkit. It is evident that there need to be regular reviews of accident data and in many circumstances how they relate to the customer/employee work base and the nature of the facilities being provided. As noted earlier in this chapter, companies that have no accident data are very rare and in the experience of the author[1], a company or organization which states it has no accidents or incidents should be carefully monitored and is certainly worth further investigation. In many respects, a review of and action upon accident data is an essential element of ensuring that a company or organization is maintaining safety standards, and in particular protecting its employees and customers from harm. Accident data can be a *barometer* for operational safety and reflective of the condition of an organization. Certainly, accident data analysis is an essential tool in the management of safety in an organization. Accident/incident data should be used in conjunction with the process of the Safety Management System (HSE, 2013) and part of a holistic system developed to ensure a MRE (a minimum risk environment) for customers and employees.

[1] Jenkins, I.S. (2014) Consultancy Notes.

9.5.2   Company policy and the development of safe operations

It is self-evident that for safety management systems to work effectively they need to have an underpinning premise or principle derived from a safety policy. This is usually the starting block for any Safety Management System (HSE, 2013). It guides the direction of health and safety within a company. It is axiomatic that all companies would like to ensure a safe and risk-free environment for their workers and customers, but this is not possible because risks are always present and need to be constantly addressed. Waring notes that '[o]rganisations with a strong safety culture enjoy a close fit between formal statements and what actually happens; official safety policy and strategy are borne out in reality' (Waring, 1996: 69). Legislation also helps guide companies and organizations in developing a safety policy; indeed in many cases the easiest action is simply to relate the policy to relevant legislation. For example, in the UK this would be the Health and Safety at Work Act 1974, or different types of standards such as British Standards (BS) or ISO standards. In addition, if a company is providing a particular activity which has a governing body, then incorporation of a code of practice from the governing body may also be necessary.

It is suggested that a company should really develop a *company ethos* reflecting the importance of safety to the organization (see Box 9.3). It has previously been mentioned that some companies base their whole product on the priority of safety (e.g. Disney). Certainly, injury and risk should always be minimized, as the psychology of leisure and tourism is one in which exposure to danger is unacceptable, unless an individual has chosen freely and with clear knowledge an activity incorporating such risks. Maslow's model of hierarchy of needs succinctly demonstrates this, identifying safety as one of the first priorities of survival.

Box 9.3. Common safety themes in safe operations

- Company performance.
- Company image.
- Worker confidence.
- Customer awareness.
- Open environment for safety issues.
- Whistle-blowing if needed.
- Good communication.
- Designation of personnel.
- A controlling mind (often deliberately overlooked due to fear of one/few individuals being held responsible).
- Appropriate training and resources.
- Regular review of accident data.
- Regular risk and hazard assessments.

Any safety policy should be similar to that of a marketing/product strategy or business plan and treated with equivalent gravitas; it should be recognized as part of the service/good of the company. Examination of some common safety themes reveals elements that should be included in such a policy.

Within this context the safety policy should be considered within the premise of a 'safety climate' and 'safety culture'. The two are not the same but overlap. Evidence suggests that a *safety culture* should be embedded and accepted within an organization, with the aim of a safety policy being to ensure safety throughout the organization. However, a *safety climate* is changeable and affected by circumstances. Glendon and McKenna (1995: 295) note that cultural features are complex, shared characteristics of a group dynamic'. They further add, 'the safety culture of an organisation is the product of individual and group attitudes, perception competencies and patterns of behaviour that determine the commitment to, and the style and proficiency of, an organisation's health' (Glendon and McKenna, 1995: 296).

A *safety policy* should set the foundations for developing the safety culture of a company or organization; in effect it controls the safety climate, which will inevitably alter due to circumstances such as personnel vicissitudes and resource allocation. Accident investigations of the 1980s and 1990s identify that some of the more notorious accidents from these years highlight a lack of a clear and appropriate safety culture. For example, the report into the sinking of the *Herald of Free Enterprise* noted a poor safety culture within the organization. What is often forgotten by management is that Sod's Law is often the cause of accidents, because 'sh*t happens' often when you least expect it! Safety is frequently overlooked or ignored by companies due to its intangible and invisible nature and is really concerned with people and their reaction to risk. Therefore employees are in essence a 'safety system in action'. A safety policy without employees has no effect and employees without a safety policy are increasing, exponentially, the risks to the company and its customers. Once again the importance of the safety policy being effectively acted upon, with its employees clearly understanding its key elements and engaging with its principles, cannot be overemphasized.

9.5.3   Conflict between personal responsibility and corporate responsibility: safety programmes

It is vital to have a safety system in place; however, the nub of the question is: 'Does it work?' Having an extremely elaborate system involving lots of paperwork and tick boxes is perhaps a start, but the real test lies in whether injury or death to workers and the public is prevented (HSE, 2013). As noted in the previous section, the effectiveness of a system really rests with the employees of a company. On several occasions, the author has been engaged in field research and, having been briefed by a manager or instructor on safety in his/her organization, found that safety procedures were often not being undertaken. This was usually confirmed by a tour of a facility often with the manager. Frequently, the author observed contraventions to the safety policy or ineffective actions being taken by staff. In many cases this was to the dismay and embarrassment of the manager, who usually exclaimed 'that shouldn't be happening, why is this there?', etc., which seems to indicate that although there were established safety procedures they were not being adhered to by employees. Safety policies and systems must be operational if they are to be effective, as well as requiring regular testing. If the policy or system states an action should be carried out, then it *needs* to be done. A simple solution would be regular *unannounced/mystery inspections* and more frequent training, resulting in a reduction/minimization of contraventions to safety policy. The author has been involved in a number of negligence cases in which the defendant lost the case, simply because the system in the safety policy was not being adhered to. It is advisable to be careful of what is stated in a safety policy and to ensure that what it states is being acted upon.

It is also necessary to have an effective communication system and a team (or individual) who organizes and coordinates safety training. Often personnel are under so much pressure to succeed that the safety aspect of their work is not considered or seems rather tenuous to their job. But safety actions that are not carried out properly or not carried out at all can result in catastrophe for a company. Recent UK accident history is littered with examples of poorly performed safety procedures resulting in tragedy. The case of the *Herald of Free Enterprise* is a perfect example of this. How could an employee/s forget to close the bow doors on a ship? As simple as it may seem, the evidence indicates a lack of procedures or procedures not being properly enacted. In addition, reporting of near misses, ignoring potential dangerous practices, when combined with low staff morale is a recipe for disaster. The Zeebrugge tragedy could have been prevented by installing warning lights and ensuring that crews were not overworked, as well as management acting on 'near miss' data.

It is emphasized that safety is every employee's responsibility, not just those designated to coordinate or manage it. However, the ultimate duty for safety lies with management, because it is management's role to devise and establish systems that work and to ensure that those systems are followed. If an employee fails to act safely, then management needs to resolve this immediately. ICT (information communications technology) appears to be a useful tool in helping keep employees aware and up to date with policies/procedures. Web-based safety tests, taken on a regular basis, can provide management with some assurance of the staff knowledge base and, as mentioned earlier, use of a mystery guest or spot checks is a very helpful method of ensuring that employees are acting safely.

9.6 CURRENT SAFETY ISSUES

Much has changed since the introduction of the Health and Safety at Work Act in the UK in 1974. The last 50 years have seen the development of the post-modernist age, where there has been a massive change in technology, complexity of systems and information, together with the introduction of new sport and tourism activities. In addition, the customer has become all important (Cadario, 2012) and payment for consumer products/activities means also increased protection against risk. Furthermore, this new technology has made the customer far more aware of risks when participating in tourism and leisure activities, changing the risk and safety management paradigm. There have also emerged new risks to customers when purchasing leisure products, perhaps the most prominent being terrorism; certainly 9/11 has emphasized the vulnerability of people/tourists to terrorism. In many ways this has introduced another paradigm in terms of safety assessment and safety management, adding to the already heavy agenda of managers to ensure that customers remain safe during their purchase of a holiday or sports product/activity.

9.6.1 Terrorism and safety management

The 9/11 attacks still reverberate around the world in terms of risk to tourists and other travellers (Jackson *et al.*, 2005; Bonham and Edmonds, 2006; Okamoto and Bladek, 2011). It was a seismic shift in potential targets for terrorism and although not specifically aimed at tourists, its indirect effects reverberated across the tourist industry. As a direct result of this attack, the number of tourists travelling to the USA dropped substantially and several airlines reduced scheduled flights across the Atlantic; however, some sceptics believe that there was already excess capacity in the airline market and this tragedy was used as a good excuse to reduce oversupply on these transatlantic routes. Also the 7/7 attacks on London (2005) further enhanced the perception of tourists as soft targets. Tourism, in its normal sense, cannot exist without ensuring safety for its customers. Safe destinations and transport are expected norms for most tourists. However, there is now an increasing trend for tourists desiring to visit war zones to experience the *real thing* rather than using the media to access information. This could be viewed as positive risk taking in order to experience the reality of risk.

The Mumbai attacks of 2010, the Egyptian bus attacks (*The Guardian*, 2014) of which the latest was in 2014 and the attacks on tourist hotels, together with the 2013 attack in Kenya on a shopping mall (Howden, 2013), are all examples of the vulnerability of tourists to terrorist action. Planning for and protecting tourists from threats in holiday areas is not easy. However, with the increasing frequency of such attacks, perhaps there is also an equilibrium effect of the tourist to such events and it is further suggested that many tourists now accept a partial risk of attack by terrorists at some resorts. Evidence to support this can be seen through the context of how quickly tourism recovers; for example, it took three months for the London tourist market to pick up after the 7/7 attacks. Sharm el-Sheik (see Chapter 11 for more case studies) is another example of a resort under threat and the increased level of security that is required to ensure the safety of tourists. It is reassuring to know, however, that tourists are still visiting there in large numbers, despite several attacks on the resort.

Why terrorist attacks on tourists occur is easy to understand: Western tourists are considered easy targets resulting in high media interest, as well as ensuring diminishing economic returns at destinations where such attacks take place. But this is not limited simply to Islamic fundamentalism as other hotspots also occur such as previously in Spain, related to the Basque separatist movement ETA. Sometimes, simply the threat of an attack is enough to ensure a decrease in tourist demand for the destination (terrorism's raison d'être). The security of hotels against attack is a considerable problem, especially as they need to have unrestricted access for their customers. Additionally, many resort hotels have large annexes and complexes attached to them which magnify security issues exponentially.

The very idea of a terrorist attack heightens tourist tensions, but facts show that the risk of an attack is low when matched against the number of tourism visits (1 billion tourist visits during 2012) and how many people are actually injured or killed; statistically the risk is very low. However, as we have seen, risk is a component of a number of different milieus and hence there are clearly destinations that are riskier, with a higher potential for attack. A look at basic tourist statistics yields an interesting picture of where tourists are *not* thinking of travelling and where they are actually going (Table 9.3).

The other aspect is of course who is being targeted? Are all tourists being targeted and are they all at risk? Evidently the answer is no, and perhaps this is an ethnocentric question, heavily skewed towards the West and capitalist regimes. Certainly with the rise of Islamic fundamentalism (Haroon, 2012; Mullins and Young, 2012) Western tourists are often the main focus because of the ideologies they represent (Ness, 2005). It is of interest to note that many Western tourists avoid certain regions because of the threat of terrorism or where their cultural norms are unwelcome; Saudi Arabia is one such country that seems to fit this assertion. The majority of its tourism is religious tourism where Western values and styles of dress are unacceptable.

However, as stated earlier there are now changes in the market and more tourists are visiting countries involved in armed conflict, but usually to areas that are more or less devoid of active military action although still involved in war. This is certainly a new development in the assessment of risk and tourist destination management.

Table 9.3. Twenty top-ranking countries in terms of total terrorist attacks and fatalities, 1979 to 2007. (From LaFree, 2010.)

Most frequently attacked		Most fatalities	
Country	Frequency	Country	Frequency
Colombia	6,767	Iraq	17,754
Peru	6,038	Sri Lanka	14,272
El Salvador	5,330	India	13,434
India	4,318	Colombia	13,009
Northern Ireland	3,762	Peru	12,822
Spain	3,165	El Salvador	12,496
Iraq	3,161	Nicaragua	11,324
Turkey	2,691	Algeria	8,545
Sri Lanka	2,611	Philippines	6,304
Pakistan	2,536	Pakistan	5,540
Philippines	2,490	Guatemala	5,135
Chile	2,287	Turkey	4,674
Israel	2,140	Burundi	4,084
Guatemala	2,023	Afghanistan	3,764
Nicaragua	1,986	USA	3,339
South Africa	1,921	Rwanda	3,200
Lebanon	1,913	Lebanon	3,093
Algeria	1,650	Russia	3,057
Italy	1,487	Angola	2,861
USA	1,362	Northern Ireland	2,842

One of the key principles in reducing risk is knowledge and experience of hazard through the accessing of up-to-date information. For British citizens, the UK FCO website is the main site to find information on where it is safe or unsafe to travel. Citizens of Canada, Australia and New Zealand also have similar systems in place; Australia has 'Smart Traveller' (Smartraveller, 2013), New Zealand has 'Safe Travel' (Safe Travel, 2013) and Canada has a government website that conveys travel information for different countries (Travel. gc.ca, 2013). These sites do differ in the information for their tourists and it is interesting to note that the risks faced by different nationalities also alter. Another key indicator of risk is the insurance industry which underwrites travellers. It is often unwilling to insure high-risk ventures or when it does, premiums are often prohibitively expensive.

Currently, by far the most frequent attacks on tourists are by Islamic fundamentalists (Table 9.4). The 7/7 attacks of 2005 in London demonstrated that national citizens are willing and able to attack their own state, wreaking havoc on an unsuspecting public as well as affecting the tourism industry. Since 9/11 and the Gulf War, Islamic attacks on tourists have increased exponentially. The last global threat was that of liquid explosives being smuggled on board planes, which was successfully foiled in 2008 by UK counter-intelligence (BBC, 2013a,b). A more recent atrocity related to terrorism was that of November 2013 with the attack on a Kenyan shopping mall; all the evidence suggests that it was related to Islamic terrorists. However, perhaps it is pertinent to stress here that most acts of terrorism emanate from a small group of extremists and it is further evident that most Islamic states still wish to welcome tourists to their countries, because they provide a major source of income for many of their citizens.

Kidnapping is another aspect of terrorism which has featured prominently over the last few years, especially in Africa (Keenan, 2006; Wanjiru, 2006; Forest, 2012). It is not necessarily linked to any particular religion or ideology but more related to pirates and criminal gangs. A spatial analysis of these areas reveals that most of the troubled hotspots are to be found in less developed destinations of the world, with the attacks again focused on Western tourists and their locales.

The UNWTO (United Nations World Travel Organization) regards terrorism as one facet of crisis management (natural disasters also feature prominently) and terrorists as just one

Table 9.4. Top-ranked terrorist locations (extreme threat), 2014. (From McElroy, 2014.)

1.	Iraq
2.	Afghanistan
3.	Pakistan
4.	Somalia
5.	Nigeria
6.	Yemen
7.	Syria
8.	Philippines
9.	Lebanon
10.	Libya
11.	Colombia
12.	Kenya

of the risks that tourists face while travelling. Minimizing the risks of terrorism is somewhat difficult; location and state information services seem to be the best knowledge system for making informed decisions of where to travel in the world to reduce the risk of terrorist attack. Currently, this is dictated by geography and the evaluation of information freely available from government websites. It is interesting to note that some of these websites actually use micro-geography to locate certain areas and regions within a country to avoid, the principle being that micro-geography is able to locate hotspots where the likeliest threats are. There are some basic principles that can be identified here. Unfortunately, tourist destinations do provide concentrated groupings of tourists as well as prominent targets including aeroplanes, buses and trains, all of which have had some form of attack in recent years. Hotels and accommodation have also proved to be easy targets, as the Mumbai raids of 2009 demonstrated. Other concentrated targets are those centres offering leisure and relaxation, such as theme parks and waterparks.

9.7   CONCLUSION

It can be seen that health and safety management has developed steadily from its emergence in the 1970s. Instrumental in employee and customer safety has been the development of legal and executive frameworks ensuring that safety regulations within organizations are adhered to, safeguarding both employees and customers. The Health and Safety at Work Act 1974 in the UK was intrinsic to this, with other English-speaking countries following the UK lead. Consumers and society at large have become far more sophisticated and aware of safety issues, and it is now unacceptable to experience sudden death or suffer injury while using a company or organization, especially while at leisure or on holiday. New practices have been introduced to ensure a safe working and consumer environment; however, new issues continue to emerge to challenge 'safe' environments. Certainly from a tourist and leisure perspective this is evident in the growing problem of terrorism and the issue of tourists being easy and attractive targets. This chapter is designed to whet the appetite on issues such as how litigation works when negligence occurs and how accident data can be used in a preventive way to help improve a company's safety record; these are explored in more detail in Chapters 8 and 10.

DISCUSSION QUESTIONS AND TASKS

1. With an increasing number of tourists becoming terrorist targets, what measures can companies implement to protect their customers?

2. Do you consider current health and safety legislation has been effective in reducing accidents at work and protecting customers?

3. The notion of a controlling mind is critical to a company's safety and responsibility but do companies actually have such a position?

REFERENCES

BBC (2012) Zeebrugge Herald of Free Enterprise disaster survivor still grieves. Available at: http://www.bbc.co.uk/news/uk-england-kent-17260649 (accessed 9 December 2013).

BBC (2013a) Terrorism plot size of 7/7 attacks 'foiled every year'. Available at: http://www.bbc.co.uk/news/uk-21878867 (accessed 10 December 2013).

BBC (2013b) On This Day 17 November 1997: Egyptian militants kill tourists at Luxor. Available at: http://news.bbc.co.uk/onthisday/hi/dates/stories/november/17/newsid_2519000/2519581.stm (accessed 14 December 2013).

Bonham, C. and Edmonds, C. (2006) *The Impact of 9/11 and Other Terrible Global Events on Tourism in the US and Hawaii. Working Paper No. 87*. East-West Centre, Honolulu, Hawaii.

Cadario, B. (2012) Drug Safety and Postmodernism: The Rise of the Patient? Available at: http://dpic.org/article/professional/drug-safety-and-postmodernism-rise-patient (accessed 31 July 2014).

CCOHS (2008) OH&S Legislation in Canada – Introduction. Available at: http://www.ccohs.ca/oshanswers/legisl/intro.html (accessed 1 July 2014).

CCOHS (2014) About CCOHS. Available at: http://www.ccohs.ca/ccohs.html (accessed 1 July 2014).

Coleman, C. (2009) The legal case of the snail found in ginger beer. Available at: http://news.bbc.co.uk/1/hi/business/8367223.stm (accessed 31 July 2014).

EU-OSHA (2014a) European Directives. Available at: https://osha.europa.eu/en/legislation/directives (accessed 10 December 2014).

EU-OSHA (2014b) European Safety and Health Legislation. Available at: https://osha.europa.eu/en/legislation/index_html (accessed 10 December 2014).

Forest, J.F. (2012) Kidnapping by terrorist groups, 1970–2010. Is ideological orientation relevant? *Crime & Delinquency* 58, 769–797.

Glendon, A.I. and McKenna, E.F. (1995) *Human Safety and Risk Management*. Chapman & Hall, London.

The Guardian (2014) Egyptian bus bombing kills Korean tourists and driver. Available at: http://www.theguardian.com/world/2014/feb/16/egypt-bus-bombing-koreans-sinai (accessed 31 July 2014).

Haroon, A.I. (2012) Why are terrorists attacking tourists? eTN Global Travel Industry News, Available at: http://www.eturbonews.com/28797/why-are-terrorists-attacking-tourists (accessed 31 July 2014).

Howden, D. (2013) Terror in Westgate mall: the full story of the attacks that devastated Kenya. *The Guardian*, 4 October 2013. Available at: http://www.theguardian.com/world/interactive/2013/oct/04/westgate-mall-attacks-kenya-terror#undefined (accessed 31 July 2014).

HSE (2013) Health and safety management systems. Available at: http://www.hse.gov.uk/managing/health.htm (accessed 10 December 2013).

Jackson, B.A., Baker, J.C., Chalk, P., Cragin, K. and Parachini, J.V. (2005) *Aptitude for Destruction, Volume 2: Case Studies of Organizational Learning in Five Terrorist Groups*. Rand, Santa Monica, California.

Keenan, J.H. (2006) Security and insecurity in North Africa. *Review of African Political Economy* 33, 269–296.

LaFree, G. (2010) The Global Terrorism Database: accomplishments and challenges. *Perspectives on Terrorism* 4, 24–46.

McElroy, D. (2014) Global terrorist death toll soars as attacks become deadlier. *The Telegraph,* 23 July 2014. Available at: http://www.telegraph.co.uk/news/worldnews/middleeast/iraq/10985470/Global-terrorist-death-toll-soars-as-attacks-become-deadlier.html (accessed 31 July 2014).

Mullins, C.W. and Young, J.K. (2012) Habituation model to terrorism cultures of violence and acts of terror: applying a legitimation. *Crime & Delinquency* 58, 28–56.

Ness, S.A. (2005) Tourism–terrorism: the landscaping of consumption and the darker side of place. *American Ethnologist* 32, 118–140.

Okamoto, K. and Bladek, M. (2011) Terrorism: a guide to resources. *Collection Building* 30, 39–46.

Safe Travel (2013) Need Travel Advice? Available at: https://www.safetravel.govt.nz (accessed 9 October 2014).

Smartraveller (2013) Travel advice. Available at: http://www.smartraveller.gov.au (accessed 9 October 2014).

Stevens, T.R. and Jenkins, I.S. (1992) *Improving the Safety of Waterslides*. SaiL, Swansea, UK.

SWA (2014a) Who we work with. Available at: http://www.safeworkaustralia.gov.au/sites/swa/about/who-we-work-with/pages/who-we-work-with (accessed 1 July 2014).

SWA (2014b) Model Codes of Practice. Available at: http://www.safeworkaustralia.gov.au/sites/swa/model-whs-laws/model-cop/pages/model-cop (accessed 1 July 2014).

SWA (2014c) Model Work Health and Safety Regulations. Available at: http://www.safeworkaustralia.gov.au/sites/swa/about/publications/pages/guide-to-the-work-health-and-safety-act (accessed 1 July 2014).

Travel.gc.ca (2013) Country travel advice and advisories. Available at: http://travel.gc.ca/travelling/advisories (accessed 9 October 2014).

Wanjiru, C.K. (2006) Kenya and the war on terrorism. *Review of African Political Economy State* 33, 133–141.

Waring, A. (1996) *Safety Management Systems*. Chapman Hall, London.

Winterman, D. (2008) The towns where people live the longest. Available at: http://news.bbc.co.uk/2/hi/uk_news/magazine/7250675.stm (accessed 10 December 2013).

WSNZ (2014a) Guidance & Information. Available at: http://www.business.govt.nz/worksafe (accessed 1 July 2014).

WSNZ (2014b) Who we are. Available at: http://www.business.govt.nz/worksafe (accessed 1 July 2014).

FURTHER READING

Bentley, T.A., Page, P. and Walker, L. (2004) The safety experience of New Zealand adventure tourism. *Journal of Travel Medicine* 11, 280–286.

Feichtinger, G., Hartl, R.F., Kort, P.M. and Novak, A.J. (2001) Terrorism control in the tourism industry. *Journal of Optimization Theory and Applications* 108, 283–296.

Ferrett, E. (2012) *Health and Safety at Work, Revision Guide: for the NEBOSH National General Certificate*. Routledge, London.

Fisher, K. (2003) Terrorism and tourism. *Leisure Management* 23(2), 36–38.

Health and Safety at Work etc. Act 1974. Available at: http://www.legislation.gov.uk/ukpga/1974/37/contents

Mewshaw, M. (2010) *Between Terror and Tourism: An Overland Journey across North Africa*. Counterpoint, Berkeley, California.

SWA (2014) Model Codes of Practice. Available at: http://www.safeworkaustralia.gov.au/sites/swa/model-whs-laws/model-cop/pages/model-cop

chapter 10

Experience, Analysis of Incidents and Accidents

The Miracle of Breathing

There are many things that harm life. As life is more unstable than an air bubble in water. It is a wonder that the in-breaths turn into out-breaths and that one wakes up from sleep. Ji Gampopa (1079–1153) Tibet (cited in TBS, 2006: 821)

CHAPTER OBJECTIVES

- To understand the importance of accident data to risk management.
- To evaluate the importance of risk models to safety management.
- To evaluate accident theory and models.
- To examine the available accident collection systems and their effectiveness.

Key concepts

Memory and experience of accidents; accident theories and causations; relevance of accident data; accident surveillance systems; cost of accidents to society and organizations.

10.1   INTRODUCTION

When one reflects on the possible accidents that could occur between birth and retirement, it is somewhat remarkable that so many of us live so long (Hillson and Murray-Webster, 2007) given the risks and hazards each one of us faces. Simply being born is a risk and when potential risks during childhood and adolescence are factored in, it is extraordinary that so many of us reach adulthood (Hillson and Murray-Webster, 2007; Brodbeck *et al.*, 2013). Furthermore, when environmental risks are included, depending on where you live in the world, potential risks multiply exponentially and help explain why the developing world has much higher mortality rates. We are *all* risk managers, constantly making decisions about risk which, if erroneous, can result in minor accidents or even death.

As we have seen risk is not a uniform concept; it can be divided into objective risk and perceived risk (Adams, 1995), and understanding risk is often viewed within the context of two different stimuli: experience and perceived knowledge. Risk and accidents are closely related, if not in juxtaposition to each other. In essence, each of us learns (usually) from past experience and when the outcome of a decision or action is detrimental, we tend to avoid it and adjust reactions for future decisions (Brodbeck *et al.*, 2013). This means that if we live without any major accidents or injuries we can be said to have managed competently critical success factors (CSF) to risk (Hillson and Murray-Webster, 2007) and our judgements have been accurate or perhaps on occasions, lucky (see Chapter 7). However, can risk really be assessed (Bradbury, 1989), with it being suggested that the concept of risk is a human invention (Adams, 1995)?

Information on potential accidents or injuries certainly influences our actions but our actions also depend upon individual perception and personality. Some individuals will take greater risks than others, even when given the same information and perhaps the same experience (Vitelli, 2013). For example, do reports of plane crashes make us reconsider whether to fly or not? Possibly, but there are so many other factors influencing that decision, including personality, frequency of flying, the flying experience, an airline's reputation, etc. It was noticeable that transatlantic flight capacity after 9/11 suddenly dropped. Yet it could be argued that from the perspective of a possible terrorist attack, this was probably one of the safest times to fly, as security, safety and risk management at airports had all been greatly increased to ensure prevention of another such incident. That said, most people perceived that flying at this time was an increased risk and that avoidance for the short term would be the safest decision, although it was not necessarily the most rational response.

Accidents are usually a consequence of poor risk management and are a commonly misunderstood concept (HSE, 2005). There appears to be an assumption that accidents happen mainly due to people taking risks; however, many accidents occur when the person usually least expects it (WHO, 2005) and when they are in a relaxed environment. The film *Open Water. Adrift 2* is a pertinent example of this and shows how small, single actions can result in catastrophe. The main narrative focuses on the lack of a ladder or any other means of access to climb back on to a sailing boat (Rotten Tomatoes, 2014). This simple act of 'omission' (not providing a ladder) results in mass fatalities. Although this is just a fictional Hollywood story it provides an excellent example of how fiction often mirrors reality. There are numerous instances of simple actions or omissions resulting in tragedy. For example, the sinking of the *Herald of Free Enterprise* in 1985 follows this accident model; the single action of not closing the bow doors led to the sinking of this ferry (BBC, 2013). Although a single action can result in catastrophe, usually these are final elements in tragedies/accidents which are generally a result of a complex 'sequence of events', often the consequence of an accumulation of unsafe actions/non-actions and poor safety culture (these are the trigger events described in Chapter 2 as part of the Anatomy of Risk Model). Furthermore, certain activities carry with them much higher risk due to environmental factors and the geographical locations of activities. An example of this is climbers on Everest (especially those using commercial companies to organize their trip), many of whom are inexperienced mountaineers. The risk ratio for death on Everest is currently 1:7, which can be regarded as relatively high; most people would not even consider getting on a plane with this potential risk statistic! Additionally, many customers pay up to US$40,000 for the privilege of experiencing this exposure to death, adding considerable monetary pressure to both the company and the customer to reach Everest's summit.

10.2   LEARNING AND EXPERIENCE OF ACCIDENTS AND RISK

It is asserted that a person's past experiences help shape future risk management skills; yet our memories are known to be unreliable and recollection of past events at best sketchy (see also Chapter 7 and the discussion of heuristics and heuristic traps). Accident statistics indicate that some of the main causes of death in the home are falls, poisoning, cuts and being struck by objects (DTI, 2003) (see Box 10.1). It is also evident that organizations also fail to learn from past experience even though they keep and analyse accident data (Stevens and Jenkins, 1993; Drupsteen et al., 2013). That said, it is evident that past experiences guide future decisions. It is often argued that childhood experiences affect how we view risk as adults. For example, fear of water is often due to a childhood incident, fear of dogs due to a bite/attack by a dog and so on. Although these scenarios may be overly simplistic, they are a means by which we develop an understanding of risk and hazard, through memory (Baron, 2014).

Recall is perhaps a problem for safety management because unless a person has experienced an adverse outcome, it becomes difficult to convey the need for risk management. Consequently it is unsurprising that many safety campaigns take time to prevent future accidents (for example, the anti-drink driving campaign) and are not always successful, sometimes requiring punitive measures to be introduced. Figure 10.1 presents a model for the process of learning from an incident/accident.

Despite this risk management and risk assessment do not have to be complicated; perhaps the most simplistic approach being the question 'what if?' This is the basis for most risk assessment programmes used by many organizations. All actions have risk outcomes and for most people the choice is to select the best outcome with the least risk; these are the often subconscious decisions we make every day. There are clearly certain actions and parameters that most people acknowledge as carrying potential risks, such as driving too fast, driving while under

Box 10.1. From accident theory to practice: leisure and sport accident databases (EHLASS, HASS/LASS)

It seems evident that accident information is an important element in the management of risks and maintenance of an MRE (minimum risk environment). With this rationale in mind it would seem sensible that governments and other quasi-state agencies have databases that can be accessed and used to monitor accidents. Such databases do exist but they are not universal and certainly in the areas of tourism, leisure and sport, information is often limited and dated. As explained previously in Box 9.1, this was a problem when deciding how risky certain tourism, adventure and leisure activities were (waterslides and adventure tourism).

In the UK, HASS (Home Accident Surveillance System) and LASS (Leisure Accident Surveillance System) (RoSPA, 2014a) reveal some interesting statistics. These statistics were produced by collecting data from 16–18 A&E (accident and emergency) departments in the UK and then projecting the figures for the population of the UK. The database was managed by the DTI (Department of Trade and Industry), which continued collecting data until 2002. It looked at 30 different elements of information and was collected for 20 years (RoSPA, 2014a).

EHLASS (European Home Leisure Accident Surveillance System) (DG SANCO, 2001) also has data on leisure activities which are collected by each member state and then submitted to the EU for analysis and summary of the data. It was trialled in 1985 and first released in 1986. It has been difficult to get EU composite reports on EHLASS; however, there are regular publications by each member state certainly until 2002. The EU does however collect accident data, the coordinating body for this being the European Agency for Safety and Health at Work (EU-OSHA, 2014). The premise for the collection of data is similar to the UK system where the main emphasis is on workplace safety.

The number of current tourism, leisure and sport accident databases is very limited. The possible reasons for this are the cost of collection and analysis, together with an appropriate system that collates and analyses the data. Proposals have been suggested to develop a more sophisticated system but these have never been fully developed. One such proposal was that of SMILE (Safety Management Information for the Leisure Industry) by SaiL in 1994, which was similar to the HASS/LASS systems of the UK but designed for a European database. It differed from previous systems by incorporating randomly selected leisure facilities together with A&E departments.

Australia, Canada and New Zealand have similar accident database systems focused mainly upon work-based accidents. As with the UK and Europe, there appear to be no specific databases specifically for the tourism, leisure and sport industries, although certain specific information can be found for sport. For example, NSW University produces

(Continued)

Box 10.1. Continued.

sports injuries reports and provides some indication on the rate and nature of the injuries (Mitchell *et al.*, 2008). They state that there needs to be a 'development of detailed routine injury surveillance systems for sport/leisure activities with high or increasing injury hospitalisation rates, to continue to monitor these injury trends in specific sports and to guide intervention priorities and evaluation' (Mitchell *et al.*, 2008: 4). This again clearly suggests that the sport and perhaps leisure and tourism industries need to be more closely monitored, so that assessments can be made on whether injuries and accidents are causing substantial economic loss through work absences and hospital treatment. As has been demonstrated through case studies, lack of pertinent accident data can cause serious disruption to companies and massively increase the economic cost of activities, resulting in reduced customer participation and increased insurance premiums. It is suggested that there is still a need for a specific tourism, leisure and sport database which providers could use to monitor accidents and, where necessary, take appropriate precautions.

the influence of alcohol, use of boiling water, not using eye protection when carrying out work that involves flying objects, not wearing a helmet when riding a motorbike, etc. But these are all risk management decisions.

Lack of risk information and accident data can also be detrimental to both customers and companies, which was the case in the UK adventure tourism industry during the 1990s. It was extremely difficult for consumers to be sure of the safety record of these companies, or find out which were safer than others (see Box 10.1). In addition, a lack of coordinated risk management information (accident data) meant that safety standards between providers could not be guaranteed and varied widely. The end result was extremely punitive with the introduction of The Activity Centres (Young Persons Safety) Act 1995, which created a statutory body to monitor and license centres whose customers were children and certain specified activities.

10.3 PREVENTION VERSUS CURE – NOTIONS OF CORPORATE SOCIAL RESPONSIBILITY AND PAST ACTIONS

The old adage, 'prevention is better than cure', is commonly accepted as a maxim for risk management. But when it comes to accidents it is often overlooked and ignored. Many of us assume that we have common sense and that each one of us views the world through similar perspectives. Yet it seems evident that this is not the case, challenging the notion of what is 'normal'. John Locke's treatise of perception argues that common sense is represented by naïve thinking (Dupré, 2007), which is perhaps evident in individual safety

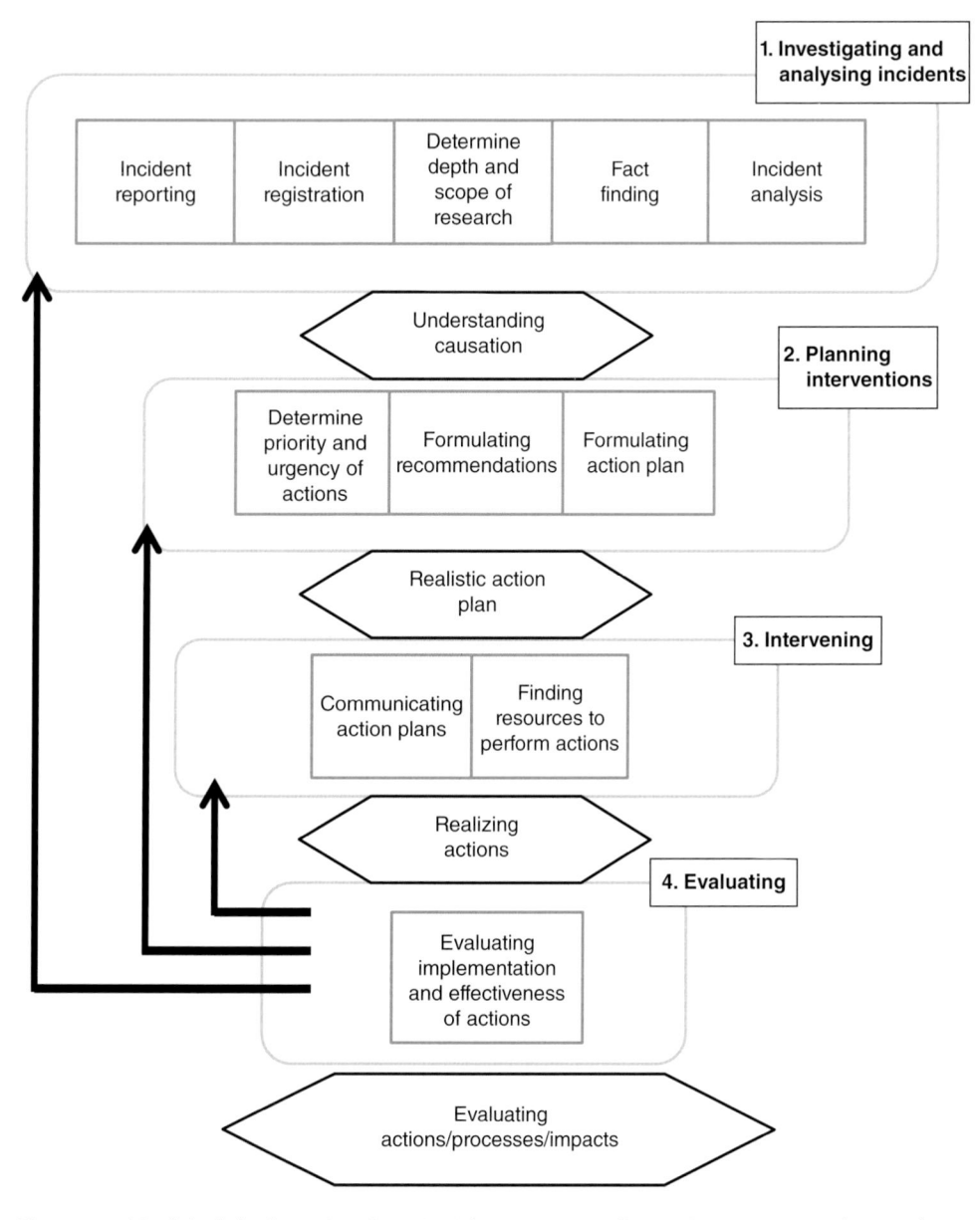

Fig. 10.1. Model of the learning from incidents process. (From Drupsteen *et al.*, 2013.)

awareness. For example, who would deliberately get too close to a cliff edge in order to fall off (see Fig. 10.2)? But it seems that people do!

Linking personal safety responsibility to organizations can be seen within the context of what is now commonly known as *corporate social responsibility* (CSR), which is linked to many areas of a company's operations such as environment, social community relations, cultural awareness and safety.

Fig. 10.2. Danger: cliffs.

Any Safety Management System should start with a safety policy linked to CSR. As has been mentioned, a number of companies regard safety as one of their primary mission statements and an integral part of the product they offer. ISO 26000 is a benchmark for measuring social responsibility and clearly within this standard there is designated an area of health and safety (ISO, 2008). It states that: 'ISO 26000 will add value to existing initiatives for social responsibility by providing harmonized, globally relevant guidance based on international consensus among expert representatives of the main stakeholder groups and so encourage the implementation of best practice in social responsibility' (ISO, 2008: 2).

In many cases health and safety will be incorporated into the main policy documents and mission statements of companies, especially those in developed countries, ensuring that both employee and customer are protected from foreseeable detrimental incidents and circumstances. ISO 26000 gives gravitas to safety and an expectation that companies will ensure that safety is part of their responsibility. It is interesting to note that safety is *part* of the system, not necessarily *apart* from the system. It is now clearly recommended that it should be embedded in the products delivered by every company. Unfortunately, as stated earlier, safety is an unseen element and often one of the first to be ignored, or receive lower priority when companies are in financial difficulties.

Health and safety information and standards should be viewed by companies and organizations as being a help rather than a hindrance; accidents and injuries do not benefit a company and in many circumstances have detrimental effects on profits, customer loyalty and workforce morale. Therefore, CSR should simply be reinforcing what health and safety procedures a competent company should already have in place. CSR should also be used as a tool for reflecting employees' attitudes and actions. A reduction in accidents will reduce liability claims, which in turn will reduce compensation costs and insurance premiums. It should also be seen as a surrogate for the quality of other systems within the company. Perhaps the biggest benefit should be seen in the communication of company ethos and a company's safety management system, which can only work if all employees are integrated within it, developing appropriate behaviour and actions. In essence the employee's action needs to reflect the company's health and safety programme. As risk is a social construct, it necessarily follows that nearly all accidents are generated by and usually occur due to human error (Hollnagel, 2012). Having a competent CSR, incorporating safety issues, ensures the reduction of risk and accidents to employees and customers.

10.4   THE ECONOMICS OF DEATH AND INJURY

It is often the case that society perceives a fatality as the worst outcome of an incident. However, this is often not a true perspective of the cost to society, leaving aside the emotional trauma of such an event. The law seems to value the outcome of an accident solely from the aspect of economics, with legal judgments appearing to reflect this stance. In addition, the law also seems to recognize the loss of economic potential as a key element when considering compensation. It is interesting to note that in the UK, compensation under criminal law for loss of life through an accident is regarded as parsimonious (see Chapter 8 on tort).

A fatality is, as the word suggests, final. The outcome is known and apart from the psychological trauma to family and friends, the actual economic costs to the individual and society are minimal (replacement of employee and compensation for loss). However, serious injuries such as paraplegic and brain injuries will result in a lifetime of economic costs to both society and the individual, which have to be borne by the taxpayer or, as in the case of New Zealand, a compensation policy. It is interesting to note that the modern strategy of warfare prioritizes injury over death, whereby injuring the enemy is perhaps more effective than killing him, as this has greater resource, strategic and psychological effects than a fatality. Indeed, many weapons are designed not to kill but simply to maim. Similarly, serious injuries can be far more costly (economically) to society than fatalities.

There are a number of schemas that evaluate the way economic costs can be calculated for injuries and treatment of accident casualties (Butchart *et al.*, 2008), see Tables 10.1 and 10.2. The design for these models is based upon injuries caused by violence but is relevant because they evaluate injury and its related costs, which are similar to injuries caused through accidents. The Criminal Injuries Compensation Scheme in the UK also uses such a system and specific injuries are compensated by relating them to loss of earnings, etc. Tables 10.3 and 10.4 provide examples of the types of payment that can be made under the Criminal Injuries Compensation Scheme 2012 (Ministry of Justice, 2012), giving an idea of how injury compensations are calculated.

10.4.1   Economic cost calculations of injuries

This section explains the rationale for the calculations and how the schemas work.

Human capital

This approach looks at the loss to the working environment; however, there are many factors involved and an accurate cost is unlikely to be obtained. The model assumes that the whole population is working, so that unemployment, voluntary work or unpaid work (e.g. housework)

Table 10.1. Typology of costing violence[a]. (From Butchart *et al.*, 2008: 7.)

Cost category	Type of cost	Components	Disaggregation options
Direct	Medical	**Hospital inpatient** **Hospital outpatient** **Transport/ambulance** **Physician** **Drugs/laboratory tests** **Counselling**	
	Non-medical	Policing and imprisonment Legal services Foster care Private security	
Indirect	Tangible	**Loss of productivity (earnings and time)[b]** Lost investments in social capital Life insurance Indirect protection Macroeconomic	*By demographic group* *By type of injury* *By mechanism* *By intent*
	Intangible	*Health-related quality of life (pain and suffering, psychological)* Other quality of life (reduced job opportunities, access to schools and public services, participation in community life)	

[a]Cost component categories in bold are the minimum requirements; those in italics are the optional modules; those not highlighted are not covered.
[b]Loss of income by the victim, the perpetrator and caring personnel are some examples. Only income lost by the victim is taken into account in these guidelines.

is difficult to adjust for (Butchart *et al.*, 2008). However, this method can give an approximation of the cost to society of an injury, formulated as follows:

Indirect cost due to injury = time lost due to injury × wage rate.

Friction cost

This focuses on the aspect of loss of output, and estimates the cost of replacing the injured or deceased individual (Butchart *et al.*, 2008). It would include items related to elements such as advertising costs, company time spent on recruitment and training of new personnel,

Table 10.2. Health policy questions that can be addressed by economic impact studies of violence. (From Butchart *et al.*, 2008.)

Level	Question
Micro	
Households	• What impact do violence-related deaths, injuries and illness have on a household's income? (Sometimes this question covers a single year, sometimes a longer period of time)
	• How much do people pay for medical or other expenses because of violence-related death, injuries and illness? (This question may cover an episode, a year or a lifetime)
Firms	• What impact do violence-related deaths, injuries and illness have on the operating costs, output or profit of a firm?
	• What is the relative impact of violence-related injury and ill-health on productivity in the workplace? (This might include impaired performance while still at work, as well as absenteeism)
Government	• What proportion of government expenditure could have been saved and directed to an alternative use in the absence of violence? (Sometimes this question covers only a subset of government, such as the health service costs that could be avoided by the prevention of violence-related injuries)
	• What impact do violence-related death, injury and illness have on the government workforce and on the government's ability to provide services?
Macro	
Society	• What impact does violence have on gross domestic product and its rate of growth?
	• How much does society pay for medical and other expenses because of violence-related death, injury and illness?
	• What impact does violence have on social welfare?

appointment fees, relocation costs, etc. It assumes that there are people available to replace the injured person, with the implied added costs to the country of training and education if there are no suitably qualified personnel.

Willingness to pay

This theory of assessment is based upon the cost of an accident to a government or company and how much people are willing to pay for acceptable outlays/safety measures to prevent

Table 10.3. Different types of injury costs. Annex E: Tariff of injuries, Criminal Injuries Compensation Scheme 2012. (From Ministry of Justice, 2012.)

Part A		Part B	
Levels of compensation	£	Levels of compensation	£
Level A1	1,000	Level B1	1,000
Level A2	1,500	Level B2	1,500
Level A3	1,800	Level B3	2,000
Level A4	2,400	Level B4	3,300
Level A5	3,500	Level B5	4,400
Level A6	4,600	Level B6	5,500
Level A7	6,200	Level B7	6,600
Level A8	11,000	Level B8	8,200
Level A9	13,500	Level B9	11,000
Level A10	16,500	Level B10	13,500
Level A11	19,000	Level B11	16,500
Level A12	22,000	Level B12	22,000
Level A13	17,000	Level B13	27,000
Level A14	33,000	Level B14	33,000
Level A15	44,000	Level B15	44,000
Level A16	55,000		
Level A17	82,000		
Level A18	110,000		
Level A19	175,000		
Level A20	250,000		

accidents happening (Butchart *et al.*, 2008). For example, perhaps the cost of lift passes on a ski piste will include the cost of safety measures to reduce the likelihood of injury (such as frequency of piste rolling, piste markers, availability of ski patrols) or on waterslides the cost of incorporating supervision at particular points or substituting this for mechanical safety measures such as traffic lights (Stevens and Jenkins, 1990).

It is evident that injuries to customers have a complex effect on society and are not solely reflected in the damage to the individual or company. This is why government and government agencies have an interest in safety and accident statistics due to the wider impacts such accidents/injuries

Table 10.4. Specific types of injury costs. Criminal Injuries Compensation Scheme 2012. (From Ministry of Justice, 2012.)

Area of damage	Type of disability	No.	£
Severe damage			
One leg	Substantial recovery	A2	1,500
	Continuing significant disability	A7	6,200
Both legs	Substantial recovery	A6	4,600
	Continuing significant disability	A10	16,500
Tibia (shin bone) fractured			
One leg	Substantial recovery	A3	1,800
	Continuing significant disability	A6	4,600
Both legs	Substantial recovery	A5	3,500
	Continuing significant disability	A8	11,000
Toe fractured			
Great toe, one foot	Substantial recovery	A1	1,000
	Continuing significant disability	A7	6,200
Great toe, both feet	Substantial recovery	A3	1,800
	Continuing significant disability	A9	13,500
Two or more toes			
One foot	Continuing significant disability	A1	1,000
Both feet	Continuing significant disability	A4	2,400
Loss of one great toe		A7	6,200
Loss of both great toes		A9	13,500

have on the economy. It is asserted that, in general, some serious injuries are more costly to the economy than fatalities, which is not to diminish the trauma that fatalities bring to families. The numerous cost elements can be summarized in the following list of areas of economic costs resulting from serious injury:

- loss of earnings;
- loss of work productivity;
- medical time and expenses;
- transport costs;
- increased insurance premiums for companies;
- increased insurance premiums for individuals;

- expert/consultancy reports;
- legal fees;
- HSE investigation time; and
- governing body/professional time.

Given the high economic cost of injuries and fatalities it is not surprising that some companies have prioritized the operation of an MRE. This is especially important for all tourism and leisure companies, where the mere thought of serious injury or death is inconceivable. 'When Walt Disney envisioned Disneyland®, he saw an environment where families could have fun together in a safe and clean atmosphere. Since then, safety has played a vital role' (Walt Disney Parks and Resorts, 2008: 1). It is evident that Disney cannot afford, not just in financial terms but also in terms of reputation, to have injuries or accidents. Safety is therefore at the forefront of the Disney product which has so far proved to be an extremely successful marketing point and, from the available data, an extremely safe company.

As mentioned earlier, companies which have frequent customer injuries or a death usually pay heavily, especially in terms of economic success. The first death attributed to a waterslide in the UK in 1987 at Richmond PLC (Stevens and Jenkins, 1990) eventually rendered the company bankrupt. It was also interesting to note that news reports at the time focused on the company's accident statistics which they believed were 'unacceptably high' and had not been acted upon, indicating that a potentially serious accident was waiting to happen.

10.5   THEORY OF ACCIDENT ANALYSIS

Accidents are a common feature of living and the word is frequently used to denote possible injury or death. In fact, many media stories use it in connection with a tragedy. The last 30 years are littered with narratives related to accidents in many sectors of the leisure and tourism industry. But this term is wrongly ascribed in many of the stories that are covered (Ridley and Channing, 1999a,b). In most cases, it is argued that a better word than 'accident' is 'incident'.

10.5.1   Definition of an accident

Accident is a commonly misunderstood word. Looking at the definition of an accident shows that it has a number of important elements. It is an event which:

- cannot be foreseen;
- cannot be prevented;
- is uncontrolled; and
- leads to a detrimental effect on or damage to person, object or phenomenon.

An unforeseen event is an accident; yet many recorded accidents can be predicted and in many cases are preventable and thus should not be defined as accidents. Few if any media-reported accidents are in fact true accidents; many relate to events that could be prevented and are foreseeable.

Furthermore, RoSPA (Royal Society for the Prevention of Accidents) notes that an accident is:

> An unplanned, uncontrolled event which has led to or could have led to injury to people, damage to plant, machinery or the environment and/or some other loss.

(RoSPA, 2014b)

The HSE provides the following definition as cited by RoSPA:

> An undesired circumstance(s) which gives rise to ill health, injury, damage, production losses or increased liabilities.

(RoSPA, 2014b)

Evaluation of accident statistics and their causes would demonstrate that most accidents do not fall under the definition of an accident. Most are in fact incidents that have a preventable, foreseeable cause, given competent safety management. However, the relevance here is not the definition, but the management actions required to prevent such events/phenomena occurring. In terms of management it is suggested that the most important constituent in accident prevention is *foresight*, and as we have seen in Chapter 8 on tort, *foreseeability* is a key element in deciding whether negligence has occurred. The concept of foresight is certainly one upon which UK law and much of UK tort legislation focuses.

This is also an interesting concept as 'foreseeability' is a perception rather than a reality. Consequently it is somewhat difficult to measure a person's capability of foresight, even though the law uses the benchmark of a 'reasonable and prudent person' or put simply, what an average person would have done. Companies are therefore not being asked to provide anything more than reasonable care and judgement. Foresight can also be linked to the likelihood of occurrence; in other words it is a statistical computation. Although many companies calculate economic performance, they may not to be as diligent when it comes to calculating indices for customer safety.

How then can foresight be defined? A common understanding might be our own estimation of the risk of possible actions/non-actions. Examples might include: an unguarded open fire increases the risk of being burnt, slippery floors increase the potential of falls, going off-piste increases the risk of avalanche, skiing has a higher risk of injury than walking, etc. Consequently foresight is recognizing what might happen and then deciding on preventable actions to avoid certain results. Unfortunately, foresight seems to be based upon 'common sense' and as discussed earlier, not everyone appears to have this.

Foresight can be defined as the perception of future consequences and what preventive actions or non-actions were made; it helps to focus a manager's thoughts on possible risks and likely consequences. However, it is perhaps interesting to note that it does not necessarily follow that the greater the risk the greater the number of accidents. This is because the more we are exposed to risks, usually the more avoiding/precautionary actions we take. Most of us will die in our homes, not because they are higher risk but simply because the longest risk exposure time on average is in this environment. However, homes are also full of potential hazards which give rise to risks (WHO, 2005) and serious accidents. In many ways accident data are useful for indicating the level of risk and the need to improve safety in certain areas. It must also be remembered that an accident is not a singular outcome; it has degrees of severity and there is evidence to suggest that the degree of severity can be used to predict likely future accidents. For example, a collection of near miss and minor accident data could be used to predict more serious accidents. Unfortunately accident data are historical, a *reactive* form of management, where the person or item has already been detrimentally affected. Risk assessment, on the other hand, is *proactive management*.

Nevertheless, even though accident data represent reactive management, they are a useful tool for management as an indicator of areas where the performance of safety management can be improved. In addition, it must be remembered that there are different types and grades of accidents, ranging from minor to fatal/catastrophic. Major or fatal accidents are perhaps those that need to be prevented, whereas those considered minor or inconsequential have little lasting impact on an individual. Yet it would be unwise to dismiss information related to the lesser category. Safety management systems have found that this information is perhaps the most useful in terms of predicting future or potential accidents, providing proactive management information. In addition, it is important to add *near miss* data, as these can be of great value to industries where accidents are unacceptable, such as the air transport industry. However, such information is also important for other industries such as tourism and leisure, where near miss data could help avoid future serious accidents. Near miss data have been recognized by the UK HSE and included in its risk assessment procedures.

A review of some of the major tragedies in the UK over the last 30 years reveals that there were, in most cases, portents from the data suggesting the potential for more serious consequences. That said, the total number of accidents is not necessarily an indication of poor safety management, but it *can* be. The important point is how the data are used and acted upon, not necessarily the total number of accidents. The analysis and review of accident statistics can provide management with a clear picture of the effectiveness of the safety management systems and indicate where improvements may be needed.

As discussed above, perhaps the most beneficial development of the last 30 years has been the introduction of 'near miss' data, which are not really accident data but 'potential' accident data. A 'near miss' is an incident where there was no actual detrimental effect, but that may have the potential to cause a detrimental effect in the future. It is necessary to review the 'near miss' to assess the future risk and perhaps take action to improve safety management.

10.5.2 Accident pyramids

One model for representing accident data is related to the concept of a pyramid (Ridley and Channing, 1999b), where the most serious accidents and fatalities are found at the apex and the more common, frequent accidents at the base (see Fig. 10.3). The importance of the theory is that common accidents/near misses can be used to possibly predict major ones.

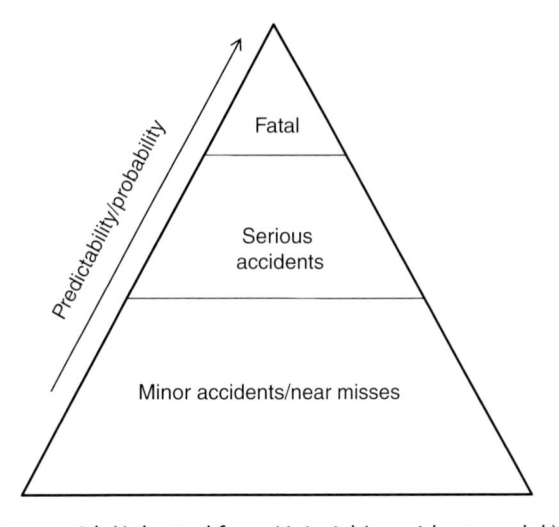

Fig. 10.3. Accident pyramid. (Adapted from Heinrich's accident model.)

This is a simplistic analogy of the use of accident data which some authors argue may not be good predictors of major or fatal accidents. However, an appropriate collection and analysis of accident data is an essential tool in identifying where future serious/fatal accidents might occur and should be used to assist managers in taking preventive measures.

10.6   THEORY OF ACCIDENTS

There are a number of theories (Ridley and Channing, 1999b; SIA, 2012) relating to the sequence of events resulting in an accident. Understanding such theories can be helpful, allowing managers to recognize possible ways accident sequences are generated and finding possible interventions to stop the sequence, through the development of barriers and prevention methods. But like most theories they are somewhat abstract and difficult to mimic in practice. The number of theoretical models has grown exponentially and a few better known examples are presented below.

10.6.1   Accident models

This section outlines and discusses a number of different accident models and in particular the theories of how accidents actually happen and the causes that give risks and hazards to them:

- *Domino effect*. This relates to the simplest form of accident theory whereby a series of events leads to the final one, eventually resulting in an accident. By examining the sequence, a manager may be able to isolate key components of the sequence of events that resulted in the injury or loss. The theory relates to Heinrich's Axiom of Industrial Safety Theory and was one of the first to link safety management to industry and the workplace. It asserts that by removing the hazard in the sequence, an accident will be prevented. However, this is now viewed as too simplistic given the complexity of many industrial processes and organizations that exist today (Waring, 1996; Ridley and Channing, 1999b).

- *Chain reaction.* The chain reaction theory relates to the concept that each part of the accident sequence results in a reinforcement of the next stage, an elaboration on the domino effect. The emphasis here is that each stage reinforces its potential for damage before the next sequence begins. Reinforcement chains act upon each stage of the sequence, emphasizing that there are a number of hazards contributing to the sequence at each stage and unless action is taken at each stage, the accident sequence will increase the potential for a detrimental outcome.

- *Multi-causal/chaos theory.* This suggests that companies and products are now so complex that attributing blame solely to one causal factor is not enough given the complexity of some operations and services. It incorporates a number of hazard elements acting in different ways, not necessarily sequential, such as operational issues, human perception and decisions, mechanical failure and poor design, all of which affect the detrimental outcome (Ridley and Channing, 1999b; SIA, 2012).

- *Catastrophe theory.* This model uses the thesis that at some point in an accident sequence, the situation starts to evolve into a state where prevention and control are virtually impossible; at this point nothing can save the situation. Recent events, such as the BP oil well disaster in the Mexican Gulf, the sinking of the *MS Estonia* and other previous disasters over the last 30 years, support aspects of this theory where beyond a certain 'tipping point' nothing could stop the inevitable detrimental outcome. Prevention of getting to this point is the essence of risk management and accident prevention.

The above theories are somewhat passé in terms of model construction but they were the basis of more current, complex modelling, providing the reader with a basic understanding of how accident sequences possibly work. Table 10.5 provides a summary of model types, with one of the latest models discussed more fully in Section 10.6.2.

10.6.2   Example of an accident model: Functional Resonance Accident Method (FRAM)

Hollnagel (2004) was one of the first to propose that the accident sequence could be explained by a three-dimensional perspective and to realize that many organizations are extremely complex and difficult to manage. His thesis is that there will always be variances in the system and this is normal for any organization; but when these variances reach a strain perspective then 'fictional resonance' occurs, leading to an accident or accidents (SIA, 2012). The complexity is focused on the social and technical perspective combined with four elements: (i) human; (ii) technical; (iii) latent conditions; and (iv) barriers (SIA, 2012). This modelling was a clear move away from the linear perspectives of other models and perhaps also tries to deal with the notions of many organizations having chaos systems (complex variances). He also examines the notion of efficiency versus accuracy and the problems of trade-off between these two functions,

Table 10.5. Typology of accident models. (From SIA, 2012.)

Type of model	Date	Summary
Linear		Earliest type of accident theory, simple linkage of hazard elements which gives rise to accident/detrimental outcome
Heinrich's Domino Model	1931	This was one of the first models. It was the first attempt to try and link theory to output. It is linked to time aspects of accident statistics. It is quite simplistic in explaining how accidents occurred
Bird and Germain's Loss Causation Model	1985	This model was an adaptation of the Domino Model. It incorporates the need for management to control the safety of products
International Loss Control Institute Causation Model	1985	This model was further adapted and became known as the International Loss Control Model
Linear-complex		Realization of complex interaction between competing hazards, no singular cause but multifactorial interactions
Energy Damage Models	1961 and 1991	The complexity of linear models was recognized and a new type of model developed identifying the importance of energy as a critical variable in causing injury or accident. When energy exceeds acceptable levels to the recipient, a detrimental output occurs
Time Sequence Models	1975	An adaptation of the Domino Model. Introduced four new aspects: (i) beginning–end; (ii) time series; (iii) structured facts; and (iv) charting events
Generalized Time Sequence Model	1991	An adaptation of Time Sequence Model, embellishing some new stages such as time zones creating opportunities to stop accidents
Epidemiology Models	1949	Adaptation from disease modelling. Accidents through three aspects: (i) host; (ii) agent; and (iii) environment

(Continued)

Table 10.5. Continued.

Type of model	Date	Summary
Systemic Models	1990s	Systems failures as well as human failures also contribute to accidents. Also emphasizes the importance of human error, increased importance of psychology
Reason's Swiss Cheese Model	2008	Increased importance of psychology and human errors: active and latent variables. Not simply one person's error, systems allow these, lack/failure of defence barriers. However, the types of barriers and holes in system not specified
The Sharp and Blunt End Model	1994	A change of emphasis away from individual blame, towards systems and human behaviour, incorporating aspects of safety culture rather than individual fault
Non-linear		
Systems-Theoretic Accident Model and Process (STAMP)	2004	Dynamic systems model that assumes safety variables are continuously changing within a system and a need for tasks and controls to change also. Its main emphasis is upon barriers and defences, linked to performance of safety indicators. Not really related to accident data and analysis. Limited practicality
Functional Resonance Accident Model (FRAM)	2004	This uses a three-dimensional perspective relating to accident causation. Sources of accidents come from four variables: (i) humans, (ii) technology, (iii) latent conditions; and (iv) barriers, which all interact creating a very complex web of accident control and prevention within an organization

especially when under pressure. An interesting perspective of safety is one of it being an unseen product that is intangible for customers and employees with the need perhaps for performance indices to make safety management visible. This clearly is a model emphasizing the safety culture of an organization (see Fig. 10.4), changing the perspective from blame of an individual or controlling mind. Clearly all aspects of a product being operated are human and the need for a more holistic approach to safety management is clearly evident in this model.

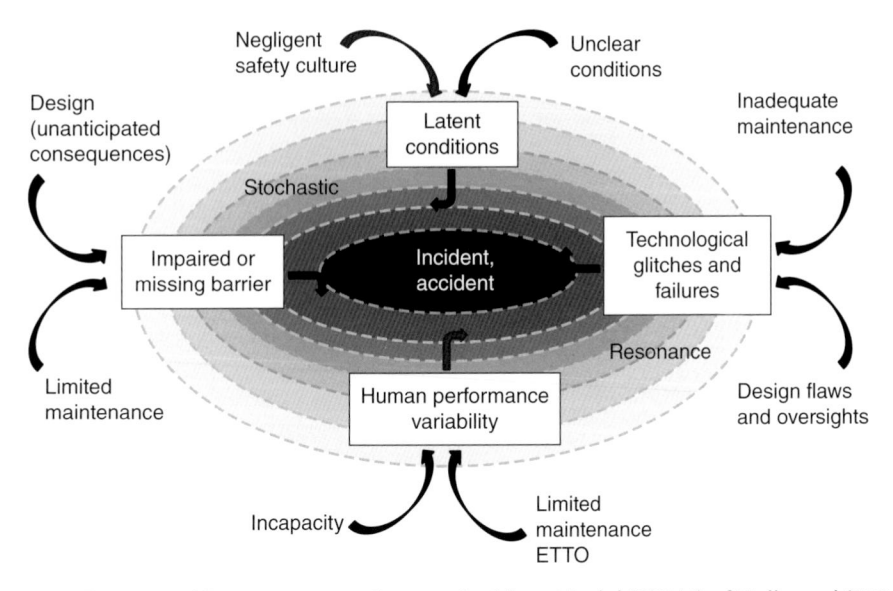

Fig. 10.4. Functional Resonance as a System Accident Model (FRAM) of Hollnagel (2004) (ETTO, efficiency-thoroughness trade-off). (From SIA, 2012.)

10.7 ACCIDENT RECORDS

As can be seen from the above, accident data are an important element (Ridley and Channing, 1999b) of safety management and there is a clear necessity for management to ensure the company has a competent accident recording system that is regularly reviewed and analysed. The frequency of acting upon these data will depend on the size of the company and the nature of its activities.

In the UK it is a statutory requirement to record certain types of accidents which can be located under RIDDOR – Reporting of Injuries, Diseases and Dangerous Occurrences Regulations 1995, amended in 2013 (HSE, 2013). The following list identifies the basic requirement for accident reporting; however, it is suggested that far more detail and information beyond these categories would be beneficial for managers (RIDDOR, 2012). The reporting of accidents to the HSE includes the following circumstances (RIDDOR, 2012):

- deaths;
- major injuries;
- over 3-day injuries (where an employee or self-employed person is away from work or unable to perform his/her normal work duties for more than three consecutive days);
- injuries to members of the public or people not at work (where they are taken from the scene of an accident to hospital);
- some work-related diseases;
- dangerous occurrences (where something happens that does not result in an injury, but could have done); and
- Gas Safe-registered gas fitters must also report dangerous gas fittings they find, and gas conveyors/suppliers must report some flammable gas incidents.

Table 10.6. Typical accident information.

Date and time	Name of person reporting incident
Location of incident	Description of accident
Who was on duty/supervision	Name of the injured or object/building area
Address	Gender
Age	Nature of the injury
Where on body	Rating scale of injury
Action taken	Follow-up action
Where on the body/building	Witness statements if relevant
Include names and addresses	Photographic evidence if appropriate

The RIDDOR 2013 regulations (HSE, 2013) detail the legal requirements of an employer to record certain accidents and incidents. Changes have been made to previous regulations, but the maxim 'more is best' is one that is needed for accident data. Although the HSE provides guidance as to what data it requires, a more comprehensive accident report would not be detrimental to an organization.

Table 10.6 provides an example of the type of accident information that needs to be kept and reviewed. The HSE has introduced an electronic entry system, meaning that the reporting of accidents is simplified and immediate. With advances in information technologies, computer record-keeping allows easier entry and analysis with a number of systems providing such information. For example, one advertised on the RIDDOR site is that of Assessment UK, which appears to be an interactive system evaluating the overall safety of an organization (Assessment, 2013).

In the author's opinion and experience[1] the more information kept the better, even if this is not a statutory requirement (RIDDOR accident reports should be considered a minimum requirement and refer to serious incidents). The aim is to improve the overall safety of employees and customers and more information is not detrimental but advantageous to this aim. However, there also needs to be a balance made between the needs of the company/organization and the time taken to record and analyse the accident data. Immediacy is the keyword for accident reporting.

[1]Jenkins, I.S. (2014) Consultancy Notes.

10.8   CONCLUSION

It is evident that accidents are an important tool in risk management. There are a number of reasons for this. First, accident data are historic and therefore reflective of a risk being realized.

Second, it is difficult to collect and coordinate databases, especially those relating to leisure, tourism and sport accidents. Most accident databases available are generally run by government safety organizations, whose main aim is to collect data related primarily to work accidents. Attempts have been made to coordinate data relating to leisure, tourism and sport accidents but these have eventually failed, ELASS being an example. Third, reporting systems that include minor accidents and near misses have not been legally required in the past and are therefore seen by many organizations as an onerous task. This has changed and it is now recognized that these accident/incident statistics can be a rich source of predicting future serious accidents, providing data for proactive management.

Clearly accidents usually occur as a result of a complicated sequence of events. Within large organizations safety culture is now more important than ever before and CSR should ensure that safety is an integrated process and that employees reflect it. Furthermore, serious accidents are one of the most expensive workplace costs and therefore prevention has a large economic benefit both to society and employers.

Accident data that are competently compiled and analysed can be an excellent source of risk reduction and good safety management and in the author's opinion far more emphasis should be placed upon this area. There is a pressing need now for 'Big Data' sets to be created so that management can assess how the company is performing against national and international organizations.

DISCUSSION QUESTIONS AND TASKS

1. To what extent do you consider accident data to be an important part of safety management?

2. Do governments consider accidents to now be one of the most important areas of safety management?

3. How relevant are accident models in helping the manager understand and reduce risks?

4. Explain the importance of near miss data in helping reduce accidents.

REFERENCES

Adams, J. (1995) *Risk*. UCL Press, London.

Assessment (2013) Assessments. Available at: http://www.assessnet.co.uk/ (accessed 12 April 2013).

Baron, R. (2014) Pilots and Memory: A Study of a Fallible Human System, http://airlinesafety.com/editorials/PilotsAndMemory.htm (accessed 25 August 2014).

BBC (2013) On This Day 8 October 1987: Zeebrugge disaster was no accident. Available at: http://news.bbc.co.uk/onthisday/hi/dates/stories/october/8/newsid_2626000/2626265.stm (accessed 10 January 2014).

Bradbury, J.A. (1989) The policy implications of differing concepts of risk. *Science, Technology, & Human Values* 14, 380–399.

Brodbeck, J., Bachmann, M.S., Croudace, T.J. and Brown, A. (2013) Comparing growth trajectories of risk behaviors from late adolescence through young adulthood, an accelerated design. *Developmental Psychology* 49, 1732–1738.

Butchart, A., Brown, D., Khanh-Huynh, A., Corso, P., Florquin, N. and Muggah, R. (2008) *Manual For Estimating the Economic Costs of Injuries due to Interpersonal and Self-directed Violence.* World Health Organization, Geneva, Switzerland.

DG SANCO (2001) *Final Report, Transformation of EHLASS Data for 1997–1999 and for Latecomers for 1986–1996, Institute of Public Health, North Rhine–Westphalia.* European Commission, Directorate-General for Health and Consumer Protection, Brussels.

Drupsteen, L., Groeneweg, J. and Zwetsloot, G.I.J.M. (2013) Critical steps in learning from incidents: using learning potential in the process from reporting an incident to accident prevention, UK. *International Journal of Occupational Safety and Ergonomics* 19, 63–77.

DTI (2003) *24th (final) Report of the Home and Leisure Accident Surveillance System 2000, 2001 and 2002 Data.* Department of Trade and Industry, London.

Dupré, B. (2007) *50 Philosophy Ideas You Really Need to Know.* Quercus, London.

EU-OSHA (2014) About us. Available at: https://osha.europa.eu/en/about (accessed 7 January 2014).

Hillson, D. and Murray-Webster, R. (2007) *Understanding and Managing Risk Attitude,* 2nd edn. Gower, London.

Hollnagel, E. (2004) *Barriers and Accident Prevention.* Ashgate, Farnham, UK.

Hollnagel, E. (2012) *FRAM: The Functional Resonance Analysis Method Modelling Complex Socio-technical Systems.* Ashgate, Farnham, UK.

HSE (2005) *Inspectors Toolkit (Draft). Human Factors in the Management of Major Accident Hazards. Introduction to Human Factors.* Health and Safety Executive, London.

HSE (2013) *Reporting Accidents and Incidents at work. A brief guide to the Reporting of Injuries, Diseases and Dangerous Occurrences Regulations 2013 (RIDDOR).* Health and Safety Executive, Bootle, UK.

ISO (2008) *ISO 26000 – Social Responsibility.* ISO Central Secretariat, International Organization for Standardization, Geneva, Switzerland.

Ministry of Justice (2012) *Criminal Injuries Compensation Scheme 2012. Scheme laid before Parliament under section 11(1) of the Criminal Injuries Compensation Act 1995.* The Stationery Office, London.

Mitchell, R., Boufous, S. and Finch, C.F. (2008) *Sport/Leisure Injuries in New South Wales, Trends in Sport/Leisure Injury Hospitalisations (2003–2005) and the Prevalence of Non-hospitalised Injuries (2005).* NSW Injury Risk Management Research Centre, University of New South Wales, Sydney, Australia.

RIDDOR (2012) What is Riddor? Available at: http://www.riddor.info/about/ (accessed 9 January 2014).

Ridley, J.R. and Channing, J. (1999a) *Safety Law: For Occupational Health and Safety (Safety at Work).* Butterworth-Heinemann, Oxford.

Ridley, J.R. and Channing, J. (1999b) *Risk Management.* Butterworth-Heinemann, Oxford.

RoSPA (2014a) HASS and LASS Home & Leisure Accident Surveillance System. Available at: http://www.rospa.com/homesafety/resources/statistics/hass-lass.aspx (accessed 9 October 2014).

RoSPA (2014b) What is the definition of an accident? Available at: http://www.rospa.com/faqs/detail.aspx?faq=255 (accessed 9 January 2014).

Rotten Tomatoes (2014) Open Water 2 (Adrift) 2006. Available at: http://www.rottentomatoes.com/m/open_water_2/ (accessed 9 January 2014).

SIA (2012) *Models of Causation.* Safety Institute of Australia, Tullamarine, Australia.

Stevens, T.R. and Jenkins, I.S. (1990) *Improving the Safety of Waterslides.* SaiL, Swansea, UK.

Stevens, T.R. and Jenkins, I.S. (1993) *'Managing a Safer Product' – Safety in Activity Holidays.* SaiL, Swansea, UK.

TBS (The Buddhist Society) (2006) *1001 Pearls of Buddhist Wisdom.* Duncan Bard Publishers, London.

Vitelli, R. (2013) Taking Risks: Why do we take more risks as adolescents than we do when we get older? Media Spotlight, *Psychology Today,* 16 September. Available at: http://www.psychologytoday.com/blog/media-spotlight/201309/taking-risks (accessed 9 October 2014).

Walt Disney Parks and Resorts (2008) *Report on Safety.* Walt Disney Parks and Resorts, Burbank, California.

Waring, A. (1996) *Safety Management Systems*. Chapman Hall, London.

WHO (2005) *Preventing Child Accidents and Improving Home Safety in the European Region. Identifying Means to Make Dwellings Safer. Report of a WHO Expert Meeting, Bonn, May 30–31, 2005.* WHO European Centre for Environment and Health, Bonn, Germany.

FURTHER READING

Baron, R. (2014) Pilots and Memory: A Study of a Fallible Human System. Available at: http://airline-safety.com/editorials/PilotsAndMemory.htm (accessed 25 August 2014).

Hillson, D. and Murray-Webster, R. (2007) *Understanding and Managing Risk Attitude*, 2nd edn. Gower, London.

Hollnagel, E. (2004) *Barriers and Accident Prevention*. Ashgate, Farnham, UK.

Hollnagel, E. (2012) *FRAM: The Functional Resonance Analysis Method Modelling Complex Socio-technical Systems*. Ashgate, Farnham, UK.

chapter 11

Learning from the Past – Case Study Analysis

CHAPTER OBJECTIVES

- To apply the key theoretical concepts to a range of case studies.
- To show the value of researching and analysing past incidents to help identify hazards and risks.
- To illustrate the benefits of case study analysis of past incidents to identify causation factors that can then be used for future scenario writing.
- To show the value of comparative analysis of cases between sectors, countries and levels of management.

Key concepts

Many of the key concepts used in previous chapters will be highlighted here in relation to the case studies analysed.

11.1   INTRODUCTION

This chapter reflects on the many theoretical concepts, models and tools discussed in all of the previous chapters in relation to a variety of incidents and accidents. When reading the case studies, encouragement is always given to consider the causation factors and how they exist in a complex web of factors or variables, whereby the activity may be constantly operating on the edge of chaos when a trigger unleashes the risk event. The cases are also designed to be provocative, highlighting what can often be some catastrophic failures in imagination, in order to help students, practitioners or managers try and avoid such failures in their own working environments. Encouragement is also made to read the case studies beyond a person's particular area of interest, or sector operated in, in order to consider what can be learnt and adapted from those mistakes.

11.2 HOW TO ANALYSE CASE STUDIES

While statistical analysis of past trends and data is an important part of any risk approach, this can always be complemented by a deeper analysis of more specific case studies. When examining the following cases, consideration should be given to the causation factors and whether any clues or pieces of data can be gleaned to help anticipate future events. These are the warning indicators used in the monitoring process discussed in Chapter 5. The cases can also be used to explore 'what if' scenarios to avoid experiencing the unexpected 'black swan' type of event discussed in Chapter 3. They offer a way to fire-up the practitioner's imagination to what is possible, learning from the cases where so often there was a catastrophic failure in imagination.

In terms of analysing the cases many of the key concepts discussed in this book will be considered. These key concepts are summarized in Table 11.1 and are based around the key themes relating to the anatomy of risk concepts, hazard categories, risk exposure and causation factors.

11.3 SPORT INJURIES AND VIOLENCE

Playing and watching sport can bring numerous benefits. It can deliver many health benefits, in terms of physical health, mental well-being and social belonging. It also is a lucrative commercial activity and an integral part of the global economy. These benefits, which are promoted and supported by governments, commercial organizations and many other key agencies, can at times blind or hide the fact that sport also has the potential for many negative risks, encompassing death, injuries, violence, drug abuse, corruption and abuse of athletes. A variety of examples relating to these areas are looked at here.

11.3.1 Spinal injuries in sport and the case of Ben Smoldon (rugby)

In 1991, during an under-19 rugby game, a 17-year-old rugby player, Ben Smolden, broke his neck during a scrum, resulting in him becoming permanently paralysed. The background to the incident and the court ruling are worthwhile exploring because of the ramifications it had on rugby and beyond. During the court case, evidence was given that the scrum had collapsed a number of times, with the touch judge warning the referee that unless he did something, someone in the front row of the scrum was going to be injured; this was further corroborated by a spectator who gave evidence. During the game, Ben was moved from the wing to hooker after the regular hooker complained of a sore neck after several of the scrums had collapsed.

Table 11.1. Examples of key concepts checklist of factors for case study analysis.

Key risk benefits	Financial, health and well-being, customer satisfaction, enjoyment, reputation, learning, flow experiences/ self-actualization
Anatomy of risks	*Hazard* (source of risk when people/organizations interact or bisect with the hazard)
	Causation factors (the many factors or variables that can be connected and combined in a number of complex ways and that can create the potential for risks)
	Risk (measured in terms of likelihood of an event and the consequences of the event, which can have upsides or downsides)
	Trigger (the event which triggers the risk events to become unleashed)
Hazards categories and examples	*Political*: political instability such as demonstrations, riots, protests, strikes; government change; regime change; security related to terrorism, war
	Economic: unemployment; inflation; recession; depression
	Social/human: criminality; transport accidents; industrial accidents
	Technological: computer system failures; hacking; new technologies
	Legal: new legislation; case law; international rulings; industrial accidents
	Environment (natural): atmospheric (cyclones, tornadoes, storms, floods, frosts); earth/geological (earthquakes, tsunamis, landslides, volcanoes, erosion, fires); temperature (extreme heat, extreme cold, snow)
	Biological/disease: human diseases (e.g. blood-borne pathogens); human epidemics; plant epidemics; plagues
	Operational conditions: people (crushing, violence, collisions, frustrations, etc.); buildings (collapse, atmosphere, visitor experience); machinery/ equipment (failures, breaks, noise); animals (attacks, bites, scratches, disease); play spaces (includes playing surfaces and terrain); natural hazards (e.g. lakes, rivers, mountains); built environment hazards (e.g. roads, barriers, buildings); game play (e.g. tackling, running, etc.); staff (e.g. coaching abuse, violence, poor customer service); medical conditions of participants (e.g. diabetes, asthma, heart conditions); transport/vehicular accidents; drugs (aggression, domestic violence, increased performance, health, ethical and reputational issues)

(Continued)

Table 11.1. Continued.

Risk exposure dimension	*Assets exposed to risk:* key stakeholders (customers/fans/clients, staff, managers, trustees, sponsors, local community, investors, shareholders); buildings, equipment; finances, reputation and brand
	Risk impact areas (consider scale of exposure): psychological impacts (e.g. trauma, flow); physical objects (e.g. equipment and buildings); reputation (e.g. brand and associations, credibility); finances (e.g. losses and gains); competition (e.g. rankings); ethical (e.g. moral dilemmas, issues of right and wrong, ethical principles compromised); operational (e.g. cancellations and delays); financial (e.g. losses, bankruptcy, profit warnings, share prices)
	Modifiers: scale of financial investment; degree of captive investment; type of client, etc.
Trigger examples	Electrical fault or dropped cigarette for fires; death of key political leader; financial collapse of a key institution; equipment failure; actions of people; environmental conditions, such as strong winds or storms; structural failure, etc.
Causation categories (agents or variables)	*Cultures and paradigms*: relates to the culture, attitudes, views and beliefs of some of the key stakeholders which can be critical factors shaping risk taking, safety cultures and what Elliot *et al.* (1997: 91) describe as the extent they are 'crisis prepared, or crisis prone'. Is it a culture of profit over safety? Do they have a desire or ability to analyse causation and incubating events? Difficulty to break with existing cultural practices, locking practices which can be dangerous?
	Poor leadership: key individuals can set the tone for the adoption of risk and safety cultures, whereby if they do not lend their support, or lead by example, many risk processes can be undermined. It also relates to what individuals do at the time, during a crisis situation
	Communication systems/procedures: many disasters occur because at some point there has been a breakdown in communication, whether this is information not being communicated down the line, blocked or simply key information not accessed

(Continued)

Table 11.1. Continued.

	Quality of physical controls: this can be when the mechanisms to prevent exposure to a hazard or risk fail, such as collapse of a barrier stopping people from falling from a height
	Quality of procedures: this is where the procedures for managing hazards and risks fail, such as those stopping people from entering or interacting with a hazard, or failing to stop dangerous play
	Equipment failure/technical failures: this can relate to failures in equipment, such as safety equipment, warning systems, technology failures or things simply breaking apart
	Weakness of research and analysis: when reviewing the cases it can be quite striking how there was a failure to identify, analyse and learn from previous incidents, such as near misses and actual accidents, from within the organization, the sector or in even in other countries. There is a failure to use such theories as the incident triangle or build up frequency profiles. It is also noticeable how there can be a poor analysis of various operational or external business environmental conditions to try and anticipate the events
	Human failings: while human errors can often be cited in accidents, the preference is to use this term 'very rarely', such as those quite specific instances when people may have died or fallen asleep at the controls of a machine. Elliot *et al.* (1997: 85) note that to just cite 'human error' is to ignore the full complexity of the events and the 'family of causal agents', meaning human error is a gross oversimplification
	Poor training: sometimes the failure is from poor training, sometimes because of money, sometimes because practices are not updated, even failing to do thorough scenario exercises
	Heuristic traps: this can relate to the term 'human error' and the work cultures, but has a number of more specific attributes. These traps (see Chapter 6) can be summarized as: inexperienced; habituation; poor learners; scarcity of opportunity; consistency of alignment; halo effect; acceptance; social facilitation/impacts
	Risk homeostasis: with safety equipment, experience does not necessarily reduce risk, but leads to increases in risk taking

In Ben's third scrum of the afternoon the incident occurred. Previously the scrum had collapsed twenty-five times, with evidence of aggression in the game.

The legal action that subsequently took place in 1996 was based on the referee having failed to properly control the game, with laws consistently contravened, and warnings of possible injury ignored, thus failing in his *duty of care*. The RFU fought the case but, after a number of appeals, the High Court ruled that the referee was liable for the crippling injuries, awarding Ben over £1 million in damages.

Despite the concerns of governing bodies at the time that the ruling might unleash a wave of litigation against referees, this has not turned out to be the case. What it has done is lay down an important precedent of the duty of care a referee has to players. Furthermore, while spinal injuries are rare, the following examples of research can give some interesting insights if one reflects back to the incident triangle discussed in Chapter 3 and the number of serious accidents in relation to near misses:

- When reviewing and comparing spinal cord injuries in Australian footballers between 1997 and 2002, Carmody *et al.* (2005) found the incident level of spinal injuries was 3.2 per 100,000 for rugby union (with the scrum the key variable); 1.5 per 1000 for rugby league; and 0.5 and 0.2 per 100,000 for Australian rules and regular soccer, respectively.
- Fuller (2007) noted how despite rule changes in rugby union, there was no sustained reduction in injuries, with forwards the most likely to suffer a catastrophic injury in the scrum.

A summary of the key risk concepts which can be applied to the case study is presented in Table 11.2.

11.3.2 Spinal injuries in sport and the case of Kevin Everett (American football)

Everett played for the NFL team the Buffalo Bills. During a game in September 2007 he suffered a severe spinal injury in a tackle that at first looked little different from many tackles which take place during an American football game. Everett was initially given a bleak prognosis with his condition life threatening. After a great deal of surgery, Kevin made some recovery, but has never achieved full recovery. Although spinal injuries are rare, Rihn *et al.*'s (2009) research can help put them into perspective. They observed that in American football, despite changes to rules, medical care and tackling and blocking techniques designed to reduce the risk over the decades, spinal injuries still continued. They note the incidence of spinal injuries is 2 per 100,000 at college football level, with the catastrophic spinal injury being 0.5 per 100,000, but with variations between high school and college level. This can be compared with rugby and other sports to help put the risk in perspective and to try and learn what can be done in an attempt to reduce this risk. A summary of the key risk concepts that can be applied to the case study is presented in Table 11.3.

Table 11.2. Application of the key risk concepts to a rugby incident.

Summary			
Trigger: scrum collapse *Hazards*: players; game play; conditions	*Key risks*: catastrophic injury; reputational damage; financial costs Rule changes to try and reduce risks are possible upsides, but with variable results	*Causation*: referee not enforcing rules/poor communication; game play and scrum; culture of the game and tolerance of aggression; poor leadership; heuristic trap of habituation; poor analysis of the risks and past incidents by governing body; hyper-flexion or crushing of neck Tackling can also be a key variable in other sports, such as a spear tackle or high tackle around the neck	*Other points*: warning incidents ignored (incident triangle theory and the number of near misses ignored); advice ignored; precedent set of duty of care of referees as in any aspect of work; decision did not deter referees as RFU asserted; also what is deemed as reasonable (ALARP) High-profile spinal injuries have continued: e.g. Daniel James who took his own life in a Swiss euthanasia clinic in October 2008 after becoming paralysed in a training accident in March 2007; Mat Hampson who became paralysed in 2005 after a scrum collapsed. Not only are these personal tragedies, but they should set some important questions for the governing body of the sport as to how to reduce the likelihood and severity of outcome

RFU, Rugby Football Union; ALARP, as low as is reasonably practical.

Table 11.3. Application of the key risk concepts to an American football incident.

Summary			
Trigger: collision *Hazards*: players; game play; conditions; equipment	*Key risks*: catastrophic injury; reputational damage; financial costs	*Causation*: tackle and angle of challenge Other factors to consider: culture of strong aggressive tackles; risk homeostasis and false assumption that helmet and pads reduce risks; tackling too low; pressures to win	*Other points*: in itself this is a regrettable accident, but when considered in relation to the wider issue of spinal injuries it reveals some worrying issues about the safety of the game and the risk of spinal injuries, many of which do not receive such publicity While the risk of occurrence may not always be reduced, the severity of outcome can still be altered based on medical training and use of equipment such as spinal boards

11.3.3 Sudden death in sport and the case of Frabrice Muamba (UK soccer)

The case of Frabrice Muamba, an English premier league soccer player, is worthwhile exploring in relation to the problem of a sudden death of a player, which all sports are exposed to. In March 2012, while playing for Bolton Wanderers, Muamba collapsed suddenly during the game. Attempts to revive him and start his heart using cardiopulmonary resuscitation and a defibrillator all failed; but, with the attention of the paramedics who were on hand, and a cardiac doctor who emerged from the crowd to help, they continued to work on him in the ground, ambulance and hospital. Eventually, after 78 minutes, they managed to restart his heart. His subsequent recovery is a remarkable case study, showing how equipment, emergency staff availability and revised training and procedures for dealing with cardiac arrest can affect the outcomes. Frabrice's case also helps draw attention to the sudden death and collapse of people playing any sport, of which there have been a number of high-profile incidents over the years in various sports. A summary of the key risk concepts that can be applied to the case study is presented in Table 11.4.

Table 11.4. Application of the key risk concepts to a sudden death football incident.

Summary

Trigger: complex physiological factors, exertion *Hazards*: hidden medical condition	*Key risks*: death; loss of career; cancellation; reputational enhancement because of effectiveness of measures Improved medical care in football is an upside result (example of dealing with a low likelihood, high severity dread risk)	*Causation*: complex physiological factors, where the science is still developing; exertion; undiagnosed heart defect Sudden death can relate to other factors like heat, exertion and medical conditions such as those relating to the heart or diabetes	*Other points*: the case of Fabrice is not unique, but his survival is. There have been many high-profile sudden deaths, such as Marc-Vivien Foé playing for Cameroon collapsing and dying during an international soccer match in 2003, Miklós Fehér playing for Benfica and Phil O'Donnell playing for Motherwell, to name but a few. Fabrice's survival was down to the effectiveness of the control measures in place, which has prompted further revision of medical procedures: the English FA working with the British Heart Foundation has introduced 900 defibrillators to English soccer clubs. Contrast this with the FA's reaction on the issue of concussion, where it has been slow to take decisive action; concussion is an example of a stealth risk, which may not initiate the same dramatic response from an organization Calls for more comprehensive medical screening (as occurs in Italy) to pick up on any risk factors have also been put on the agenda

11.3.4 The risk of concussion in soccer and American football

Jeff Astle played for West Bromwich Albion in the top division of English soccer. He was a renowned goal scorer and header of the ball. In 2002 he died aged 59, with the inquest ruling that his death resulted from an 'industrial disease', namely dementia brought on by repeatedly heading the ball. After he died, the FA promised to investigate more into the risks of heading the ball, an investigation that it failed to honour, eventually issuing a public apology for its failure to the family in March 2014. An apology no doubt prompted by court actions in the USA against the NFL and the settlement of US$765 million for the players and families who brought the law suit based around the risks of concussion and the negligence of the NFL to deal with the risks.

The case of Jeff Astle can easily (and indeed should) be compared with the risk of concussion in other sports, particularly: (i) American football, such as the case of Mike Webster, the investigation by journalists Mark Fainaru-Wada and Steve Fainaru and their damning exposure of the NFL covering up or denying the risks in their book the *League of Denial* (2012); (ii) boxing, such as the cases of Micheal Norgrave, Becky Zerlentes and Pedro Alcazar and how the governing body has responded; and (iii) rugby, where a number of people have died from concussion, such as Jordon Kemp in New Zealand or 14-year-old Ben Robinson who died from second-impact syndrome concussion (repeated head injuries during a game). A summary of the key risk concepts that can be applied to the case study is presented in Table 11.5.

11.3.5 Coaching abuse in sports

Abuses by coaches can be categorized around four key areas: (i) physical abuse; (ii) emotional abuse; (iii) neglect; and (iv) sexual abuse, the main focus in this section. A number of cases illustrate some important and worrying issues about coaching abuses in sport. For example, Alan Roberts, a leading coach and figure in the sport of judo in the UK, who had been involved with Olympic teams, was barred for life by the British Judo Association (BJD) in 2011 when the BJA panel decided that, over four decades, Roberts had manipulated his position, influence and experience for the purposes of his own sexual gratification. Other cases such that of Harry Cook, a well-established and well-known figure in karate, a senior coaching figure and having published works on martial arts, has also given further exposure to the issue in the UK. It is easy to find examples in other countries. For example, Kayla Harrison, who won a gold medal at the London 2012 Olympics and became the first US gold medallist in judo, revealed that she had suffered years of sexual abuse at the hands of her childhood coach; or in Australia, where although Scott Volkers, a prominent swimming coach, was committed to trial for indecent treatment of girls in the 1980s and 1990s, he has continued to work as a swimming coach in other countries, such as with the elite swimming squad in Brazil.

What the research reveals is the worrying scale of abuse in all sports, in all countries. Reviewing the many cases that can be found in different countries can show a shocking culture by the governing bodies of sport, where the abuse was ignored, not taken seriously, or even had a degree of acceptance and was not viewed as a criminal act. Another worrying aspect about

Table 11.5. Application of the key risk concepts to concussion sport injuries.

Summary			
Trigger: complex physiological factors; blow to the head or sudden stopping (e.g. tackling producing whiplash effect) *Hazards*: ball; players; game play; equipment	*Key risks*: death; loss of quality of life for individual and family; reputational damage for the sport; impact on participation levels; legal actions For other sports: the reputational impact for the NFL has been profound, with the cover up and the various legal actions. It is an issue which all sport governing bodies must be seen to be dealing with	*Causation*: complex physiological factors, relating to the whiplash of heading the ball; old leather footballs were much heavier, particularly when they became waterlogged; culture of the game to be 'first to the ball' and win the header; position as striker and heading goals; poor medical safeguards, such as no rehabilitation time between injuries; culture of the governing body For other sports: culture of the game to get pumped up, tackle hard, win the game; protective gear such as shoulder pads and helmets could in fact have contributed to the problem (homeostasis); glancing blow can be more dangerous than the direct impact; protective gear may have little reduction on the risks (e.g. issues as to how effective protective headgear is in amateur boxing)	*Other points*: this is an example of a stealth risk, with catastrophic implications. The time delay of the illness means it can be less dramatic and harder to generate actions for change, which is in contrast to the case of Fabrice Muamba. It also shows the value of not just looking at incidents within a particular sport, but also between sports, countries and other incidents, such as those related to domestic violence. The recording of an 'industrial disease' should be noted There are many more cases now being brought to court in many countries, with the research giving more insights into the problem Part of the problem is the vital need to change the culture of some coaches, who may be so embedded in past practices they may find it difficult to change. It's the 'it never did me any harm' brigade Aspects of prospect theory can be used here in relation to parents and fearing that they could lose the health of their child

these cases is the timespans over which coaches abused young people, in some instances going back decades, but only now coming to light. A summary of the key risk concepts that can be applied to the case study is presented in Table 11.6.

11.4 ADVENTURE

It has been frequently stated that of all the sectors looked at in this book, the perceived need for risk is the most intimately related to adventure. The perceived element really does need emphasizing here, as it is about balancing the challenge with the skill level, as safely as is reasonably practicable. Furthermore, it is important to recognize that adventure is a diverse industry, with adventure tourism a key and growing sector.

This means that the risk assessments often need to move beyond the physical dangers to assessing the environmental and political conditions, particularly for overseas ventures. For example, for UK operators who are doing any overseas expedition, fieldwork or adventures, there is a quality standard (BS 8848:2014) that can be followed whereby a number of important conditions are highlighted as points of good practice; standards which have applicability for any organization, in any country, doing an overseas venture. The standards include considering such things as: (i) identifying a 'competent' person to lead the assessment exercise; (ii) clarifying the purpose of the venture; (iii) collecting key information on the participants; (iv) ensuring third party providers meet required specifications (e.g. checking their risk analysis and management system, safety policy, public liability insurance); (v) conducting proper research, such as the degree of compatibility of the location with the activities, or the foreign office advice; (vi) presenting pre-trip literature to help the participants make informed decisions; and (vii) ensuring the venture's integrity, such as proper insurance being taken out by participants.

11.4.1 Lyme Bay

In 1993, four schoolchildren drowned in a canoeing disaster in Lyme Bay, Dorset. A party of eight pupils, their teacher and two instructors set off in the morning to cross the bay and return to Lyme Regis by lunchtime. Early into the trip, the teacher got into trouble. While one of the instructors assisted the teacher, the other instructor rafted the other canoes together, which soon drifted away rapidly, and into waves that were getting bigger, which eventually swamped the canoes and resulted in all the people ending up in the water. The teacher and instructor were eventually rescued by a lifeboat at 17.31 hours, while the rest of the group was picked up between 17.40 and 18.40 hours. What unfolded during the court case was a whole series of 'contributory factors' that were cited as leading to the disaster. The legal action which followed saw the company, the managing director and the centre manager prosecuted, with the managing director of the centre jailed for 3 years and fined £60,000, as he was seen as the 'embodiment' of the organization. The basis of the decision was on the principle of corporate manslaughter, despite such cases in the UK having failed in the past. A summary of the key risk concepts that can be applied to the case study is presented in Table 11.7.

Table 11.6. Application of the key risk concepts to coaching abuse incidents.

Summary			
Trigger: complex physiological factors/single trigger events not always obvious; opportunity to isolate athletes; physical contact *Hazards*: coach	*Key risks*: emotional harm and trauma; loss of childhood; reputational damage to the sport; reduced grass-roots participation as trust and credibility is eroded	*Causation*: complex physiological factors; opportunities/ isolation of athletes; some sports governing bodies had a culture where a 'blind eye' could be turned to abuse; habituation and replication of past practices; competitive culture to win can create emotional pressures to perform which may be relevant for physical and emotional abuse; coach may have psychological disorder; some sports with more physical contact (e.g. martial arts) can carry higher degrees of risk	*Other points*: the length of time over which the abuse could take place indicates many failures in terms of procedures and the cultures of the organizations The scale of the abuse reveals that it is a critical issue, where risk assessments and control measures need to be put in place to try and comply with various regulations in different countries relating to child protection Illustrates how governing bodies, along with such institutions as the church, believed that they could deal with the behaviour within the organization, whereas in fact it was a criminal act

11.4.2 Surf accidents (Australia)

Matthew Barclay, a 14-year-old boy, was taking part in the Australian Surf Life Saving championship at Kurrawa Beach on the Gold Coast in 2012, but disappeared during the race. His body was found 17 hours later. During the inquest, the Australian workplace health and safety inspector said the event should have been postponed because the inflatable rescue boat was not available at the start of the race, in very rough and turbulent surf conditions. As the

Table 11.7. Application of the key risk concepts to a canoeing incident.

Summary			
Trigger: initial capsize *Hazards*: sea/water, surf conditions and wind	*Key risks*: hypothermia; reputation; business failure; increased regulation/improved safety in other centres?; prison	*Causation*: factors failing to reduce the likelihood: failure to scrutinize weather forecast and adjust activities; strong offshore winds and surf; no specific recruitment criteria to become an instructor; communication between staff and managers was poor; skill level of participants; accusations of poor safety culture; habituation *Factors that increased the severity*: did not notify the harbour master of route, time of departure and estimated time of arrival; delay in the centre manager reporting the group overdue; trip leader was a not provided with basic safety equipment, such as flares, two-way radios, tow ropes; kayaks did not use spray decks; speculation that method of rescue and lifted out of sea increased risk of death	*Other points*: this event and the media amplification of the issue meant there were some profound reverberations across the sector in terms of regulation and insurance costs. In the UK it also showed how the company director, who was not on site, could be found guilty of corporate manslaughter and be sent to prison

inquest unfolded, a litany of mistakes emerged, ranging from poor communications, where the risks and concerns raised by different people were ignored, to the poor safety procedures and equipment breaking down. The misuse and poor interpretation of the iPad risk assessment tool, whereby the rating was manipulated and interpreted to support the decision to allow the event to continue, rather than in an objective manner to cancel the event, was also a key point of criticism. A summary of the key risk concepts which can be applied to the case study is presented in Table 11.8.

Table 11.8. Application of the key risk concepts to a surf incident.

Summary			
Trigger: wave swamping surfer *Hazards*: sea/water, surf and sand bar; surf boards	*Key risks*: drowning; emotional trauma of family and friends; knocked unconscious by board (factor for Saxon Bird, but not Matthew Barclay); reputational/brand damage; future viability of event questioned; participation levels/parents' trust in the safety; criminal acts	*Causation*: large shore dump on shallow sandbank; low tide; rips; people who had concerns of dump did not voice opinion because not as experienced; habituation of organizers; halo effect of organizers; effectiveness of high-visibility vests questioned; rescue boat stranded with no crew; no back-up of jet skis; over-reliance on one person to man boat; rescue boat broke down; ignored warning signs; risk rating system inappropriately used; poor communication; safety concerns by emergency services of back-up rescue plans ignored; skill level of participants; officials did not know of their authority to suspend the event; accusations that commercial and sponsors' interests received priority over safety, to ensure the event went ahead	*Other points*: one of the aspects which showed the organizers in a particularly bad light was that there had been deaths in 2010 (19-year-old Saxon Bird) and 1996 (15-year-old Robert Gatenby), where the safety culture did not change and there was a poor analysis of past incidents The criticism that a rating system (where death was rated only as remote) was poor, which needed to be made in accordance with the conditions on the day Debate about the use of safety helmets to reduce risk of concussion and self-inflating/new flotation vests Encouragement for the organizers to schedule over more days to take into account need to cancel events because of conditions Better training and resources given (e.g. use of jet skis)

11.4.3 Death during a tough mudding event (USA)

Tough mudding involves overcoming a series of obstacles, usually focusing on personal challenges, developing teamwork and is a way of raising money for charity. The event has grown in popularity in the USA, UK, Australia and many other countries. The distances are usually about 10–12 miles, with the obstacles ranging from cold water plunges, overcoming walls, negotiating tunnels and using monkey bars. In April 2013, in the USA, 28-year-old Avishek Sengupta died while negotiating the plank obstacle, falling into the water below and drowning. The verdict on Sengupta's death was that it was accidental and did not warrant criminal investigation.

When compared with other endurance sports, such as triathlons and marathons, the number of deaths has not been as great, but such comparisons can be misleading because: (i) they are not considering the ratio of deaths per number of participants; (ii) the causation factors can be different; and (iii) it can distract from genuine concerns over other injuries, such as the higher incidence of spinal injuries. Yes, more people may die in marathons and triathlons, but many of these relate to heart conditions, rather than some of the hazards integral in the activity. The issue of injuries needs particular investigation as in the USA there have been cases of people becoming paralysed from diving or falling off obstacles and many severe limb injuries, with a number of those who have been injured taking legal action. The newness of the activity also means that fewer critical incident data have built up, so rather than just restricting the analysis to cases and incidents within the activity, comparative analysis should be done with other sports. A summary of the key risk concepts that can be applied to the case study is presented in Table 11.9.

11.4.4 Adventure World (Switzerland)

In 1999, 21 people were drowned while canyoning in Switzerland, when they were caught in a flash flood. Canyoning is the activity where people work their way down river valleys and gorges using floats and wearing wet suits. In this instance, the 19 tourists and three guides, part of a larger group of 45, were swept away when they were caught in a narrow canyon. The judge found six of the senior staff negligent and guilty of manslaughter, with a catalogue of safety measures not taken by the company, relating to poor communication, training and weak safety culture, where money could override safety concerns. It was also not the first accident the company was involved with, as an American tourist died in 2000 when given a bungee cord that was too long. As a result of this latter case the company went out of business. A summary of the key risk concepts that can be applied to the case study is presented in Table 11.10.

11.5 EVENT MANAGEMENT

Events offer many interesting challenges in relation to risk management, whereby a broader risk analysis and assessment may need to be done of the external business environment, then later doing a more detailed operational health- and safety-related risk assessment for the actual

Table 11.9. Application of the key risk concepts to a tough mudding incident.

Summary			
Trigger: slip *Hazards*: water; obstacles/falling from heights; hitting obstacles; participants	*Key risks*: drowning; concussion; spinal injuries; reputation (relate to charities); scrapes/bruising (high likelihood); broken limbs; cuts	*Causation*: level of skill versus level of challenge; tiredness; supervision; quality of medical support and equipment; less preparation in comparison with other endurance events; unfamiliarity with events; pressure to win (even though they are not presented as races); although not competitive, the dynamics can mean people can become competitive and go too quickly, try too hard	*Other points*: the newness of the activity and the lack of a governing body mean that the regulatory standards are still developing. They should be able to draw on other event regulations, such as dealing with the risks of heat stroke, spinal injuries and drowning developed in other sports and events Switching attention by saying other activities are more dangerous because more people have died in them is disingenuous In some actions, waivers were signed, but in subsequent litigation relating to injuries these were deemed as insufficient because of the dangerous design of the course which participants would not be fully aware of Although no deaths have occurred in the UK and Australia, comparative analysis should be done between the countries

Table 11.10. Application of the key risk concepts to canyoning.

Summary			
Trigger: heavy rainfall in short period of time *Hazards*: water; rocks; flooding	*Key risks*: deaths/ drowning; severe injuries; litigation; concussion; company going out of business; prison	*Causation*: flash flooding; ignoring warning signals of rising waters and thunderstorm breaking; narrow valley; people poorly prepared; poor communication; high cliff walls with no escape routes; debris washed down; speed of water; poor risk cultures ('much fun–no risk' was a mis-selling of the activities); poor consultation of weather forecasts and assessment of risks; no record kept of participants' names (difficulty establishing identities and exact numbers who were missing); profit over safety, where staff told to ignore dangers to ensure activities took place; heuristic traps relating to halo effect, habituation and scarcity of opportunity	*Other points*: the safety culture was weak, with the company failing to learn. Evidence of senior manager hubris and falling into many heuristic traps The event saw the introduction of a new code of conduct for the adventure sector in Switzerland There have been other incidents of being caught in floodwater surges, caused by not properly assessing the weather conditions

event. In addition, there can often be a range of additional legislation, such as that related to stadiums, whereby risk management is an implicit part of the process to comply with the regulations. Depending on the scale and type of event, there can be the added challenge of considering a diverse range of key stakeholders' interests, ranging from fans or spectators to venue owners, police, sponsors and the local community, together with the added complexity of events being prone to many external environmental factors, from the natural to the political.

Merna and Faisal (2005: 17) citing Thompson and Perry (1992) highlight the three key failures of all projects based on failure to: (i) keep within cost estimate; (ii) meet the required completion date; and (iii) achieve the required quality and operational requirements. In terms of the specific hazards and risks for events, Emery (2010: 159) gives a useful overview of sport event management incidents based around the categories of: ticketing (forgeries, touts, etc.); crowd (e.g. racism, violence, fireworks); legal problems (e.g. criminal negligence prosecutions for accidents, sponsorship disputes); financial problems (debt, lack of sponsorship); weather (e.g. intense heat, cold, snow); and other (political asylum, poor playing surfaces, terrorism). Interestingly, he also comments how many of these problems are known about, transcending national boundaries, yet many event organizers still fail to learn from past mistakes and incidents.

11.5.1 Key case study: Hillsborough

On 15 April 1989 during an FA cup semi-final between Liverpool and Nottingham Forest, at the Hillsborough football stadium in Sheffield, 96 people were crushed to death, with more than 400 injured. There had been a bottleneck building up outside the ground due to the combination of a large number of fans arriving late because of roadworks and fans being refused entry because they did not have a ticket, but not being able to leave the area owing to the constant flow of arrivals. Despite the congestion and the huge queues, the decision was taken not to delay the start of the game, which only contributed to people's sense of urgency to get into the ground. Outside the ground, there were growing concerns about the risks of crushing, but when some gates were opened fans began to rush through, meaning that as thousands of fans entered the narrow terrace tunnels, people soon became pressed up against the immovable fences designed to stop pitch invasions. Many were crushed to death standing up. The problem did not become evident until fans started climbing the fencing to get out, with other fans pulling people to safety. Finally, the fence broke under the pressure of people.

Not only were there numerous factors where actions to prevent the event were not taken, there were also numerous deficiencies in the handling of the crisis, which meant the severity of outcome was made much worse. These deficiencies included: inadequate escape routes or crumple zones to ease congestion; limited first aid equipment; difficulty of getting ambulances on to the pitch to administer first aid; and inadequate number of first aiders.

There are many significant legacies of Hillsborough. The Taylor Report led the way for all-seater stadiums and the removal of fencing. It also marked a significant change in terms of attitude and how fans were treated, whereby an element of dignity returned, rather than the adversarial, conflict approach where fans were seen as animals to be caged and tamed. It is a case study that anyone involved with events, in any country, should scrutinize as it shows so many failings which sadly are still evident in other countries, as subsequent stadium disasters illustrate. A summary of the key risk concepts that can be applied to the case study is presented in Table 11.11.

11.5.2 Athlete security – Monica Seles stabbed

In 1993, Monica Seles was the world's number one women's tennis player and was playing a quarter-final match in Hamburg when a spectator ran from the crowd and stabbed her in the back with a kitchen knife. Although the physical injuries healed relatively quickly, the psychological scars took much longer, with Seles not returning to competitive tennis for two years. Parche, the man who stabbed her, had an obsession with Steffi Graf (whom Seles had beaten three months earlier to win the Australian Open, and was her opponent in the match) and was found to be mentally ill. This act in theory changed some security measures, but others have disputed the lasting impacts and it is an important case study illustrating what is possible in terms of athlete safety, which in the future could have far more serious and catastrophic effects. A summary of the key risk concepts that can be applied to the case study is presented in Table 11.12.

11.5.3 Serbia versus Albania football game cancelled

During the Serbia versus Albania qualifying match for the 2016 European soccer championship in October 2014, the game was cancelled after violence occurred between the players and fans. During the game a drone flew into the stadium carrying a flag, which a Serbian player tore down, sparking a fight between players that escalated with Serbian fans invading the pitch and the Serbian players ending up trying to protect some of the Albanian players. Although Albanian fans were banned from attending because of problems in the past, this did not stop the violence. The roots of the incident relate to the political tensions over the former Serbian province of Kosovo, which declared independence in 2008. Despite a huge police presence and an awareness of the risks, this failed to prevent the violence. A summary of the key risk concepts that can be applied to the case study is presented in Table 11.13.

11.5.4 Terrorist attacks on sport

On 3 March 2009, gunmen ambushed the Sri Lankan cricket team coach and its accompanying police detail in the heart of Lahore, in Pakistan. Using guns, grenades and rocket launchers, the attackers killed six policemen and the coach driver, with seven of the cricketers and assistant coach injured. The tour had taken place amidst security concerns, with the Sri Lankan team stepping in to replace the Indian team after it had pulled out because of concerns over safety following the Mumbai terrorist attacks. In the aftermath of the attack, the International Cricket Council (ICC) removed a number of important games, such as the 2009 Champions trophy, because of concerns over safety, along with countries pulling out from cricket tours to Pakistan, with the Pakistani cricket team often being forced to conduct its tours in neutral countries such as Dubai.

Table 11.11. Application of the key risk concepts to football event catastrophe.

Summary			
Trigger: opening of gates allowing people to enter *Hazards*: people; fences; stairwells	*Key risks*: death (by crushing); injuries; emotional trauma; *The Sun* newspaper publishing stories, later proved false, of fans robbing the dead, destroyed its reputation in the City of Liverpool where its sales have not recovered and the paper is still boycotted	*Causation*: capacity of ground; demand for tickets; poor stewarding outside the ground; poor stewarding within the ground; erection of immovable fences as part of the 'war on hooligans'; crowd dynamics/ mood (sense of urgency); police culture; poor communications; club culture; football fans were not customers to be pleased, but potential hooligans to be contained; numerous near misses going back over 100 years that had been ignored (alerts to their existence, likelihood and the severity of outcome); profit over safety; adversarial politics of confrontation of Mrs Thatcher; limited staff, poorly trained; ageing infrastructure	*Other points*: it shows failings in reducing both the likelihood and the severity of outcome. The culture of the key stakeholders can be particularly striking, whereby it was not until Hillsborough that many of the old cultural paradigms for managing football were changed (Taylor Report was the ninth report on crowd safety made after previous deaths and accidents). Darby *et al.* (2005: 25) and Elliot *et al.* (1997: 16) are critical of the football cultures of complacency and reacting to previous disasters in a piecemeal fashion, reactively and unimaginatively There was a shocking failure to learn from the past: the Bradford fire disaster, Heysel and Ibrox being but a few examples. The incident triangle application can be particularly revealing. Looking back, hundreds of people had died, thousands had been injured, but this was never properly analysed as to why. Many international cases to look at: Lima stadium disaster in 1964 where 320 lost their lives; Moscow in 1982 where an estimated 340 lost their lives; rock concert by the group, The Who, in Cincinnati's Riverfront Coliseum in 1979 saw 11 people crushed to death

Table 11.12. Application of the key risk concepts to an athlete security breach.

Summary			
Trigger: difficult to ascertain in terms of the perpetrator's mindset, but an opportunity was seen when Seles was sitting there with her back to the crowd *Hazards*: obsessive fans	*Key risks*: emotional trauma; reputational damage; loss of earnings; watched by 6000 fans and the media	*Causation*: while the psychology can be difficult to fathom, the security measures can be drawn attention to, such as easy access of fans to court, no screening-off of fans or weapon searches	*Other points*: the wider point about this attack is that it reminds event organizers of what is possible, where a more serious attack (such as a terrorist attack) always remains a possibility This needs to be balanced out by the enjoyment fans have from being near athletes

Table 11.13. Application of the key risk concepts to a football event and political risks.

Summary			
Trigger: drone and flag ripped down *Hazards*: fans; seats; players	*Key risks*: physical injuries; game aborted; competitive (points loss/bans); fans excluded from games, impacting on atmosphere and competitive performance	*Causation*: political divisions and tensions played through sport; culture of political activism and violence in Serbian fans; failure to control fans and break up fights; control of flying objects	*Other points*: this event illustrates how sport is not divorced from politics, but is played through it The drone shows the art of what is possible and how a terrorist group could use it for a more serious attack, rather than just a point of protest

This attack by terrorists on sport activities, teams and events was not the first, nor has it been the last, as illustrated by the cases of: the murder in 1974 of Israeli athletes during the Munich Olympic games; the 1996 Atlanta bomb attacks during the Olympics; the 1997 IRA threat on the Grand National horse race in the UK resulting in the event's cancellation; the 2002 New Zealand cricket team abandoning its tour after a suicide bomb attack outside its hotel; a suicide bomb attack in a marathon in Sri Lanka in 2008; the attack on the Togo football team in 2010 during the African football cup; and the Boston marathon bomb attack in 2013. Although rare in terms of occurrence, it would be too simplistic to base the control measures just on frequency of past events, where a likelihood ratio it would be infinitesimal. A summary of the key risk concepts that can be applied to the case study is presented in Table 11.14.

11.6 TOURISM

Looking at the case studies, it is evident how there can be many factors making the assessment of risks potentially very complex. Tourism can be particularly vulnerable to many hazards in the external business environment, ranging from the weather, natural events to the political environment; factors which tourism companies have very little control over, beyond monitoring them to try and anticipate the events, or putting in place effective crisis mechanisms to try and reduce the severity of impact. In addition, many countries have various additional regulations whereby risk considerations may be an implicit part of the implementation of the regulations, such as those relating to bonding and package holidays.

In terms of tourists, depending on their type, they can at times be characterized as being more risk averse because of the importance attached to holidays in terms of finances and quality

Table 11.14. Application of the key risk concepts to a terrorist attack.

Summary			
Trigger: opportunity of the travel route *Hazards*: terrorist groups	*Key risks*: death; injuries; cancellation; delays; reputational damage; tourism; country attractiveness (threats can create cancellations)	*Causation*: complex political factors; opportunity; poor security measures; failing to deal with warnings; wider foreign policy actions; mobile technologies	*Other points*: looking at terrorist attacks beyond sport, such as 9/11, the attacks in Madrid and London on transport systems and the Bali nightclub attack, shows a change in terrorist tactics, where they have increasingly gone for 'soft targets' marked by increased lethality of the attacks
			The dread risks of these events means that increasing amounts of money are spent on security, but this has led to some questions about the risks to civil liberties

of life. So understanding the customer perceptions of risk is of critical importance for tourism operators, as this will influence customer behaviour, even if it is based on false information or misunderstandings.

11.6.1 Terrorist attacks on tourists

Egypt is often cited as one of the world's oldest tourist destinations, with evidence of its sites having attracted people to visit for thousands of years. On 17 November 1997, the Temple of Hatshepsut became the place that marked a significant turning point for terrorist attacks on civilians, not just in Egypt, but for the world. On that day, six men who were part of a radical Islamic terrorist group killed 68 people, most of them at the Temple of Hatshepsut. They arrived at the temple, shot the security guard, then proceeded up to the temple shooting and hacking at people for 45 minutes. The design of the temple, built into the rock, was such that the tourists had little means of escape and so were effectively trapped inside, where they were shot, stabbed or hacked to death. In all, 57 tourists were murdered there: ten were Japanese, 36 were Swiss and four were from the UK, with the dead including children and couples on their honeymoon.

Almost immediately, governments around the world issued travel warnings, advising against travel to the country, with most tour operators immediately curtailing their operations to Egypt. After a surprisingly short space of time, tourist numbers recovered, only to dip again after the 9/11 attacks on America, recovering again until Arab Spring in 2011 and the associated political turmoil that has been created. Interestingly, the terrorist attacks on the Red Sea resort of Sharm el-Sheik, in 2005, did not witness the mass evacuations that the Luxor attack had before, together with more restrained advice from the governments around the world. A summary of the key risk concepts that can be applied to the case study is presented in Table 11.15.

11.6.2 Ferry disaster

On the evening of 6 March 1987, the *Herald of Free Enterprise* ferry, sailing between Dover and the Belgian port of Zeebrugge, capsized shortly after leaving the Belgian port, killing 193 passengers and crew. This made it the worst maritime disaster for a British-registered ship since the sinking of *HMY Ioaire* in 1919. The ship was carrying over 400 passengers, with many of them having taken advantage of a cheap trip deal offered by *The Sun* newspaper.

There were various factors which contributed to the capsizing. The first was that the ship was not designed for the type of embarkation system in Zeebrugge, as it was developed for a different route and type of port. The result was that it could be difficult to load cars, made worse by high spring tides, which meant that the ship had to compensate by loading up with more ballast at the front of the ship, so that the port and the ship's loading decks were level. It was due a refit later in the year so that this problem could be resolved. The tight turnaround schedules meant that all crew members were under pressure to depart as quickly as possible, so the First Officer would often leave the car deck before it was fully loaded, leaving the responsibility for closing the doors to another crew member. The design of the ship was such that the First Officer could

Table 11.15. Application of the key risk concepts to a terrorist attack on tourists.

Summary

Trigger: no single trigger event less definable *Hazards*: terrorist group; political tensions	*Key risks*: death; injuries; cancellation; delays; reputational damage; tourism; country attractiveness (threats can create cancellations) Demand for tourism fell dramatically, but recovered	*Causation*: if one examines Egypt's political situation and the pattern of terrorist attacks, it is possible to discern a number of warning signals that a major attack on tourists was always possible. The group El-Gama'a el-Islamiya has warned foreign tourists to stay away from Cairo and upper Egypt President Bush's War on Terrorism policy gave new impetus to the groups, with attacks beginning again in 2004	*Other points*: the attacks on tourists that took place before the ones at Luxor illustrate not only the frequency of attacks, but their growing lethality or severity of outcome The crisis to the Egyptian tourism industry was exacerbated by the Egyptian Foreign Minister's (Mamdouh Al-Beltagui) handling of the situation, which is a useful illustrative example of poor crisis management Glaesser (2003: 48) framed this analysis within the context of 'cultural circles' and how the closer one could identify with the groups attacked, the greater the impact upon behaviour. In Switzerland, the country whose citizens suffered the most from the attacks, tourism demand fell by 73% (WTO, 2003)

not see from the wheelhouse whether the doors were closed or not. On the day of the incident, the crew member usually responsible for closing the doors had taken a short break, but had fallen asleep in his cabin. The First Officer, assuming that the doors would have been closed, set sail. Ninety seconds after leaving the harbour water began to enter the decks, which destroyed the ship's stability, resulting in her listing, with water soon affecting the electrics and plunging the ship into darkness, and the ship finally capsizing. The fortuitous turn at the last moment meant that the ship fell on a shallow sandbank, meaning she was half submerged, rather than in the deeper water the other side, which no doubt would have resulted in a higher death toll.

Having no communications, and the speed of the event, meant the crew could not call for help, but luckily a dredger notified the port authorities after seeing the lights suddenly disappear. The capsizing of the ship took place in less than a minute. Most of the deaths resulted from hypothermia because of the cold waters. A summary of the key risk concepts that can be applied to the case study is presented in Table 11.16.

Table 11.16. Application of the key risk concepts to a ferry disaster.

Summary			
Trigger: turn, water entering decks *Hazards*: sea and water; ship's furniture	*Key risks*: death/ drowning; injury and loss; illustrative of how a brand or reputation can be destroyed, with the Townsend Thoresen brand and logo changed to P&O Ferries; prison; financial losses	*Causation*: the extra ballast contributed to the ship sitting lower in the water, allowing the decks to flood more easily; the design of the ship/open decks, with no flood dividers meant the ship could fill more rapidly and soon become unstable in the water; poor communications; poor safety culture (Lord Justice Barry Sheen reported on the 'disease of sloppiness and neglect at every level of management'); ignoring previous near miss incidents and warnings (*Herald*'s sister ship having made it to her destination with the bow-doors open, without incident); ignored/poor analysis	*Other points*: it was found that previous concerns raised by managers had been ignored by senior managers. A fact that led to the UK Public Interest Disclosure Act 1998 which gives legal protection, in relation to dismissal or victimization, to individuals who disclose malpractice in an organization (the whistleblower) Later, civil prosecutions were brought against P&O European Ferries Ltd and several of its employees on the grounds of corporate manslaughter. In the end the judge directed an acquittal against the senior managers as it was too difficult to prove they had been reckless Despite this event, there have continued to be a number of high-profile cases of ships sinking: the *Costa Concordia* cruise ship in 2012, where 32 people died; or the South Korean ferry disaster where more than 260 died, many of them young, on an overloaded ship. The number of ferry disasters before and after the *Herald of Free Enterprise* disaster has called into question the inherent safety of ferries

11.6.3   A volcanic eruption

When the volcano Eyjafjallajökull began erupting in Iceland in 2010, many may not have given it much consideration. It was by no means the largest eruption, but it ended up have a profound impact on tourism because of its effect on air traffic, with numerous countries closing the airspace, millions of travellers affected and with millions of lost revenues occurring each day. However, the eruption proved to have upside risks for some forms of transport, such as ferries and rail, which saw an increase in usage.

Part of the concerns related to the risk that volcanic ash posed to aircraft based on a number of past incidents, such as the BA flight from London to Auckland in 1982. This aircraft flew through a volcanic ash cloud from a volcanic eruption in Indonesia, which resulted in all its engines stalling; thankfully, after gliding without engines for 15 minutes, the pilot was able to restart them. On investigation, the problem proved to be that as the ash entered the jet engines, it melted to a consistency of liquid glass, blocking up the air inlets and jamming the rotor blades. The ash also meant that the windscreen was difficult to see through and so the landing was made relying almost completely on instruments. When the engines had cooled, the molten ash became brittle, allowing the engines to be restarted after a number of systematic attempts of running through the engine restart checklist. Initially, the airspace was not restricted, with the ash cloud difficult to spot by radar; but after a similar incident with another aircraft, the airspace was closed.

These previous incidents meant that a great deal of caution was adopted during the Icelandic volcano eruption, but as the closing of airspace continued, a number of companies asked if it was an over-cautious response, running their own flights to test the safety of flying through the cloud. A summary of the key risk concepts that can be applied to the case study is presented in Table 11.17.

11.7   CONCLUSION

These case studies consider a wide range of risk factors relating not only to safety, but also to how the hazards and risks affect operational conditions, project management and strategic planning. When the individual cases are further examined in relation to both other cases and statistical data that can be obtained from reports and research, a much richer picture can be gained.

What is of particular importance is that people reading these cases remember the stories and the key factors of failures. These can then be used as key benchmarks stored in the student's, practitioner's or manager's memory to help him/her identify, analyse and assess risks, which should help in putting in place proper control measures to deal with the risks. Finally, there is encouragement to look beyond the particular sector or area of work or interest, as this can be invaluable to alert and show the art of conjecturing future scenarios of what could be, unless certain actions are taken.

Table 11.17. Application of the key risk concepts to an aviation incident.

Summary			
Trigger: flying through ash cloud *Hazards*: ash cloud	*Key risks*: engines stalling and crashing; reputational risks; financial risks; credibility; loss of visibility/damage to windscreen; cancellations; delays	*Causation*: ash melting on to components, stalling engines; elevation; design; failing to identify the ash cloud; poor route selection; capacity to glide (15 min without engines) Glass particles of pulverized rock; abrasive; erodes blades; melts and can block airflows, so stalling the engine; covers windscreen; erosion of external components Difficult to know how far cloud had spread	*Other points*: this case also shows the value and strength of the control mechanisms and training, and the power of checklists The actions taken by the pilot to deal with the engine failures caused by the ash created a new set of crisis checklist responses for pilots who may encounter a similar problem Another incident in 1989, but the closure was felt by some to be over-excessive with airlines testing planes by flying through the clouds Improved spotting technologies

DISCUSSION QUESTIONS AND TASKS

Find a range of cases for a sector or area of interest and ask the following questions:

1. How can the key anatomy of risk elements be identified and applied?

2. What have been, and still are, the implications of the incident, including any upside and downside risks?

3. Which of the key causation factors were evident and how did they combine to generate the risks?

4. What were the limitations in terms of: (i) the effectiveness of the control measures to reduce the likelihood; and (ii) the effectiveness of the control measures to reduce the severity of the outcome?

5. How many similar incidents (frequency profiling) occurred before the selected event and after the event?

6. Looking at the past incidents, was the selected case study a black swan event?

7. Has anything been learnt?

REFERENCES

BS 8848:2014 (2014) *Specification for the provision of visits, fieldwork, expeditions and adventurous activities outside the United Kingdom*. British Standards Institution, London.

Carmody, D.J., Taylor, T.K., Parker, D.A., Coolican, M.R. and Cumming, R.G. (2005) Spinal cord injuries in Australian footballers 1997–2002. *Medical Journal of Australia* 182, 561–564.

Darby, P., Johnes, M. and Mellor, D. (eds) (2005) *Soccer and Disaster: International Perspectives*. Routledge, London.

Elliot, D., Frosdick, S. and Smith, D. (1997) The failure of 'legislation by crisis'. In: Frosdick, S. and Walley, L. (eds) *Sport and Safety Management*. Butterworth-Heinemann, London, pp. 83–107.

Emery, P. (2010) Past, present, future major sport event management practice: the practitioner perspective. *Sport Management Review* 13, 158–170.

Frosdick, S. (1997) Managing risk in public assembly facilities. In: Frosdick, S. and Walley, L. (eds) *Sport and Safety Management*. Butterworth-Heinemann, London, pp. 273–291.

Fuller, C. (2007) Catastrophic injuries in rugby union: an assessment of the risk (final draft). Available at: http://irbplayerwelfare.com/pdfs/CI_Risk_Assessment_EN.pdf (accessed 20 September 2014).

Glaesser, D. (2003) *Crisis Management in the Tourism Industry*. Butterworth-Heinemann, Oxford.

Merna, T. and Faisal, F.A. (2005) *Corporate Risk Management: An Organizational Perspective*. Wiley, Chichester, UK.

Rihn, J.A., Anderson, D.T., Lamb, K., Deluca, P.F., Bata, A., Marchetto, P.A., Neves, N. and Vaccaro, A.R. (2009) Cervical spine injuries in American football. *Sports Medicine* 39, 697–708.

Thompson, P. and Perry, J. (1992) *Engineering Construction Risks. A Guide to Project Risk Analysis and Risk Management*. Thomas Telford, London.

WTO (2003) *Tourism Market Trends – 2003 Middle East*. World Tourism Organization, Madrid.

chapter 12

Conclusion

A ship is always safe at the shore – but that is NOT what it is built for. Albert Einstein

The authors' intention was to write a textbook for both industry and academia covering risk and safety management within the adventure, events, sport and tourism industry sectors. In their opinion, all of whom have considerable experience of risk and safety management, there appeared to be a dearth of current texts for both students and practitioners explaining the breadth and variety of risk management concepts and practices they might encounter. Consequently, this book seeks to encapsulate the theories and best practice in these sectors.

From the various chapters in this book, it should have become apparent that risk and safety are concepts not always fully understood by either the public or the various providers, and that over the last 50 years there has been an exponential growth in management and litigation related to accidents and injuries. What is clearly evident is that future managers in these industry sectors will, on a daily basis, be faced with making decisions concerning risk and safety related to the product or service that they are employed to deliver. Also, case studies over the last 50 years consistently demonstrate that companies having unsafe practices are also companies that are *unlikely* to be viable enterprises in the future.

When trying to define risk management and what it entails, on one level it is clear that practitioners and managers are constantly dealing with and managing risk. To reiterate a common point in this book, because something is not stated or described as risk management, does not mean risk management is not being undertaken. While risk management is an implicit part of management, there are however times when it has to be more explicitly engaged with and documented in order to comply with health and safety regulations or rules for good corporate governance.

Within the Preface, a number of broad aims were developed which can now be revisited, helping with final reflections and drawing out some of the key conclusions of this work. These aims were:

- to explain the underpinning concepts, theories and tools of risk, safety and risk management as they relate to the adventure, events, sport and tourism industries;
- for students and practitioners to develop a clear understanding of risk culture, or philosophy of risk, which can shape how they view and approach operational, project and strategic risk management;
- for students and practitioners to gain an appreciation of the variations in definitions and approaches, in order to develop more effective risk management practices that can be clearly communicated to staff, customers and other key stakeholders; and
- to enable practitioners and students to develop and implement effective risk control measures.

In relation to the key concepts and theories, it has been demonstrated how it is possible to identify a number of significant concepts that can be used for any country, sector and level of management. It was emphasized that terms or concepts may differ between practitioners and risk assessment frames but this is not because of any theoretical impediment, just usually reflective of past practices. For example, it was shown how commonly used the concept of a 'hazard' is in many countries when considering issues of health and safety, yet the concept is rarely used in project and strategic risk assessments. Instead, a variety of frameworks and tools such as PESTLE (which categorizes a variety of external business environment factors) are used, creating opportunities and threats. With a simple realignment, these can easily be framed as hazards (the source of risks), allowing a consistency of language for all types of risk assessment exercises, which in turn means there can be clarity in the communication of risks, which in turn means better decision making.

The comparison of risk terminology from different countries, sectors or levels of management was an important part of the discussion in this book. This was to give insights into variations in practice and how different terms may be used to describe what is essentially the same concept: such as the terms chance, likelihood and probability which, in essence, refer to a similar concept. While this book has certain preferences in conceptual terminology, such as viewing risk as something which can be opportunistic as well as threatening, it is not dogmatic in the insistence that these are the ways the concepts must be used. Instead, it can be used as a lexicon to help interpret a wide variety of literature and examples, in order to learn and call attention to good practice. What really matters is that a consistent language and way of approaching risk is utilized within an organization, matching best practice within the industry sector. It is an approach whereby with a few adjustments, such as not just considering *who* is at risk, but also *what* is at risk, one can move the analysis from just focusing on health and safety to consider broader operational, project and strategic risks.

There was a preference in this work to view risk as part of a fourth-age risk paradigm, which sees risk as opportunistic as well as threatening and, just as crucially, embedded within complex systems. While there is an inevitable bias to focus on the negative consequences, particularly when looking at safety risk management, the use of the fourth-age paradigm helps act as a counterweight that it is not always about the removal of risk, because very often this can destroy the essence of the activity. It is not quite the same thing saying that we are just risk seeking, rather than we often seek stimulating activities, or do activities which can bring financial or reputational gains, but that these can carry risks which can also be detrimental.

The idea of complexity was also particularly important. It was discussed how, for example, if one just considers hazards as the cause of risks, this can lend a superficial simplicity to the analysis. Much better is to use the hazard as the source of the risk, which requires a deeper analysis of the multiple causation factors that may be constantly in operation, but which may just need one triggering event for a risk to manifest itself, with the more serious risks moving into the area of crisis situations.

Another feature of this paradigm is that risk is viewed as something dynamic, ever changing, with activities and businesses often operating on the edge of chaos. For example, while the risk management process is presented as different stages, it is worth reiterating that in practice the differences between the stages are much more blurred: as you begin to identify hazards and risks as part of the context, you will inevitably begin to analyse and assess the risks; as more research is done to inform the analysis and the assessments, this will mean control measures are already being identified, with the key pieces of information recorded on forms and monitoring continually taking place, to review and make appropriate changes.

In addition, a simple comparison of risk between activities is also problematic as it relates to the complexity of the activities and hazards that are present. For example, trying to compare squash with riding a waterslide illustrates the problem in a number of ways. First, there is the time exposure factor to consider. A game of squash lasts for 40 minutes whereas a ride on a waterslide lasts, at best, 10 seconds; therefore you would have to ride a waterslide 240 times before you are exposed to the same time factor as squash! Second, there are the differing risk conditions and hazards: in squash these are the experience of the player, the type of rackets and balls and the condition of the court; for a waterslide, these hazards and risk conditions will include the design of the slide, maintenance of the slide, management of rides, and low and peak times. This example clearly illustrates that equivalent comparisons of risk between activities are difficult to make when all the complex relationships are factored in.

A number of questions also come to light in terms of practical processes. For example, how much work actually has to be undertaken when engaging with risk management? Despite the thousands of words written in this book, it is vital to reiterate that the risk process can be done remarkably quickly, with little to no paperwork, provided that what is being 'risk assessed' is a relatively simple activity, with limited risk exposure in terms of who/what is at risk, how they are at risk and the size of the stake. As the complexity and the risk exposure increase, it would be foolhardy indeed not to engage more critically with the risk management process, particularly in terms of the research conducted and tools applied in order to analyse the risks and develop some type of assessment about them.

The key purpose of all the safety tools such as accident data, risk assessments, etc., is simply to make better decisions. The decisions made should be framed around the notion of attempting to control risks in some manner, where the options available are represented as a jigsaw of measures based around the control categories selected, the resources employed and the ways to implement the controls. It is also important to recognize that the approach taken is to consciously mix up whether the hazards are managed or the risks. Practitioners need to be pragmatic when deciding on the best approach, depending on the nature of the problem they are dealing with.

It is also evident that, as with risk, safety legislation is to some extent consistent in most of the countries identified within the book. Countries tend to have a central organization that is responsible for the protection of its citizens from risks and harm. In all cases the essence of protection is based upon the aspect of workplace safety and legislation related to that; much of this reflects the UK's HSE and the Health and Safety at Work Act of 1974. Similar structures exist in Canada, Australia and New Zealand, but differ due to federal systems of government which delegate more responsibility to individual states within the country. There is little legislation relating directly to the sport and tourism industries, with the sole exception being the UK where the AALA (Adventure Activities Licensing Authority) was established after the tragic death of four teenagers (in 1993) undertaking adventure tourism activities.

Health and Safety Acts were and are designed to reduce the number of accidents and injuries, holding companies/employers accountable for unsafe or negligent actions. Although criminal negligence is seen as very important and something that any practitioner needs to be fully aware of, the alternative civil law is perhaps an area that will be more relevant to many managers and students. It has been within the area of civil law that much press coverage has focused over the last 30 years, often relating to huge financial payouts to plaintiffs who have been injured by negligent acts. Tort, a part of civil law, has warranted a separate chapter in this book as it is a significant legal premise that managers will encounter on a regular basis. Once again, the principle of common law is found in many of the English-speaking countries of the world and much of tort legislation is founded upon the original English Common Law. Evidence suggests that even the US system of law uses many of the precedents created by English judgments when making decisions. In essence, common sense should be the guide to good safety management and in many instances the law verifies this, focusing on the principles relating to a duty of care, reasonableness and foreseeability.

Concomitantly, accidents can be outcomes of poor risk and safety management, although it is now evident that accidents are incorrectly termed and in most cases should be called incidents. The term 'accident' is used in a generic sense of including incidents. As discussed in Chapter 10 the problem with accidents is that they are a reactive tool for management, whereas most safety management schemas require proactive measures. Changes to the UK health and safety regulations identified the importance of accidents as a risk measure; in particular a new category for assessment, that of 'near miss incidents', attempted to introduce accidents as a proactive tool. A 'near miss' was seen as datum that could provide the manager and practitioner with vital information for future risk control. 'Near miss' data had been used by the aviation industry for years as vital information to adjust procedures and actions ensuring safer environments and prevention of accidents. It is argued that the amendment to UK safety regulations helped place accident data on a new level; by analysing accident patterns and trends, together with acting upon this information, risk factors can be reduced. As can be seen within this book, so often many disasters had previous near misses, warnings or indications of a likely accident that were ignored by management.

The book has also demonstrated the complexity of accidents or incidents and how they relate to models of risk. The most recent accident models are now seen as complex and similar to chaos systems, especially so with the growing complexity of products and services and the increasing size of companies. It is evident that accident and risk theory are linked axiomatically, namely that a risk is normally related to a negative outcome (accident), but also in our understanding of hazards and how they affect risk, for example chaos theory of risk has also a chaos theory of accidents.

It has also been necessary to review the idea of compensation resulting from injuries sustained while participating in leisure or at-work activities. Death is usually viewed as the most serious consequence of poor risk management. However, an injury to an individual can have a far more costly outcome both for society and the individual, not only in terms of an inability to work, but also in terms of the cost of healthcare which, for more serious cases, may be for a significant number of years.

It is hoped that the case studies presented in this book clarify how risk works and what risk management strategies should be taken. It has been difficult to overemphasize the importance of risk in our lives, as most examples of risk taking reflect negative consequences, frequently reflected in research findings and available data. That said, the notion of adventure activities and outdoor recreation (inherently risky activities) is clearly an important element in school curricula, clearly benefitting children's development.

A key feature of this book has been explaining why things are done in certain ways and this will go some way in helping practitioners avoid some of the catastrophic failures in imagination that the many case studies illustrate. To do this means not only will organizations be more successful, but also customers can receive more enjoyable and satisfying experiences that will not cost them their lives or the company its livelihood.

Index

Page numbers in **bold** type refer to figures, tables and boxed text.